Privileged Attack Vectors

Building Effective Cyber-Defense Strategies to Protect Organizations

Second Edition

Morey J. Haber

Apress®

Privileged Attack Vectors: Building Effective Cyber-Defense Strategies to Protect Organizations

Morey J. Haber
Heathrow, FL, USA

ISBN-13 (pbk): 978-1-4842-5913-9   ISBN-13 (electronic): 978-1-4842-5914-6
https://doi.org/10.1007/978-1-4842-5914-6

Managing Director, Apress Media LLC: Welmoed Spahr
Acquisitions Editor: Susan McDermott
Development Editor: Laura Berendson
Coordinating Editor: Rita Fernando

Cover image by Freepik (www.freepik.com)

Distributed to the book trade worldwide by Springer Science+Business Media New York, 233 Spring Street, 6th Floor, New York, NY 10013. Phone 1-800-SPRINGER, fax (201) 348-4505, e-mail orders-ny@springer-sbm.com, or visit www.springeronline.com. Apress Media, LLC is a California LLC and the sole member (owner) is Springer Science + Business Media Finance Inc (SSBM Finance Inc). SSBM Finance Inc is a **Delaware** corporation.

For information on translations, please e-mail rights@apress.com, or visit http://www.apress.com/rights-permissions.

Apress titles may be purchased in bulk for academic, corporate, or promotional use. eBook versions and licenses are also available for most titles. For more information, reference our Print and eBook Bulk Sales web page at http://www.apress.com/bulk-sales.

Any source code or other supplementary material referenced by the author in this book is available to readers on GitHub via the book's product page, located at www.apress.com/9781484259139. For more detailed information, please visit http://www.apress.com/source-code.

Printed on acid-free paper

*Having a happy and healthy life is all
the privileges anyone in the world should ever need.*

Table of Contents

About the Author

Morey J. Haber is Chief Technology Officer and Chief Information Security Officer at BeyondTrust. He has more than 20 years of IT industry experience and has authored three Apress books: *Privileged Attack Vectors, Asset Attack Vectors*, and *Identity Attack Vectors*. In 2018, Bomgar acquired BeyondTrust and retained the BeyondTrust name. He originally joined BeyondTrust in 2012 as a part of the eEye Digital Security acquisition. Today, Morey oversees BeyondTrust strategy for privileged access management and remote access solutions. In 2004, he joined eEye as Director of Security Engineering and was responsible for strategic business discussions and vulnerability management architectures in Fortune 500 clients. Prior to eEye, he was Development Manager for Computer Associates, Inc. (CA), responsible for new product beta cycles and named customer accounts. He began his career as Reliability and Maintainability Engineer for a government contractor building flight and training simulators. He earned a Bachelor of Science degree in Electrical Engineering from the State University of New York at Stony Brook.

About the Technical Reviewer

 **Derek A. Smith** is an expert in cybersecurity, cyber forensics, healthcare IT, SCADA security, physical security, investigations, organizational leadership, and training. He is currently an IT program manager with the federal government and a cybersecurity Associate Professor at the University of Maryland University College and the Virginia University of Science and Technology, and runs a small cybersecurity training company. Derek has completed three cybersecurity books and contributed a chapter for a fourth. He currently speaks at cybersecurity events throughout America and performs webinars for several companies as one of their cyber experts. Formerly, Derek worked for a number of IT companies, Computer Sciences Corporation and Booz Allen Hamilton, among them. Derek spent 18 years as a special agent for various government agencies and the military. He has also taught business and IT courses at several universities for over 25 years. Derek has served in the US Navy, Air Force, and Army for a total of 24 years. He completed an MBA, MS in IT Information Assurance, Masters in IT Project Management, MS in Digital Forensics, a BS in Education, and several associate degrees. He completed all but the dissertation for his doctorate.

Foreword

You almost can't read a news article or watch the nightly news these days without seeing some reference to hacking. One company after the next is falling victim to cybersecurity breach incidents and data loss, and the frequency of these data breaches has been accelerating over 10 years. It's almost to the point that these news events are so commonplace, we scarcely even pay them attention. We simply just accept that our most private information, from our financial records to our likes and dislikes, and even our genetic profile, is open for the public to read.

The problem in our new overconnected world is everyone wants everything immediately available at their fingertips. We want to shop from the convenience of our couch and have the items show up at our door—sometimes within hours of making our purchase decision. Or, we want to pay our friend back for buying lunch and ship funds from one electronic source to another with the click of a button. We bank online, shop online, talk online, play games online, and perform myriad other activities too numerous to list. More and more we are interconnecting every aspect of our lives and giving away our most precious commodity, our private information.

The majority of the world's users simply don't understand the value of what is being given away. One study estimated in 2020 the average Internet user to have 207 accounts. Seven of these will be for social media platforms alone. Unfortunately, the average user doesn't really understand what it takes to protect their accounts either. During a recent rollout of an SSO platform, I discovered how many users didn't understand that it took more than using their child's name as their password to protect their information. I was even asked why it all was necessary. Didn't the hackers already have all of this anyway?

The problem is, how do we really know who we are giving all this information to? More importantly, who are these companies then giving our information to? I can't tell you the number of times I've looked up some product or service on Google only to find it being offered at a discounted price the next time I'm shopping on Amazon. How often are the things we discuss on social media, our search histories, and buying habits used to "enhance" our online experience?

From a business perspective, it's a great model. The customers do all the work, provide all the information free of charge, and the business gets to reap the rewards. It's basically the business model Google was founded on—provide other businesses with targeted marketing research based on the consumers' search habits, for a fair price of course.

We all hope that the companies we interact with will protect our information the same way we would protect it ourselves. The truth is they often don't have the resources to accomplish this goal. It seems like every day a new attack vector is discovered. A new computer virus or malware is released, or a hacker publishes a new technique to bypass a company's defensive security tools. Typically, the tools the company spent their hard-earned resources installing, configuring, and deploying to prevent such an incident. This onslaught of attacks is simply draining for companies.

Unfortunately, the anonymity of the Internet offers a playground for the unscrupulous. It was recently estimated that the global cybercrime economy generates over 1.5 trillion in profits. Every technology platform available is currently being exploited somehow by someone for their own gains. I know I get at least five calls a week either telling me my car warranty has expired or my computer has been reporting malicious activity and they want to help "fix" it. Every piece of personal information I've shared online has somehow come back to be used against me as part of this nefarious worldwide theft.

Sadly, many organizations just don't take the necessary precautions to prevent the theft or misuse of the information we provide. Since the information security industry evolved from information technology (IT), there is a tendency to focus on the physical systems and networks while neglecting to adequately address the users and system admins. You might think, in today's world, information security professionals would be ten steps ahead. The inexplicable truth is many just simply aren't. I'm not sure if it's caused by too much work, a lack of time, or the simple lack of understanding, but the impact is the same; everyone's private information is at risk.

If you read any modern breach report, you'll find that some percentage of every data breach around the world involves some sort of account compromise. Most of these reports estimate between 80 and 95% depending. No real big surprises there. If you want to steal information, you're going to need access to it. However, the big surprise is how often it's the compromise of an IT administrator's credentials that lead to the loss.

Long gone are the days when we can think of the "hacker" as some mischievous or disaffected teenager in their basement, using an acoustic coupling modem to dial up NORAD and start World War III. They're not even hanging out in a wine cellar with Halle Berry, watching a green screen graphic cube "hack" into a bank to siphon $9.5 billion from government slush funds. Today (2020), it's more likely to be some sophisticated organization gaining access through an unprotected supply chain and infecting the downstream product, or, alternatively, some company employee who ends up with more access to information than they need.

If we really take a precise look at the problem, we find that administrative privilege is commonly exploited in most modern "hacking" practices. If the threat actor can find a way to give a user more access than needed, or create a new account on a system they can use, these often go unnoticed by system administrators. In 2019, the average time it took to identify a data breach was 206 days. That means the "hacker" would have more than 6 months to steal any information they want, before even being detected by the company. That doesn't include the time it would take to figure out all the access they have and remove it from all the systems.

The legitimate use of admin privileges is a business necessity in today's technologically dependent environments. However, exploits to misuse privileges tend to outpace the innovations to protect against them. For example, many legacy applications that are still used by companies can't support modern authentication practices to ensure administrators are valid. Many systems don't protect user accounts with encryption or other general functions used to protect administrator access. Even some administrators don't want to be burdened with two-factor authentication or any restrictions they perceive would impede their ability to support their organization in times of need.

Today's businesses are a complex set of technologies, people, and processes. They simply can't update everything and everyone to the most modern solutions available all the time. There is always going to be something, an old operating system, a custom application, or a long-standing process, that will need to be maintained.

In this second edition of *Privileged Attack Vectors*, Morey will help you understand the current threats to privileged accounts and why properly managing them is so important. This book will provide a road map to understand how to protect against a breach, protect against lateral movement, and improve the ability to detect hacker activity or insider threats in order to mitigate the impact. There is no silver bullet to guarantee you'll have all the protection you need against all vectors and stages of an attack, but this *Privileged Attack Vectors* will arm you with the tools and strategy necessary to stand a fighting chance.

David Tyburski

Vice President of Information Security and CISO

Wynn Resorts

Acknowledgments

Contributions by:

Contributing Editor: Matt Miller

Product Management: Brian Chappell

Deputy CTO: Christopher Hills

Illustrations and Graphics:

- Angela Duggan

- Hannah Reed

- Greg Francendese

Marketing:

- Stacy Blaiss

- Liz Drysdale

And a special thank you to Daniel DeRosa, the Chief Product Officer at BeyondTrust, for his contributions on PAM strategy and machine learning.

Introduction

In quantum mechanics, the observer effect[1] theory asserts that the mere observation or measurement of a system or event unavoidably alters that which it is observing/measuring. In other words, the tools or methods used for measurement or observation interfere with the system or event they are interacting with in some way.

As one example, consider the measurement of voltage across a circuit or battery. A voltmeter must draw a very small, but measurable, amount of current in order to make the calculation. This lowers the overall current (I) ultimately available to a system. If the measurement was intrusive or did not have a sufficiently high resistance (R) (Ohm's law—voltage equals current multiplied by resistance), the available current and potential voltage (V) would be impacted as well.

While the effects of measurement are commonly negligible, the object under observation or utilization may still experience a change. And sometimes, these changes can alter our perception of the entire system because the measurement itself is much more intrusive than anticipated, or initially designed. This effect can be found in domains ranging everywhere from physics to electronics—and even digital marketing.

This concept is fundamentally important in the world of privileged attack vectors because the more a privileged account is used, exposed, or made readily available, just like a measurement, the higher risk it has to an environment. To that end, let's begin by diving into the role the observer effect plays in the realm of cybersecurity and home in on the importance of keeping privileges secure.

---

[1]The Observer Effect in Quantum Mechanics—www.scienceabc.com/pure-sciences/observer-effect-quantum-mechanics.html

The Cybersecurity Observer Effect

Every measurement used for a cybersecurity check impacts the overall system. This is true for a simple antivirus check, all the way through resources used for logging. CPU, time to load, memory, network traffic, and others can each be altered in the course of providing a security measurement for some activity.

Ideally, a security measurement should operate with little to no impact, but how often is this really the case? Can frictionless, no-impact security actually be successfully implemented within an environment? The answer may surprise you and the observer effect plays a big part.

As we have established, every IT security measurement does alter a system and, in so doing, consumes resources and potentially changes the risk surface for an environment. If all of the measurements are serial, elongated by time, each one adds a piece of information to the overall measurement to calculate an observable outcome. The total resource consumption becomes cumulative and is calculated by storage, authentication time, changes or elongation in workflow, transmission of data, and auditing of all data logged as a part of the assessment.

However, when measurements and logical decisions are performed in parallel (provided the system has enough resources to perform them simultaneously), then the amount of time needed to perform a measurement can be reduced and the perceived impact to the user minimized because the measure is in a finite timeframe and is not persistently reoccurring. This is basically parallel processing. To achieve no-impact security (truly, we're talking about minimal-impact or as-frictionless-as-possible security), security measurements and operational logic should occur alongside regular processes in parallel, and *only when needed*. This is contrary to typical measurements that might occur at fixed intervals or batches where anomalies or security incidents like an unauthorized remote session could occur between measured intervals. These could be potentially missed unless all logs are processed for connection history (in parallel) in lieu of just checking if a session is active at a point in time. If you had to constantly monitor for a remote session, the observer effect would clearly have a resource impact vs. looking for a trigger, in parallel, to determine a remote session is active and to begin measurements.

Therefore, cybersecurity measurements are best conducted when a baseline has been established and changes occur—authorized or not. While a periodic test of the baseline is a security best practice, checking for the same thing over and over on a static resource is a waste of resources. This is true for disciplines like vulnerability management that assess for the same vulnerabilities over and over again, even though nothing has changed on the asset. Detecting that a change occurred and performing a new measurement, plus reviewing any historical logging for context, minimize the observer effect in cybersecurity measurements. When this is applied to privileged accounts, all aspects—from discovery to session monitoring—can ensure that privilege monitoring and management is low impact to the user and does not create the resource issues we have been describing (i.e., checking for privileged activity and usage over and over again).

Consider the following two real-world cybersecurity scenarios when trying to measure access.

Scenario 1

Before any multi-factor or two-factor authentication can occur to a resource, the security tool introduces new steps in the workflow to validate the user. In addition to traditional credentials, a second factor is included to provide physical validation of the user. That is, I have something in my possession to help prove that I am authorized to use an account. It does not prove the user's identity, however. That is a different discussion and another book.[2] This adds time and resources, as well as a level of

---

[2]Morey Haber and Darran Rolls, *Identity Attack Vectors* (Apress, 2019).

annoyance, to end users. Single sign-on (SSO) technology mitigates some of this annoyance by only requiring two-factor authentication once to a group of resources and passing through authentication—since the user is already considered trusted for that session.

As described earlier, the first launch of two-factor initiated a workflow to validate the user for subsequent applications vs. requiring them to repeatedly relaunch two-factor. The process of single sign-on is now running in parallel to the user's normal operations and, in fact, provides a lower impact than requiring credentials each time the application is launched—even without two-factor authentication. The user just logs in without any additional challenge and response. So, the measurement of the user's trust was done once intrusively with additional steps, but subsequently made easier because of the high confidence in the initial measurement. Logging continues to occur in parallel with each new application launch to audit for activity.

The alternative method is highly intrusive and would require credentials and two-factor authentication for every application launched by the end user in a serial workflow and based on the policy to provide multi-factor authentication for every application launch. This underscores the necessity of parallel processing and a simple model for creating a secure, frictionless environment. Measure only when needed and minimize the observer effect.

Scenario 2

Consider the password storage capabilities within a password safe or password vault technology. Enterprise versions of these solutions can automatically rotate passwords (and certificates) on a schedule or based on usage, such that they are ever-changing and not a liability if known by a threat actor—whether an insider or external. The more that they are exposed, utilized, or documented externally (measured), the higher risk they represent.

If a user or administrator needs to use these credentials, the typical workflow involves authenticating into the password safe or vault (hopefully using the two-factor discussed earlier) and retrieving the credentials needed to perform a specific task. From a workflow perspective, simply measuring when privileged credentials are being accessed by a user and providing the current password is intrusive to the end user due to the additional steps required to obtain them. For example, the user has additional mouse clicks, time, and applications to complete the task while potentially creating additional risk of copying the password into memory using the clipboard (copy/paste) or even physically exposing it by writing it down on paper. While this is the primary use case to measure privileged access by documenting when privileged credentials were requested, it provides little security if we cannot reliably determine when, where, and how the credentials are being used. This is a high-impact model that needs to change from both a resource and risk perspective. Both are negative impacts with regard to the observer effect.

Next, consider session monitoring and management. This will be discussed in detail later in this book, but the capability provides a gateway, or proxy technology, into a host for monitoring sessions, and potentially documenting, all security and user activity. Session management is essentially a low-impact method to monitor what is actually happening when a privileged session occurs, but it requires the remote connection to occur through the proxy, as opposed to a lateral connection, in order to be effective. Essentially, there has to be a man in the middle in order to perform the session monitoring, even if it is dedicated software that reports its findings to a proxy or gateway based on local or remote access.

Without proper access control lists (ACLs), a password retrieval from a safe allows for remote access without any session monitoring capabilities. This is an undesirable state as there are no measurements since the session can occur without using the proxy. When we consider password storage, retrieval, rotation, and session monitoring as a solution working in parallel, we can measure activity down to the keystroke and can create a very low-impact session management implementation. And, if this entire workflow can measure all activity and privileged access based on the account or user, then the observer effect becomes a moot point for a successful privileged account management model.

To that end, password storage solutions alone can be intrusive to the workflow for password retrieval. Session monitoring by itself is vulnerable to security flaws like lateral movement. When used together as a strategy for universal privilege management, the two solutions can operate in parallel to create a near no-impact security solution.

Mitigating the Observer Effect in Cybersecurity

The observer effect presents an ongoing concern for cybersecurity practitioners. Many solutions can have a high impact on the runtime within an environment and create undesirable delays, single points of failure, and changes that negatively impact users, operations, and productivity. The worst problems can cause even the best solutions to become shelfware since the end users push back and resist adoption.

Measuring and implementing security will always have some impact, but the goal is to make it as unperceivable as possible—especially to the end users. While zero impact is truly unobtainable, the concept of little to no impact after initial setup is definitely viable.

When you evaluate security solutions from a single vendor, or multiple vendors, ask how the solutions can operate in parallel or be used in tandem to create a no-impact environment. After all, if they all run serially or have a high impact, users will not only reject them, your ability to obtain accurate cybersecurity measurements will also suffer due to the resources required to collect necessary data. Now, let us apply this to modern cybersecurity findings.

The Observer Effect in the Real World

Each year, Verizon publishes its Data Breach Investigations Report[3] (DBIR), and BeyondTrust publishes its Privileged Access Threat Report.[4] Each report provides valuable data for information and security technology professionals around cybersecurity trends, perceptions, cyberattack methods, causes of breaches, and more—all observer-based. With both reports now available, security professionals can make further deductions about cyberthreats, particularly the most dangerous ones—privileged threats—along with the best strategies to mitigate them.

Top Privileged Threats

In June 2019, BeyondTrust published the Privileged Access Threat Report. In this report, the organization surveyed over 1000 IT decision-makers across a diverse set of industries throughout the United States, EMEA, and APAC to gauge the perceived threats facing organizations and the risks of privileged attack vectors. The survey generated some noteworthy data around breaches and poor cybersecurity practices:

- About **64%** of respondents thought it is likely that they've suffered a breach due to employee access, and **58%** indicated that they likely suffered a breach due to vendor access.

---

[3]Data Breach Investigations Report (DBIR)—https://enterprise.verizon.com/resources/reports/dbir/

[4]Privileged Access Threat Report—www.beyondtrust.com/resources/whitepapers/privileged-access-threat-report

- About **62%** of respondents were worried about
  the unintentional mishandling of sensitive data by
  employees based on the following poor security
  practices:

    - Writing down passwords (**60%**)

    - Downloading data onto an external memory stick
      (**60%**)

    - Sending files to personal email accounts (**60%**)

    - Telling colleagues their passwords (**58%**)

    - Logging in over unsecured Wi-Fi (**57%**)

    - Staying logged on (**56%**)

- About **71%** of respondents agreed that their company
  would be more secure if they restricted employee
  device access.

But what are the attack vectors that drive these opinions—and fears?

According to the 2020 Verizon Data Breach Investigation Report
(DBIR), **use of stolen credentials** is the second most common threat
activity attackers leverage to breach an environment, just below
phishing. In addition, the DBIR also reveals that over 80% of breaches
classified as hacking involve brute force or the use of lost or stolen
credentials.

Stolen credentials are most often used on mail servers, leading to
a variety of identity-based attack vectors. Unfortunately, the actual
techniques used for obtaining and applying stolen credentials are not
covered in the Verizon report. But that doesn't mean the answers are
beyond our grasp and something we cannot measure.

According to the PATR, it is reasonable to conclude that well more than half of employees and vendors have been the source of a breach and also that poor cybersecurity hygiene for credentials and passwords is the prime cause for these breaches.

Combining the Verizon and BeyondTrust data points, we can deduce the following as the top privileged attack vector techniques used, as well as why they are an unacceptable risk for any business:

- Password guessing

- Dictionary attacks or rainbow tables

- Brute force attacks

- Pass the hash (PtH) or other memory-scraping techniques

- Security question social engineering

- Account hijacking based on predictable password resets

- Privileged vulnerabilities and exploits

- Misconfigurations

- Malware, like keystroke loggers

- Social engineering (phishing, etc.)

- MFA flaws using weak 2FA, like SMS

- Default system or application credentials

- Anonymous or enabled Guest access

- Predictable password patterns

- Shared or unmanaged, stale credentials

- Temporary passwords

- Reused passwords or credentials

- Shadow or obsolete (former employee) credentials

- Various hybrid credential attacks (i.e., spray attacks) based on variations of the above

These two reports alone are supported by analysts like Forrester. Forrester Research[5] estimates that privileged credentials are implicated in over 80% of data breaches.

Mitigating Privileged Attack Vectors

Now, the question becomes, "What can organizations and users do to resolve these privileged attack vectors?"

To begin, consider the following universal cybersecurity best practices regarding credential and password management:

- All privileged accounts (administrator and root) should be monitored for appropriate activity and have proper certifications based on roles and ownership.

- Users should always perform their daily computing activities as a Standard User and only use a privileged account when absolutely necessary and appropriate.

- When possible, administrative privileges should be removed or eliminated, and end users, administrators, DevOps processes, and RPA (robotic process automation) should operate using the concept of least privilege.

---

[5]Forrest Wave—www.beyondtrust.com/resources/whitepapers/
the-forrester-wave-privileged-identity-management-q4-2018

- All accounts, regardless of operating system or application, should have a unique password whenever, and wherever, possible. The credential rotation and management practices should be based on policy and guided by considerations such as regulatory compliance and other security best practices, like NIST.

- All sessions, locally initiated or remotely started, should honor all of the best practices listed and, when possible, avoid the implementation of always-on privileged accounts. The concept of just-in-time-privileged access can help implement these best practices.

While the implementation of these concepts may seem daunting and unachievable for many organizations, these goals are practical and well within your reach, but they do require your adoption of a formal privileged access management (PAM) program. This is often referred to as a PAM journey. In addition, when PAM is implemented correctly, it can mitigate threats illustrated by the observer effect in the real world and, most importantly, provide a frictionless approach to securing your universe of privileges. That is the key. If any of this journey introduces measurements that impact resources or provide a poor user experience, it will fail.

Therefore, here is what a successful PAM journey within an organization encompasses, and what we will detail in great lengths through the remainder of this book:

- Password management for rotation and check-in and checkout of passwords.

- Session management for recording, indexing, filtering, and documenting of all interactive sessions.

- Endpoint privilege management to remove administrative or root privileges on any platform including Windows, MacOS, Unix, Linux, and even network devices like routers, switches, printers, and IoT devices.

- Secure remote access to establish sessions based on personas (i.e., vendors or help desk staff), with least privilege credentials and the need to share credentials with approved operators.

- Directory bridging to consolidate logon accounts across non-Windows systems, like Unix and Linux. This enables users, regardless of persona, to authenticate using their Active Directory credentials in lieu of local accounts.

- Management of next-generation technologies from ICS to IoT and all of the automation technologies in between, from RPA to DevOps.

- User behavior analytics and reporting to provide complete attestation reporting, certifications, and alerting on inappropriate behavior based on privileged usage.

- The cloud, just-in-time administration, and zero trust all play a major part in the strategy for almost every modern organization. Embracing PAM as a journey with these tactical concepts will help ensure the observer effect for privilege management does not impact their deployment.

- The complete integration of all the preceding capabilities within an organization's established ecosystem for change management, ticketing, operational workflow, identity governance, and security information and event managers (SIEMs).

These practices ensure that privileged credentials and passwords are vigorously resistant to hacking attempts. In addition, should the credentials ever become compromised, the risk and damage from any exploit can be mitigated by keeping them unique among resources and having the least privileges necessary—and for a time-limited duration—to perform necessary, authorized actions. One key piece of least privilege involves reducing the privileges of the credentials to those of a standard user, which makes it exceedingly difficult for a threat actor to use privileged attack vectors (stolen credentials) as a method of compromise.

Finally ask yourself one honest question, "How confident are you in your own organization's PAM abilities?" If you have any doubts about your PAM posture, then this book is for you and will guide you along a safe and successful PAM journey.

CHAPTER 1

Privileged Attack Vectors

We see it in the news and on social media nearly every single day—another cybersecurity incident, breach, hack, or attack. From a forensics perspective, the vast majority of attacks originate from outside the organization and, therefore, are initiated by external threat actors. While the specific tactics may vary, the stages of an external attack are similar (see Figure 1-1).

1. **Infiltration—Insiders and External Threats**:
   The days of a threat actor attempting to penetrate the perimeter directly are no longer the primary threat to an organization. It is more than likely they will execute a successful campaign via attacking misconfigured resources with compromised privileged accounts, or launch a phishing attack to compromise a user's system, and establish a beachhead inside of an environment. Their goal is to do this all while flying "under the radar" of security defenses and maintain a persistent presence. The days of "smash and grab" attacks have faded away, just like attacks on the perimeter. And, with the expanding remote workforce, infiltration can occur through a combination of attack vectors, leaving an organization exploitable via methods outside of their management controls.

© Morey J. Haber 2020
M. J. Haber, *Privileged Attack Vectors*, https://doi.org/10.1007/978-1-4842-5914-6_1

2. **Command and Control Through the Internet**: Unless it is ransomware or self-contained malware, the attacker quickly establishes a connection to a command and control (C&C) server to download toolkits and additional payloads and to receive additional instructions. This allows them to assess the environment and plan their next move.

3. **Identify Privileged Accounts and Attempt Privileged Escalation**: Threat actors begin to learn about the network, infrastructure, privileged accounts, key identities, and the assets performing daily and critical functions. They start looking for opportunities to collect additional credentials, upgrade privileges, or just use the privileges that they have already compromised to access resources, applications, and data.

4. **Lateral Movement Between Assets, Accounts, Resources, and Identities**: Threat actors then leverage the stolen credentials and knowledge of the environment to compromise additional assets, resources, and identities (accounts) via lateral movement. This continues their campaign of propagation and navigation through the victim's environment.

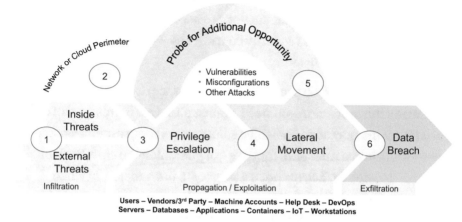

Figure 1-1. *Stages of an External Attack*

5. **Probing for Additional Opportunities**: While
    continuing to ascertain other weaknesses like
    vulnerabilities, misconfigured hosts, and additional
    privileged credentials, a threat actor's goal is to
    remain undetected. If their movement or presence
    is identified, most organizations will immediately
    strive to mitigate the incident. Therefore, operating
    in a stealth mode, the threat actor can identify
    more targets, install more malware or hacking
    tools, and expand their presence using additional
    attack vectors, from vulnerabilities to compromised
    identities.

6. **Data Exfiltration or Destruction**: Finally, the threat
    actor collects, packages, and eventually exfiltrates
    the data or, in the worst case, typically destroys
    your assets and resources based on their mission
    (i.e., ransomware). It is important to review that
    this entire attack chain can be performed by an

insider or external threat, as mentioned in step 1. The knowledge of an insider can accelerate all these steps and bypass security controls since they may be considered trusted.

There is no one single product in the cybersecurity industry today that will provide the protection you need against all stages in this type of attack. And while some new and innovative solutions will help protect against, or detect, the initial infection, they are not guaranteed to stop 100% of malicious activity. In fact, it's not a matter of if, but a matter of when you will be successfully breached. And, privileged accounts and their associated attack vectors will always be at the foundation of any successful breach outside of a vulnerability and exploit combination. You can read more about that in *Asset Attack Vectors*.[1]

Therefore, you will always need to do the basics—vulnerability management, patching, endpoint protection, threat detection, and so on. But you also need to protect, control, and audit the privileges in the environment. Properly managing privileges can help at all stages of the attack. From reducing the attack surface to protecting against lateral movement, to detecting a breach in progress, to actively responding and mitigating the impact of that breach—this is why I wrote this book. This book examines where these privilege vulnerabilities exist, how attackers can leverage them, and more importantly, what you can do about it. First, we need to understand what privileges really are and who is trying to leverage them for malicious intent.

---

[1]Morey J. Haber and Brad Hibbert, *Asset Attack Vectors* (Apress, 2018).

Threat Personas

Before we get into the gory details about privileges, let's spend a few minutes on who we are protecting ourselves from. An attack can originate from outside or inside an organization. They may be opportunistic, or well planned and targeted. They may be perpetrated by individuals or groups of individuals. To categorize their motives and tactics, we may refer to the perpetrators as hacktivists, terrorists, industrial spies, nation-states, cybercrime syndicates, or simply hackers.

There are subtle differences between a hacker, an attacker, a threat actor, and the malicious activity that they conduct that warrants proper definitions to be stated for daily conversations. Many times, security professionals will use the terms interchangeably and with little distinction between the definitions. As security professionals, we study recent breaches, we scour over forensic investigations, and, ultimately, wait for the arrests that will follow. Rarely do large-scale breaches go long unsolved. However, these cybercrimes can take years to prosecute based on extradition laws and whether a nation-state was involved. During these events, we learn about incidents, breaches, and whether it was a threat actor, hacker, or an attacker that caused the malicious activity.

The question is: What is the difference? After all, don't they all basically mean the same thing? The truth is they do not, and many times the various terms are misapplied in reporting a breach or cybersecurity incident. The proper definitions for each of our threat personas are as follows:

- **Threat Actor**: According to TechTarget, "A threat actor, also called a malicious actor, is an entity that is partially or wholly responsible for an incident that impacts – or has the potential to impact – an organization's security."

- **Hacker**: According to Merriam-Webster, "a person who illegally gains access to and sometimes tampers with information in a computer system."

- **Attacker**: In cybersecurity, an attacker is an individual, organization, or managed malware that attempts to destroy, expose, alter, disable, deny services, steal, or obtain unauthorized access to resources, assets, or data.

Based on these definitions, a breach or incident is typically conducted by a hacker. An attacker can also be a hacker and typically adds a layer of destruction to the situation. A threat actor, compared to a hacker or attacker, does not necessarily have any technical skill sets (see Table 1-1). They are a person or organization with malintent and a mission to compromise an organization's security or data. This could be anything from physical destruction to simply copying sensitive information. It is a broad term and is intentionally used because it can apply to external and insider threats, including their missions, like hacktivism, without actually performing a hack or an attack.

Table 1-1. *Threat Actor Examples*

Threat Actor	Example
External	Nation-State Sponsored
	Political Activist
	Organized Crime
	Opportunistic, Financially-Driven Attacker
	Terrorist Organization
Insiders	Administrators
	Developers
	Systems Users
	Data Owners
	Contractors
	Trusted Third Parties

Therefore, hackers and attackers are technical by nature and intentionally targeting technology to create an incident, and hopefully (for them, not you), a breach. They can be lone-wolf actors, groups, or even nation-states with goals and missions anywhere in the world. Their objectives may be to destabilize a business, create distrust between governments and citizens, disseminate sensitive information, or seek financial gains in the form of profiting from stolen data or ransomware.

The difference between an attacker and hacker is subtle, however. Hackers traditionally use vulnerabilities and exploits to conduct their activities. The results may be intentionally damaging, or they may just stem from curiosity. Attackers can use any means necessary to cause havoc. For example, an attacker may be a disgruntled insider who deletes sensitive files or disrupts the business by any means to achieve their goals. Remember, as these insiders have access to the target systems and data, they can simply use their granted access (privileges) to accomplish their goal. A hacker might do the same thing, but they use vulnerabilities, misconfigurations, stolen credentials, identity theft, and exploits to compromise a resource outside of their acceptable roles and privileges to gain access and accomplish their mission.

I believe it is important to grasp the distinctions between attacker, threat actor, and hacker. Security solutions are designed to protect against all three types of malicious personas, and the results will vary per organization:

- To defend against a **threat actor**, privileged access management (PAM) solutions can manage privileged access, log all activity in the form of session recordings and keystroke logging, monitor applications to ensure that a threat actor does not gain inappropriate internal or remote access, and document all sessions just in case they do (insider threats).

- To defend against a **hacker**, vulnerability management (VM) solutions are designed to identify vulnerabilities such as missing patches, weak passwords, and insecure configuration across operating systems, applications, and infrastructure to ensure that they can be remediated promptly. This closes the gaps that a hacker can use to compromise your environment. Most vulnerability management solutions help organizations measure the risk associated with these vulnerabilities such that they can prioritize remediation activities to reduce the attack surface as quickly and efficiently as possible. It is important to note that hackers can also use techniques associated with privileged attack vectors when the credentials used to secure a resource have been compromised.

- To defend against an **attacker**, least privilege solutions and network and host intrusion prevention solutions can be used to reduce the attack surface by removing the level of privileged access threat actors have to resources. This includes the removal of unnecessary administrator (or root) rights on applications and operating systems. These solutions can also perform detailed access and behavior auditing to detect compromised accounts and privilege misuse.

A combination of these solutions not only prevents outsider attacks, but limits privileges to assets and identities, thereby inhibiting lateral movement. This is the basis for protecting against the privileged attack vector and will be discussed in detail in later chapters. In addition, it is also modeled at the highest level as the three pillars of cybersecurity: asset, privileges, and identities. All security products can be classified in one of these pillars, and the most effective solutions gravitate toward the center, with functional overlap in each area. Figure 1-2 illustrates this in the form of a basic Venn diagram.

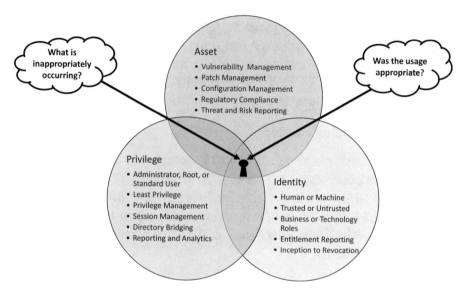

Figure 1-2. *The Three Pillars of Cybersecurity*

However, let us not get ahead of ourselves. This concept is more about the solution chosen to solve the problem vs. an understanding of the problem and attack vectors themselves. Let's start with a review of the basic elements of privilege before formulating our defense.

Regardless of their motives—from financial to hacktivism to nation-state, threat actors, hackers, and attackers will almost always take the path of least resistance to commit their malicious activity. While this path may sometimes leave obvious trails for forensics, the art of the hack is to be subversive without detection (if possible) and perpetuate the activity under the radar of the implemented security defenses. Attackers, like most people, will choose the path of least resistance. Fortunately, the methods for gaining user and application privileges are well known due to various attacks and exploits. This leads us to a formal definition of what is a privilege:

> *A special right or permission granted, or available only to, a particular person or group to perform special or sensitive operations upon or within a resource. These are typically associated within information technology as administrator or root accounts or groups and any accounts that may have been granted elevated entitlements.*

And what is an attack vector:

> *An attack vector is a path or means by which a hacker, attacker, or threat actor can gain access to a computer or network resource to perpetrate a malicious outcome. Attack vectors enable the exploitation of resources based on privileges, assets, and identities (accounts) and can include technology and human elements.*

Now it is time to explore these malicious activities and potential defenses so that privileges do not become a successful attack vector for anyone against your organization. The strategy to protect against them is commonly referred to as privileged access management (PAM). However, in the eyes of the security community and some analysts, you may see this discipline referred to as PIM or PUM (privileged identity management or privileged user management). While similar, there are subtle distinctions, just as with the different types of adversaries we reviewed earlier.

CHAPTER 2

Privileges

Today, privileges based on credentials are one of the lowest-hanging fruits in the attack chain. They are currently the easiest method for a threat actor to own a resource and, ultimately, the entire environment. These threats include

1. Insiders having excessive and unmonitored access to accounts, opening the potential for misuse and abuse

2. Insiders that have had their accounts compromised through successful phishing, social engineering, or other tactics

3. Accounts that have been compromised as the result of weak credentials, passwords, devices, and application models, allowing attackers to compromise systems and obtain privileges for malicious activity

To recognize how privileges can be used as a successful attack vector, a better understanding of the definition of privileges needs to be established above what has been previously discussed. In plain English, a privilege is a special right or an advantage. It is an elevation above the normal and not a setting or permission given to the masses. An example is the relationship to education. "Education is a right, not a privilege."[1] Everyone has the right

---

[1]www.globalpartnership.org/blog/education-right-not-privilege

© Morey J. Haber 2020
M. J. Haber, *Privileged Attack Vectors*, https://doi.org/10.1007/978-1-4842-5914-6_2

to education and, thus, in the information technology world, is analogous to a Standard User. A standard user has the same basic rights as almost everyone else; they are not privileged. Therefore, in a typical organization, standard users have rights that are global to all authenticated users—just like an education. As these user accounts are created and provisioned, they are granted these standard rights. This could be basic access to company-wide applications, the ability to access the Internet or intranet, or productivity applications, such as email. A privileged user has rights above that. This may include the ability to install other software, change settings within their local machine or application, or perform other routine tasks like adding a new printer. This does not mean they are an administrator. It means they have been granted privileges, at a granular level, above the baseline of Standard User to perform these tasks. This granularity can have as many levels as an organization deems necessary based on the roles and job responsibilities for its users. The most basic interpretation contains only two levels:

1. **Standard User**: Shared rights granted to all users for trusted tasks.

2. **Administrator**: A broad set of privileged rights granted for managing all aspects of a system and its resources. This includes installing software, managing configuration settings, applying patches, managing users, and so on.

However, most organizations will define privileges across five fundamental levels:

1. **No Access**: This means you do not have a user account, or your account has been disabled or deleted. This is the denial of any form of privileged access, even anonymously.

2. **Guest**: Restricted access and rights below a standard user. Often, this is associated with anonymous access.

3. **Standard User**: Shared rights granted to all users for trusted tasks.

4. **Power User**: A power user has all the entitlements of a standard user, plus additional granular privileges to perform specific tasks. They are not an administrator or root, but have been trusted to perform specific tasks that are typically associated with administrators.

5. **Administrator**: Authorized permissions (in the form of privileges) to alter or abuse the asset's runtime, configuration, settings, managed users, and installed software and patches. This can also be further classified into local administrator rights and domain administrative rights affecting more than one resource.

While this perspective of privileges is at a macro-user level, it is essential to understand the micro-level of permissions down to the token and file to formulate a proper defense. It is myopic to consider privileges are only a part of the application you are executing. Privileges must be built into the operating system, file system, application, database, hypervisor, cloud management platform, and even network via segmentation to be effective for a user and application-to-application communications. This is true if the authentication is granted by any mechanism ranging from a username and password to a certificate key pair. The resource's interpretation of the privileges cannot be just at any one layer to be truly effective. It must be available across the entire stack. To that end, let's explore privileges based on each level, excluding no access.

Guest Users

As a Guest User, your privileges are strictly limited to specific functions and tasks you can perform. In many organizations, guests are restricted to isolated network segments with basic access—perhaps access to the Internet for visiting vendors. If these unmanaged computers are, or become, compromised, the risk is mitigated by limiting access to the organization's resources, especially via lateral movement. For example, a network scan from a compromised guest machine will not (or at least should not) provide the attacker direct access to corporate systems and data, regardless of whether they are connected via Ethernet or wirelessly.

Standard Users

As a Standard User, you have select privileges beyond that of a Guest to perform additional tasks and to fulfill the mission that is associated with your job and role. While organizations may forego implementing Guest Users, it is typical to have granular levels between a Standard User and a Full Administrator. These are often referred to as power users. Typical organizations may have 100s or 1000s of different standard user roles designed to balance access and efficiency with risk. Each role has been granted access to specific systems, applications, resources, and data required for their specific job. In many cases, a user may be a member of multiple groups, depending on their specific job requirements. For example, low-access roles (also called basic roles, basic entitlements, and birth rights when discussing identity governance) are typically provided to each organizational user (employee, contractor) to provide basic access. As an example, this could provide access to email and the corporate intranet. Next would be specific roles that would add more access based on the job function or role itself. See Figure 2-1 for a very basic example of a role hierarchy in a typical environment.

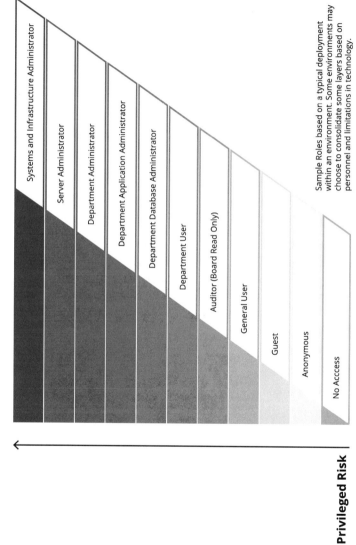

Figure 2-1. Example of a Role Hierarchy in a Typical Environment

15

In this example, the banding and nesting of granular permissions within business roles may allow specific users access to a web server, but not access to a database, or vice versa. From the perspective of a threat actor, compromising accounts with elevated privileged rights is typically the target as these credentials are the ones that have access to sought-after systems and data. As a rule of thumb, the more administrative functions you are required to perform, the more administrative privileges you have. In addition, as you go up the hierarchy from sole contributor to executive, the fewer privileges you should have. Unfortunately, in many organizations, that is not always the case, and it is bad security practice when navigating on your PAM journey.

With this in mind, malicious activity does not require full-domain administrative or root rights (even though that reduces technical barriers and makes it easier for them to conduct nefarious activity). For example, if the user is a manufacturing floor worker, their potential privileges are limited by their job role (barring a vulnerability and successful exploit). If the target user is an information technology administrator, such as a server administrator, desktop administrator, database administrator, or application administrator, the associated privilege risk will be higher as these employees have been granted additional access as defined by their role. This makes them desirable targets for a threat actor. Take, for example, a threat actor who wants to gain access to a corporate database or file system with sensitive unstructured data (see Figure 2-2).

Threat Actor

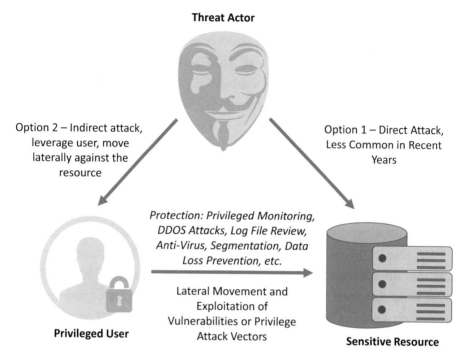

Option 2 – Indirect attack, leverage user, move laterally against the resource

Option 1 – Direct Attack, Less Common in Recent Years

Protection: Privileged Monitoring, DDOS Attacks, Log File Review, Anti-Virus, Segmentation, Data Loss Prevention, etc.

Lateral Movement and Exploitation of Vulnerabilities or Privilege Attack Vectors

Privileged User

Sensitive Resource

Figure 2-2. *Example of an Attacker Who Wants to Gain Access to a Corporate Database or File System with Sensitive Data*

Does the threat actor:

1. Attempt to directly attack the hardened database or system housing the sensitive data. This is a system that is likely patched and monitored and incorporates advanced threat detection and attack shielding technologies due to its sensitivity and regulatory compliance requirements.

2. Use a phishing attack to compromise the system/ database administrator and steal those credentials to log directly into the target system, impersonating a legitimate user.

Having privileged access to an application, its database, or supporting file system is all that is needed to extract information once an internal beachhead has been established. This attack vector can also potentially allow the threat actor to execute commands, perform lateral movement, and exfiltrate the data regardless of whether they are an external or internal threat.

Additionally, many organizations grant more privileges than are required for a specific job, which leads to increased risk from both hackers and attackers. For example, many organizations still allow users to have administrative control over their desktops simply for convenience or due to legacy applications that require administrative rights.

It is also important to note that recent attacks are beginning to focus on nontraditional assets that may lack the flexibility and control required in today's sophisticated threat environment. With some systems, the access options are very Boolean. You have access, or you do not. When you do, you are an administrator and have complete control. This is primarily true for consumer devices that do not have any concept of role-based access, but it's also true for many Internet of Things (IoT) devices, legacy systems, and even next-generation technologies used for manufacturing, automation, and robotic control.

Power User

A power user is an elevated use case of a standard user that engages with applications and resources that need unique, sensitive, or advanced features that are not entitled to be used by the average standard user. A power user may not have extensive technical knowledge of the resources they operate, but have the competence or role to operate within privileged guidelines to perform specific tasks.

Also, within an organization, a power user may be a formal role given to an individual, and they may be considered the specialist for a particular software, role, or resource. Often, these are people who are trained to perform advanced functions above their typical job role, and, thus, given privileges to do so. Power users represent the universe between standard users and full-blown administrators based on explicit privileges granted to perform specific tasks. Again, they are not administrators, but based on the privileges they have been granted, they can be a source of privileged attack vectors. This is especially true if they are overprovisioned, unmonitored, or the entitlements they have been granted abused since their privileges allow them access to potentially sensitive tasks.

Finally, some common roles that are associated with power users are typically found within development, help desk staff, application and database administrators (even though they are not granted administrative or root privileges), and even engineering.

Administrators

As an Administrator or Root User, you "own" the system and all its resources. All functions, tasks, and capabilities are potentially within your control, and even if technology is deployed to block an administrator, being an administrator means there is still likely a way, or backdoor, around the restrictions. This leads to the premise that once you are an administrator, the security game is over. An administrator can circumvent any protection designed to protect against an administrator, even if the results are destructive to the processes themselves.

Obtaining administrator or root access represents privileged access that is considered the crown jewels to a threat actor. Once the threat actor has root access and can operate undetected, then any system, application, or data is potentially within their reach. Gaining privileges is the ultimate attack vector for breaching an organization, government, or even end-user–based computing device. Again, in this case, organizations tend to grant too many unmanaged administrator privileges, which leads to significant risk posed by threat actors and insiders. One of the primary use cases for PAM is to remove these unnecessary privileges and only grant the ones that are explicitly needed, and just for the moments in time they are required. This will be discussed in more detail later in the book.

Identity Management

The process of defining, managing, and assigning these roles to ensure that the "right" people have the "right" access at the "right" time is known as identity and access management (IAM). It is a specific solution family within identity governance. These "rights," including role-based access and permissions, are called entitlements. Privileged access management (PAM) typically complements traditional IAM processes and solutions with additional layers of control and auditing for "privileged" accounts. These are the accounts that pose the greatest risk to the organization. Figure 2-3 shows the relationship of PAM to identity governance as defined by the Identity Defined Security Alliance (IDSA).

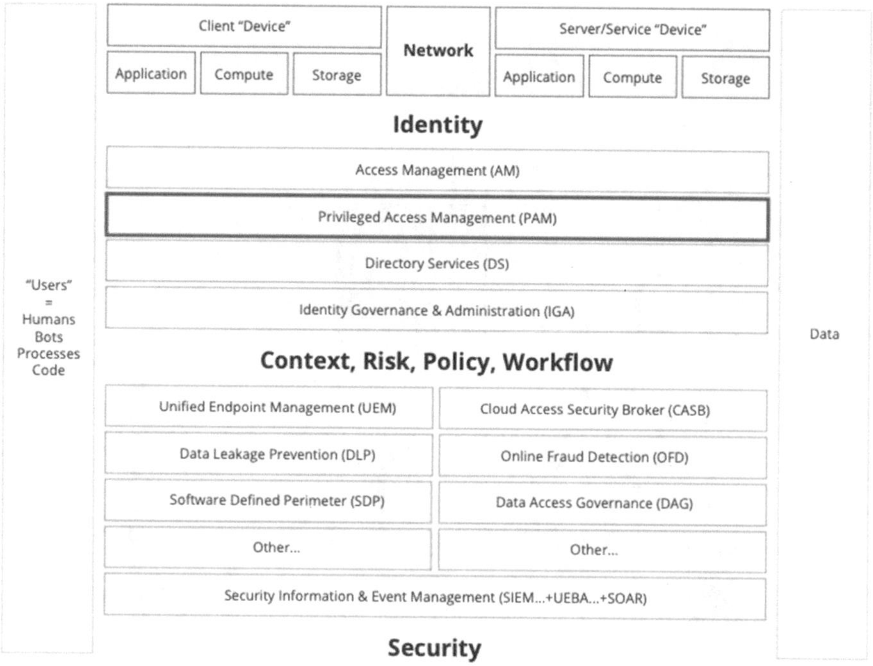

Client "Device"			Network	Server/Service "Device"		
Application	Compute	Storage		Application	Compute	Storage

Identity

Access Management (AM)

Privileged Access Management (PAM)

Directory Services (DS)

Identity Governance & Administration (IGA)

"Users"
=
Humans
Bots
Processes
Code

Data

Context, Risk, Policy, Workflow

Unified Endpoint Management (UEM)	Cloud Access Security Broker (CASB)
Data Leakage Prevention (DLP)	Online Fraud Detection (OFD)
Software Defined Perimeter (SDP)	Data Access Governance (DAG)
Other...	Other...

Security Information & Event Management (SIEM...+UEBA...+SOAR)

Security

Figure 2-3. *Identity Defined Security Alliance Framework (IDSA), 2019*

To better understand the scope of privilege risks, please reference Figure 2-4. In many situations, a lack of visibility and control over privileged accounts, users, and assets could leave you exposed to a damaging data breach. That visibility often begins with a simple discovery exercise through all assets within an organization. Ergo, let's first take a look at where these privileged accounts exist. Then, once we get a complete picture of the scope of the challenge, we can discuss some strategies to address it.

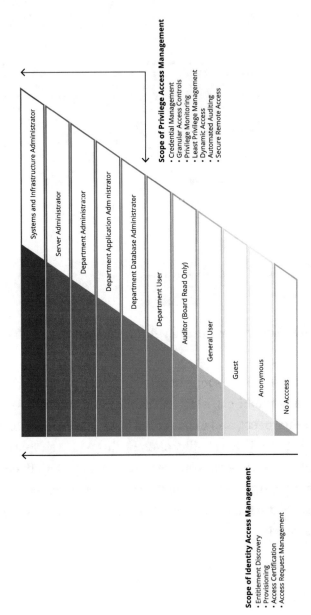

Figure 2-4. *Lack of Visibility and Control Could Lead to a Data Breach*

Although this perspective of privileges is at a macro-user level (identity management), it is imperative to understand the micro-level of permissions down to the token and file to formulate a proper defense. It is again a mistake to consider privileges are only a part of the application you are executing. Privileges must be built into the operating system, file system, application, and even network via segmentation (often zero trust) to be effective for a user and application-to-application communications. The resource interpretation of the privileges cannot be just at any one layer to be truly effective. Thus, identity management only provides access to the resource by scope or role. In contrast, privileged access management provides the granular permissions needed when the operating system or application is incapable of providing these privileges itself. It is fair to state that PAM is a subset of IAM and an extension to protect privileges at every level.

Identities

For the sake of definitions, and commonly misused within the industry, an identity is simply a carbon-based life form (and a quick shout-out to all my fellow Star Trek fans. Spoiler alert—Decker and V'ger created the Borg, and it was all Kirk's fault for allowing it to happen). It is any human being or user that interacts with resources, from applications to operating systems. This includes physical and electronic access and is a convenient way of saying I am a person. "I think; therefore, I am," and I have an identity. A user should only have a single identity.

In addition, in modern computing environments, an identity can also be assigned to a piece of information technology. These are typically devices like mail robots or other technology that interacts with the real world in a physical nature. Electronic identities are not software or applications, but rather devices that can take on human traits. It is important to note that any technology assigned an identity can have multiple accounts, just like a human identity, but they also have a unique attribute to designate its owner. That is the human identity (or group) that is responsible for the electronic identity by reference of an owner tag.

For human identities, security best practices become blurred when people assume different names, including having maiden names, and they may have duplicate identities referenced electronically in an organization. To be clearer, they still have only one identity, but may have electronic instantiations to multiple identities, which should not be confused with having multiple accounts. Organizations should only have one identity for a person, like their social security number (which is a bad practice due to personally identifiable information), or preferably an employee number—one person, one identity, and one electronic reference linking them. Then, they can have multiple accounts. As an additional security best practice, the number of accounts should be minimized and easily linkable back to the proper identity.

Accounts

An account is an electronic representation of an identity or reference for a set of permissions and privileges needed for an application or resource to connect or operate within the confines of the system. While the definition of an account is evident for an identity, it can take on a variety of forms when used electronically for services, impersonations, and application-to-application functions. Accounts can have a one-to-many relationship with identities, be defined locally, grouped, or managed via directory services. Accounts can have role-based access applied at the account level, group level, within a directory, and these can range from disabled (denied access) to privileged accounts such as root, local administrator, or domain admin. The level of privileges and role-based access is dependent on the security model of the system implementing them and can vary significantly from one implementation to another.

Therefore, accounts linked to identities are how we gain access to information technology resources. For technology itself, accounts are a vehicle to authorize their usage, provide development automation, and supply operational parameters. Too much privilege given to any type of account can introduce risk, and accounts can literally be named and referenced to almost anything, and are subject to limitations within any system. For example, some systems may not allow the renaming of an administrator account even though it is a security best practice to do so. Accounts are literally a reference field to provide authentication, and an account may or may not have a password or key. When a password is assigned, regardless of its strength, type, or security, it becomes a credential.

Credentials

A credential is an account with an associated password, passcode, certificate, or other type of potentially secret key. Credentials can have more than one security mechanism assigned for dual or multi-factor authentication, or be basic Guest credentials for anyone to access— without the need for a secret key or by using a common, known key. Credentials are just a mere representation of the account-password combination needed for authentication. They are, nonetheless, the crown jewels for any threat actor to begin an escalation of privileges.

When an attacker indicates that they have "hacked" an account, what they mean is that they have hacked the credentials associated with the account. Literally hacking an account would only yield a username. Both the username and password are needed to compromise a system, and potentially its data, successfully. Thus, for the sake of simplicity in the remainder of this book, hacking an account means the same thing as hacking credentials. It is difficult enough to manage privileges in an environment rather than worrying about the semantics used every day in describing the threat. Security professionals and the press will probably never change in saying one million accounts were compromised, when, in fact, one million credentials were compromised. See the difference? (And another shout-out to sci-fi fans, what credentials did R2-D2 use to hack the Death Star?)

Default Credentials

Whenever you purchase or license a new resource, whether it is a device, application, or even a cloud resource, it comes with a default credential scheme used for initial access and configuration. The resource is typically in a pristine state, not fully hardened, and vulnerable to a variety of password attacks, especially to the default root or administrator account that could own the entire system. If this account is compromised, a wide range of persistent privileged attacks could occur by a threat actor and go undetected for years since the defaults governing the solution have not been managed and, more consequently, not maintained or monitored. These default credentials are required so that an organization can consistently perform the initial configuration. Logically, using security best practices, the default credentials should be changed, but many times they are not. This exposes these default accounts as a privileged attack vector. Today, manufacturers have six choices for passwords when they ship a device, application, or other resource:

1. **Anonymous Access**: Full, unrestricted, default access with no credentials

2. **Blank Password**: Default username, but no password

3. **Default Password**: Default credentials with predictable username and password

4. **Default Randomized Password**: Default username with a fully randomized password

5. **Pattern-Generated Password**: Default username with predictable password

6. **Forced Password Change**: Default credentials with a forced password change required before normal operation

If the default passwords are not changed, it's just a matter of time before the device, application, or resource will be owned. These are the basics for privileged management: changing the predictable or easily obtained to something that requires knowledge to access.

Note that the California Consumer Privacy Act implemented in 2020 requires scenarios 4 and 6 to be implemented on all new consumer devices to prevent privileged attacks. All other methods are now considered illegal for consumer device sales. This does not necessarily hold true for devices targeting businesses or noncommercial sales, and it is still unclear how adoption will be enforced across all network-enabled devices. In addition, even though this is a California state law, all geolocations will benefit from this legislation since it is highly unlikely device manufacturers will produce two versions targeting the rest of the world and the fifth largest economy in the world, the state of California.

Anonymous Access

Anonymous access is simple and absolute. No authentication is needed to begin the setup of the resource, including advanced settings that may be used to secure the asset from future attacks. While this method seems completely ludicrous in today's security climate, it is often the only way to configure a resource for the first time. Consider the purchase of a new cell phone or mainstream tablet with either iOS or Android. Its initial configuration allows for anonymous access to set up Wi-Fi. The initial user can connect to any Wi-Fi network, including ones for which they may have

WPA2 keys. This is typically not required to complete the configuration, but if misconfigured, initially or not, it could lead to a man-in-the-middle attack if the setup is not performed in a secure location.

In addition, the primary administrator user account on the device can be set with a null password, basically allowing full, unrestricted access to the device at any time. This even holds true for devices that have biometrics, like facial identification or fingerprint recognition. These devices can be configured to not enforce a password even though it is recommended, and it may be required later to access corporate resources via a mobile device management solution or management profile. If the device was compromised in the first place, adding these restrictions later is a moot point.

What makes anonymous access an absolutely horrible security threat are the instances when it is not disabled or changed after the initial configuration. Surprisingly, there are plenty of information technology resources that only support anonymous access. These include, but are not limited to, SCADA sensors like thermocouples, children's IoT toys, and digital home assistants (after their configuration) that rely on voice commands. In the end, these are devices that have minimal-to-no programmatic concept of accounts or role-based access, and every user that interacts with the device has the same level of privileges. To that point, Figure 2-5 displays how even a file share can be granted anonymous access for anyone, at any time, to gain access.

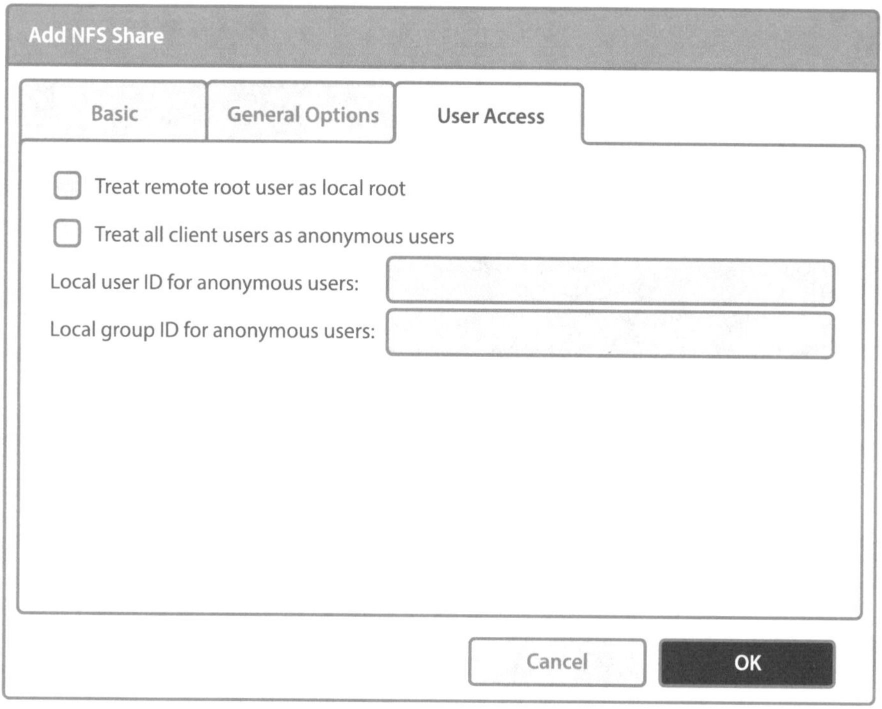

Figure 2-5. *Anonymous Option for Adding an NFS Share*

Blank Password

Blank passwords are commonly used in resources that have multiple accounts but have a null password by default. The security and initial configuration of the resource may require that a password be assigned; however, many technologies, including older databases, do not even prompt for a password assignment after the solution is installed and operating. The risks are apparent. Accounts are present, not properly configured, and, depending on the privileges, are easy targets for a threat actor. Figure 2-6 illustrates this for a website where the credentials have not been set.

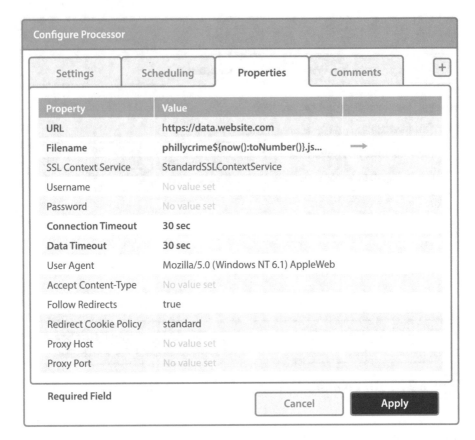

Figure 2-6. *No Account or Password Settings*

Blank passwords (credentials) are not anonymous accounts but rather credentials that have not been assigned and, in many cases, just a bad misconfiguration that should be mitigated when hardening the device. People commonly confuse accounts that have blank passwords with anonymous access. However, two significant differences should be well understood. With anonymous access, the identity of the user is not considered, and such access is typically reserved for low-risk activities. With an account with a blank password, the identity of the user is considered, but the security of the authentication process is diminished, usually an oversight that creates undue risk. The most common, and widely used, blank password solutions are systems that support Guest accounts. Anonymous access is independent of whether the guest account is enabled and is typically reserved for all to access. My point is that unauthenticated access is typically purposeful and required for operations, while a blank password is usually an indicator of a privilege vulnerability and bad configuration.

Default Password

For many years, manufacturers released solutions with default passwords. Every model series of the device had a unique password, and, for some manufacturers, the default password is the same for every new resource they produce. Although this is a common practice, it is a glaring security issue. There are volumes of lists publicly accessible on the Internet of these default passwords for every vendor, and all a threat actor needs to do is try them. Also, regulatory mandates (discussed later) prohibit the existence of default passwords (of any type) to be used in production due to the risk. These devices are susceptible to an attack as soon as they are connected to a network or the Internet. This is particularly dangerous if the device is not properly configured and still has the default credential after the resource is placed in production. However, some devices may not actually allow for the default password to be changed. This represents a privileged attack vector that is extremely vulnerable, just like anonymous or blank password access to the root account.

However, blank passwords (as defaults) are not just a threat to endpoints and networking devices. In many cases, application vendors will place the onus of implementing security controls on the application users and developers. For example, MongoDB is a popular NoSQL database used by organizations to perform big data and heavy analytics workloads. The default installation of MongoDB on older releases does not actually require authentication to access the database. This resulted in a widespread attack in early 2017 in which application and database administrators were not enabling authentication to the database. To make matters worse, many of these databases were directly accessible to the Internet. For these reasons, the importance of communicating security best practices at all levels of the organizations, including secured coding by the development and application teams, is critical. Figures 2-7 and 2-8 illustrate real-world, commercially available technologies that have poor default password implementations.

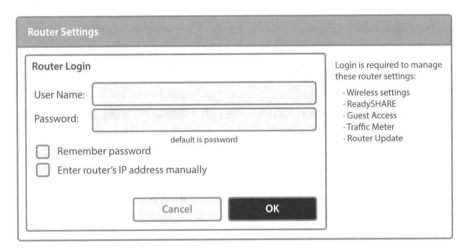

Figure 2-7. *Home-Based Router with Actual Text in the User Interface Stating the Default Password*

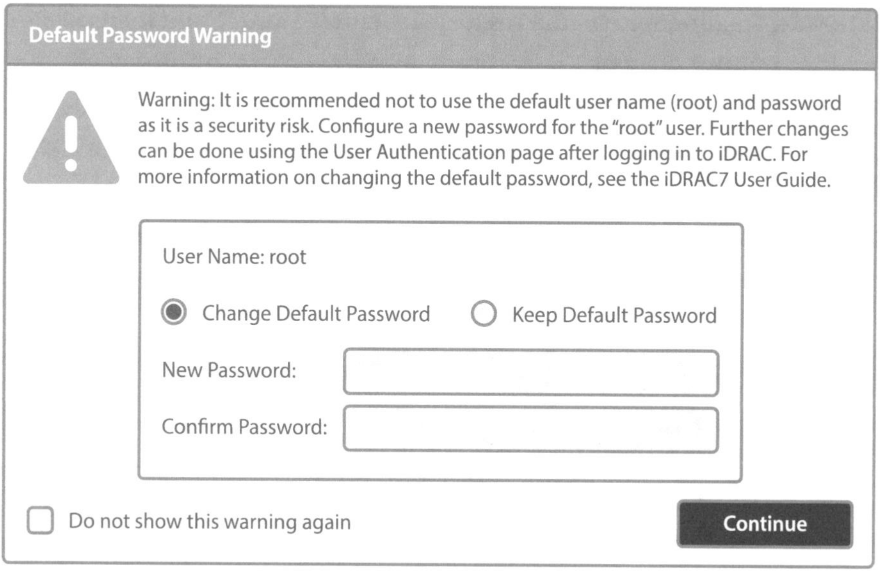

Default Password Warning

⚠ Warning: It is recommended not to use the default user name (root) and password as it is a security risk. Configure a new password for the "root" user. Further changes can be done using the User Authentication page after logging in to iDRAC. For more information on changing the default password, see the iDRAC7 User Guide.

User Name: root

◉ Change Default Password   ○ Keep Default Password

New Password: [   ]

Confirm Password: [   ]

☐ Do not show this warning again   **Continue**

Figure 2-8. Commercial-Based Server Solution with an Option to Keep Default Credentials

Default Randomized Password

In today's world, the most secure default password is one that is unique and randomized for every single resource that is produced, licensed, or sold. This password needs to be securely conveyed to the administrator or organization for the initial setup and should be changed upon the initial configuration. Unfortunately, some manufacturers have taken this concept to a level that makes the devices unsecure if physical access to the device is available. Along with the serial number, these vendors have printed the default passwords on the device for anyone to retrieve (see Figure 2-9). A simple press and hold of the reset button restores the password to the default and, depending on the device, the configuration too. Once reset, a threat actor now has access to compromise the asset. Mitigation for this type of threat is relatively simple. Copy (photo, scan, or type) the default password documented on the resource, securely store it, and then destroy, mask, or remove the label. In addition, physical access to any device that allows for a soft or hard reset, or password reset remotely, should be secured to prevent this threat. Most compliance regulations mandate this as well. Randomized passwords are currently one of the most secure methods to distribute default passwords, but they also may present risks depending on how that password is initially distributed.

Figure 2-9. *Factory Serial Number with Weak Default Credentials and Randomized SSID Password*

Pattern-Generated Passwords

Identity governance requires sound, documented, and repeatable processes for onboarding new users, creating new identities and accounts, deleting identities and accounts, providing certification reports for access, and providing access for them to perform their jobs. When not managed properly, these accounts can create a significant security risk.

Have you ever worked for a company where an automated system creates the default login account and password based on something that everyone knows—like your name? Often, this is how an IT/help desk sets up the default access for new employees or reset passwords upon some form of authentication or login failure. For them, it is easy to document, potentially automated, and can be similarly communicated to users as a password for them to gain access.

For example: If I have a new user named "John Titor" (and, before I go any further, I am not John Titor,[2] the time traveler from 2036—sorry to disappoint you). I may have an algorithm that generated the login account and credentials by extracting components of his name. Here my provisioning process is to create the login account using the "first initial of his first name + last name" with a default password of "New" + "first initial first name" + "first initial last name" + "!!!2036$". This paradigm results in the following account:

> Login Account: JTitor
>
> Password: NewJT!!!2036$

To successfully compromise this account, all I need to know is the new user's name and the algorithm to define the default password. And if I am an insider who went through this process, I would have a pretty good idea of what it is. Now, you may indicate that this is not really a risk, as these accounts would typically be set to require a password change upon first login, and that is true. However, there are three things to consider:

1. This account would certainly be exposed from the time it is created and the hacker changed the password upon login to the time the new employee realized that they could not access their pre-created account and has their password reset by the IT team.

---

[2]Who is John Titor? https://en.wikipedia.org/wiki/John_Titor

2. In some cases, the organization may not enforce "change after first logon" for these default passwords, and the employee may continue to use it!

3. The process may be used to reset locked or disabled accounts, making the passwords highly predictable.

Of course, to overcome these issues, more secure best practices can be implemented to reduce these risks, including the enforcement of "change password on next login" and multi-factor authentication. Figure 2-10 shows how to enforce a password reset during the next logon. This should be used regardless of whether or not you use a pattern-generated password to keep the password secured only to the account and the appropriate user.

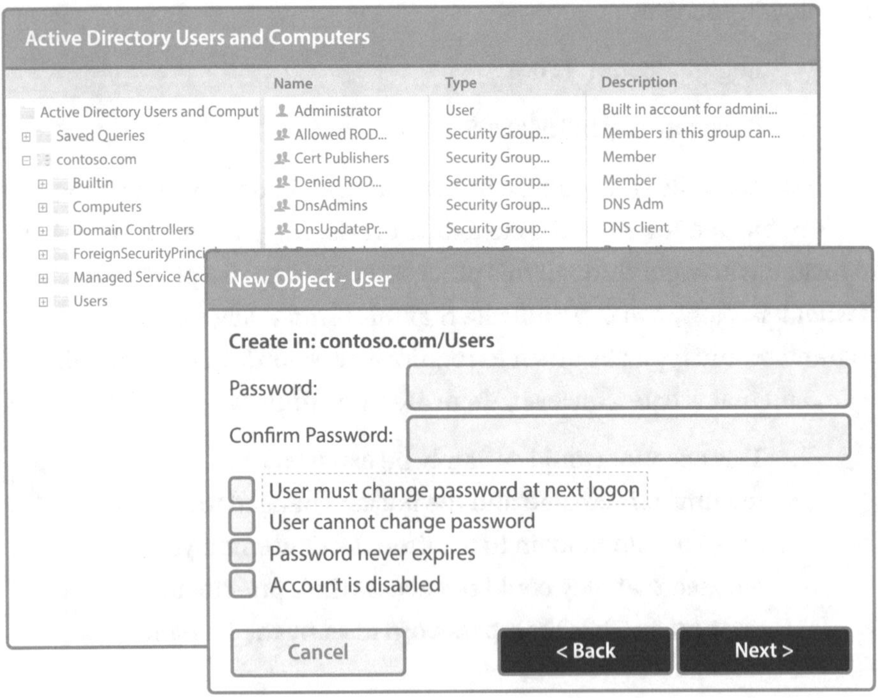

Figure 2-10. *Force a Password Reset During the Next Logon*

Forced Password Change

Forced password changes are a natural extension to forcing a password reset upon the next login. The major difference is that this setting is enforced upon the initial setup of the device or application, and the product will not function correctly until it is completed. Unfortunately, even though this has the best of intentions to protect against default credential attacks, it does not:

1. Have a mechanism for more than one device to share or reuse the same credentials. This makes them more susceptible to lateral movement, or other privileged attack vectors discussed later.

2. Have a mechanism to enforce password complexity, common passwords, or other password mistakes that can be used as attack vectors.

3. Provide a mechanism to centrally manage credentials upon an initial forced change. In other words, there will always be a local administrative account, potentially not under management, that can be leveraged as a backdoor.

CHAPTER 3

Credentials

In practice, credentials are the evidence of authority to rights, entitlements, privileges, or similar permissions. They are usually presented in written or typed form like an account name and password, and only those accounts, applications, services, scripts, and the like with properly validated credentials are permitted to proceed.

Shared Credentials

One of the cardinal rules in cybersecurity is never to share your password (credentials) with anyone. Whether it is a colleague or contractor, there are no sound use cases when it should be done, ever! That said, many employees continue to share passwords in times of emergency, due to simplicity and ignorance, to delegate tasks, or to overcome issues in planning with sick leave and vacation.

The problem with shared credentials is that once they are out of your control, how fast and far could they propagate before they are in the hands of a threat actor? This could be anything from a real hacker with malicious intent, to a suspicious spouse or memory-scraping malware. If multiple users are using the same credential, for example, a local or domain administrative account, how can an organization reliably associate access and change events to an individual identity? Unfortunately, even though these risks and challenges exist, there are real-world use cases where shared credentials are absolutely required for an application to work in a multitier architecture, for devices to connect to a network, and

© Morey J. Haber 2020
M. J. Haber, *Privileged Attack Vectors*, https://doi.org/10.1007/978-1-4842-5914-6_3

multiple users to administer the same resources. Shared credentials, or the act of sharing credentials, is a real privilege problem because once the information is shared, limiting its exposure and measuring the risk of that exposure becomes a difficult threat to quantify. Minimizing privilege risk, or privileges as an attack vector, requires knowledge of all the different places shared credentials can exist. And, what can be done to mitigate inadvertent propagation of them? It includes documenting any time that shared credentials are used, which individual requested them, what actions they performed, and changing the password periodically to ensure it does not become stale. Shared credentials should also be rotated when organizational events occur, such as employee changes and contractor access. The concept of credentials to provide access and the intentional or unintentional sharing of them is a core use case for privileged access management.

Account Credentials

Users expose their account information in a variety of ways: some intentionally and some inadvertently. The most common methods outside of authenticating to a resource include verbally, through email, and through text messages. Outside of a hot microphone, the latter leaves a permanently documented paper trail in backups, log files, and text message history. Most likely, these texts are completely outside of your organization's control, and the credentials have technically been exposed to unmanaged resources. People forget that deleting an email or text from a device does not mean the message is truly eradicated. It is just removed from the user's local view. If a password was sent via one of these methods, it still exists out there somewhere. Where it exists, and the subsequent exposure to risk, is dependent on how the password was stored. For a human-based identity, password storage and retrieval can take many forms, including the following:

1. **Mentally**: Only memorized in the human brain.

2. **Documentation**: Written on paper. These can be secured in a physical safe or inappropriately written on paper like a Post-it note or bulletin board.

3. **Flat File**: Documented in an electronic file like a spreadsheet. These can be secured on a file system or encrypted with a password to prevent basic tampering.

4. **Password Manager**: A technology solution for the storage and retrieval of credentials and their associated passwords. Advanced versions of this technology can also randomize the passwords and automatically rotate them according to policies.

While storing the information solely within your head is presumably the most secure, it has risks that degrade this as a best practice. This is where the expression, "If you got hit by a bus," becomes painfully relevant. Documenting and creating specific accounts for emergency privileged access is a good method for Break Glass and for use case–based sharing, but represents risks if the files are shared, copied, or placed in an unsecure location. In this case, a threat actor could have unhindered access to your password, and to resources you have access to as well. To reduce this risk, many end users utilize password managers for storage and retrieval of passwords. This represents one of the best solutions for managing privileged access to mitigate this attack vector.

It is important to note that there are two classes of password managers. One class is strictly for personal password storage and the other for enterprise password storage. Neither should be used across both use cases. In other words, do not use a personal password manager to store business credentials and vice versa. A business should never store your personal credentials, like for banking or personal social media accounts, and a personal password manager is inadequate to manage and audit business privileged access. As a rule of thumb, keep the two classes of password management solutions separate unless the solution and strategy your organization chooses has distinct provisions for both use cases. This will be discussed in detail later in this chapter and has special relevance for users that tend to use the same passwords both at home and at work ("I have a bad feeling about this"—Han Solo).

Shared Administrator Credentials

Most applications, embedded solutions, networking devices, Internet of Things (IoT), and appliance-based solutions ship with and rely on local accounts to perform management functions. In traditional environments, multiple system administrators will use these accounts (shared credentials) to perform specific tasks for configuration and maintenance. The sharing of these accounts and their related passwords, vs. creating a unique login for each administrator, may be due to the limitation of the device and/or application. Therefore, these credentials may be shared across administrators due to management overhead, complexity, and cost of implementing unique credentials across the environment for a system that natively does not support it.

Take, for example, an environment that has ten administrators managing 1000 systems, as shown in Figure 3-1.

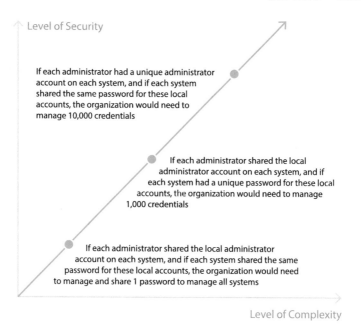

Level of Security

If each administrator had a unique administrator account on each system, and if each system shared the same password for these local accounts, the organization would need to manage 10,000 credentials

If each administrator shared the local administrator account on each system, and if each system had a unique password for these local accounts, the organization would need to manage 1,000 credentials

If each administrator shared the local administrator account on each system, and if each system shared the same password for these local accounts, the organization would need to manage and share 1 password to manage all systems

Level of Complexity

Figure 3-1. *Administrator Environment, Number of Credentials Mapped Against Complexity and Security*

As such, for efficiency's sake, many organizations will choose the less secure, less complex, but easier alternative. Let's examine the risks associated with each option in our model:

1. Using the same account on each system with each system account using the same password is the easiest solution, from an operational perspective, as administrators only need to share and coordinate a single password. However, this option is clearly the most insecure approach. If an administrator's password is compromised, the hacker can easily gain access to all 1000 systems via lateral movement.

2. If the managed systems each had a unique password for the shared account, it reduces the risk and impact of a potential breach. In this case,

if an administrator's password was compromised, it would only grant the hacker access to that one system. All other systems would have their own unique password. The only challenge with this approach, as with all shared accounts, is that you cannot isolate specific account activity to an individual. In this example, all activities across all administrators would be tracked as "administrator" and not tied to the particular person who performed the action. Also, note that when using a shared account, the password can only be changed if such updates are efficiently coordinated and communicated with everyone that uses the account. The more accounts and passwords, the more complicated this coordination exercise can become. In this example, we need to update 1000 passwords across 1000 systems and appropriately notify the ten administrators when these password updates occur. The result is that, many times, in addition to sharing these passwords, they are infrequently updated, which further increases the risk of compromise. Of course, an automated Password Management solution provides an effective and efficient way to frequently update these 1000 local accounts with unique and complex passwords.

3. The third option is the most complex option. In this option, users do not use a shared local account. Instead, each user is granted access through their own account. This enables all activities to be logged and tied to a specific user for accountability. However, in our example, that would either require

that ten accounts (one for each admin, if possible) be created on each local system or that each local system relies on a directory service or centralized identity solutions to perform the authentication process. We will discuss identity solutions and directory services later in this book.

4. The fourth option is the most common for a privileged access management solution, and local accounts on the system are leveraged in the design. The systems are managed and have unique passwords that are automatically managed and rotated by an enterprise password management solution. Access control lists (ACLs) are implemented on the system or network to limit lateral communications and rogue session requests. All activity is performed through an authorized bastion host or gateway that authenticates the user first for auditing and reporting and then brokers the connection. This translated into 1000 managed passwords and unlimited administrators that are provisioned through the password management solution. In today's world, this is currently the best approach.

Temporary Accounts

Temporary accounts are commonly associated with interns, vendors, contractors, temporary employees, or other identities that will require transient access. These accounts should never be shared by users in the same job function—like temporary workers that leverage a shared kiosk, contractors working on plant machinery, professional services contractors, auditors, or other temporary workers that need to have an account readily available when they start. Each temporary account should be unique per individual. The risks for temporary accounts include the following:

- Lack of accountability over who performed which task with the accounts (if shared).

- Workers may end up having access for longer than they should have if the accounts are not disabled or removed after their tasks are complete.

- Uncontrolled access in environments where these passwords are not frequently changed, or the accounts use a patterned password template model.

- Accounts not managed or disabled, allowing for unsanctioned access after an appropriate time period has ended. These are gaps in the deprovisioning process.

SSH Keys

Secure Socket Shell (SSH) keys are a special network protocol leveraging public-key cryptography to enable authorized users to remotely access a computer or other device via access credentials called SSH keys. Normally, SSH keys are used to access sensitive resources and perform critical, highly privileged activities. It's vital to manage SSH keys as you would other sensitive credentials correctly. While SSH keys are standard, and more frequently used, in Unix and Linux environments, they are also used in Windows systems.

Overview of SSH Key Security Authentication

The Secure Shell, and the public-key cryptography (an encryption schema using two keys: one public, one private), that SSH keys use is designed to provide strong, encrypted verification and communication between the user and a remote computer. SSH technology is based on the client-server model and provides an ideal way to access remote devices over unsecured networks, like the Internet. Administrators typically use the technology for several functions including

- Logging into remote systems and resources for support and maintenance

- Transferring of files from computer to computer

- Remote execution of commands

- Offering support and updates

- Authorizing devices to participate in network communications (Wi-Fi as an example)

Today, Telnet, one of the Internet's first remote login protocols and in use since the 1960s, has largely been supplanted by SSH, owing to the latter protocol's enhanced security and encryption features. Telnet, for example, performs all communication in clear text and is an easy target for threat actors.

Benefits of SSH Key Authentication

The SSH network protocol encrypts all traffic between the client and the server while it is in transit. This means that anyone eavesdropping on the traffic, such as by packet sniffing, would not be able to access and decrypt transmitted data properly. SSH is also resistant to brute force attacks and protects against specific attack vectors being used to gain access to remote machines. Public-key encryption ensures that passwords need not be sent over the network, providing an additional layer of security. Due to the massive number of SSH keys that may be in use or exist across an enterprise at any time, SSH key management in the form of privileged access management can significantly lower the overhead and risk of manually managing and updating keys.

Generating SSH Keys

SSH keys are always generated in pairs. These pairs consist of one "public" SSH key and one "private" SSH key. These keys are paired using powerful algorithms, making it infeasible to guess or "fake" a private key, even if you know the public key. While private keys should be kept secret by the authorized person wishing to gain access to a system, public keys may be freely shared. SSH keys are usually generated by a user entering a passphrase or other information. Typically, public and private keys will be generated from phrases of a few words.

SSH Key Access

A remote computer identifies itself to a user using its public key. When an account attempts to connect, the remote system issues a "challenge" derived from the public key, for which only someone possessing the paired private key could correctly decrypt and respond. Once the challenge is correctly answered, the remote system provides access. In almost all cases, generating keys, sharing public keys, issuing challenges, answering them, and gaining access can be automated such that the process is transparent to end users.

SSH Key Sprawl Poses Security and Operational Risk

SSH key sprawl exposes organizations to considerable risk in the form of privileged attack vectors, especially considering that they can provide such a high level of privileged access, such as root. With typically 50–200 SSH keys per server, organizations may have upward of a million SSH keys deployed within their environment. While many of these SSH keys are long dormant and forgotten, they can provide a backdoor for threat actors to infiltrate critical servers. And once one the server and SSH key is compromised, a threat actor could move laterally and find more hidden keys. As with other types of privileged credentials (or passwords in general), when organizations rely on manual processes, there is a proclivity to reuse a passphrase across many SSH keys or to reuse the same public SSH key. This means that one compromised key can then be harnessed to infiltrate multiple servers. It is the same problem as a reused password.

SSH Key Security Best Practices

As with any other security protocols, it is imperative to maintain strong standards and best practices around SSH network protocols, keys, and passphrases. NIST IR 7966[1] offers guidance for government organizations, businesses, and auditors on proper security controls for SSH implementations. The NIST recommendations emphasize SSH key discovery, rotation, usage, and monitoring. In even modestly complex environments, manual SSH key rotation is infeasible. For instance, you could identify accounts set up to use SSH keys, you could manually scan

---

[1]Security of Interactive and Automated Access Management Using Secure Shell (SSH)— https://nvlpubs.nist.gov/nistpubs/ir/2015/NIST.IR.7966.pdf

through authorized keys file in the hidden.SSH user folder, but this falls short of helping you identify who has the private key matching any of the public keys in the file. Organizations who recognize the risks posed by SSH key sprawl typically take a proactive cybersecurity posture, use a dedicated SSH key management or automated privileged access management solution, and generate unique key pairs for each system to perform frequent key rotation. Automated solutions dramatically simplify the process of creating and rotating SSH keys, eliminating SSH key sprawl, and ensuring SSH keys enable productivity without compromising security.

Personal and Work Passwords

We all have dozens of passwords to remember, and forgetting them seems to be commonplace. To reduce the risks and frustrations of forgotten passwords, many users have turned to Password Management solutions, which inventory and secure all their passwords, requiring that they only remember the master password to gain entry. As discussed earlier, there are personal password managers and enterprise password management solutions. Both are good strategies. What is not a good strategy is to reuse the same password for multiple applications, services, and other resources across home and work, nor to cross-use personal and enterprise password solutions for each other's use cases. Recent breaches in which millions of consumer passwords were disclosed to hackers are not damaging just because they allow access to the already compromised system, but the impact has a multiplier because they can often be reused in other attacks. Those passwords could also unlock access to your other email accounts, banking applications, social media, and more. If the same password was present at work and home, the ramifications could be devastating to your identity in both realms.

With this in mind, there are some security best practices that should followed in this category:

- Don't share and reuse passwords across both personal and corporate accounts, as a compromise in either one could put yourself, employer, and business partners at risk too.

- Never use the same account name for personal and business functions. If work has standardized on first initial and last name for your account (i.e., "jtitor"), do not use it for accounts at home or even personal email. It is an easy way for a threat actor to link personal and business accounts to your identity.

- If you use social media for work, consider creating multiple accounts for personal and professional posts. If this is undesirable because you are considered a public figure, then learn how to set up groups in social media to target your postings to family, friends, and the public at large. Obviously, the account names and passwords should be sufficiently different too.

- Do not use a personal password manager to store business passwords and do not use an enterprise management solution to store personal passwords. This is true for any use case, including Break Glass (covered in detail later in this book) or any type of vendor, backdoor, or unique accounts.

Applications

Another cardinal rule of cybersecurity is that users should have a unique password for every application, and no two distinct applications should share the same credentials unless required to communicate. This is another form of password reuse and presents one of the largest privilege problems in information technology security today. People use the same password among multiple applications, systems, resources, infrastructure, and others. Should any one of them be compromised, the same reused password can be leveraged against any other device, application, resource, etc. with the same password. This is why centralized directory stores, single sign-on, password management, and multi-factor authentication are so important to mitigate the risk. This is true for standard user accounts as well as for privileged administrative accounts.

Unfortunately, and contrary to this, there are valid use cases where shared passwords between applications are required and represent a unique attack vector. To communicate, some applications require the same credentials, and if they are out of sync, the resources fail to function as a desired solution. If one of the resources is compromised, the same problem as password reuse can occur via lateral movement allowing authentication with the same shared credentials. The most common places these shared passwords are used are service accounts, scripts, and application-to-application authentication, including DevOps. There is no simple method to mitigate this problem, but there are methods to ensure the risk is appropriately managed.

- Do not hard-code passwords in scripts, applications, or driver connections—even if the application compiles the source for runtime.

- Map all services, applications, and accounts that use shared credentials for visibility and risk management.

- Never place passwords in clear text files or files that can be easily decrypted. If a legacy application requires passwords in a file, make sure they are properly hashed, and the keys are not stored on the same system for decryption.

- For end-user interaction, authenticate users against a directory store like Active Directory when possible.

- To minimize the observer effect for end users, consider using multi-factor authentication with single sign-on.

- For applications that can only use local role-based access, enforce periodic password rotation.

- Educate team members on the risk and importance of *not* reusing passwords.

While this short list may sound daunting and exhausting to implement, mitigating these risks is not unsurmountable. Enterprise password management solutions provide a vehicle to remediate these risks via an application programming interface (API). In lieu of hard-coding the password, an API call is made to a password safe, or password manager, as a part of a privileged access management (PAM) solution to retrieve the correct password. The PAM solution understands the linkage and mapping of solutions that need the same passwords and either distributes them correctly upon an API call or automatically changes them based on the same relationships. In addition, for end-user interaction, the same API can drive unique credentials per application and per user using single sign-on technology to make the end-user experience frictionless. This entire process is secured from a threat actor using its own authentication mechanisms, covered later in this book.

A password storage solution (password safe, lockbox, or vault) is, therefore, the best-practice recommendation for application-to-application password storage vs. coding passwords in the solution.

Figure 3-2 illustrates an application that uses credentials to secure communications for future application-to-application interaction. This technique avoids coding or storing passwords in a separate file and minimizes the risk of password theft by a threat actor by obfuscating and securing passwords from any end users.

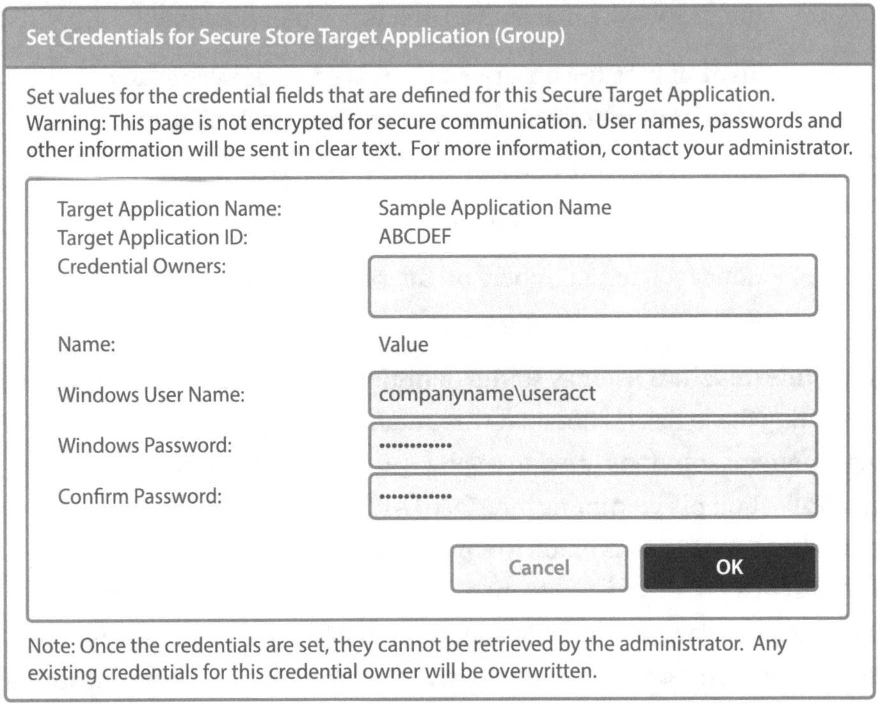

Set Credentials for Secure Store Target Application (Group)

Set values for the credential fields that are defined for this Secure Target Application. Warning: This page is not encrypted for secure communication. User names, passwords and other information will be sent in clear text. For more information, contact your administrator.

Target Application Name:	Sample Application Name
Target Application ID:	ABCDEF
Credential Owners:	
Name:	Value
Windows User Name:	companyname\useracct
Windows Password:	•••••••••••••
Confirm Password:	•••••••••••••

Cancel   OK

Note: Once the credentials are set, they cannot be retrieved by the administrator. Any existing credentials for this credential owner will be overwritten.

Figure 3-2. *Static Credentials for Secure Storage Authentication Between Two Applications*

Devices

Devices that share passwords are very similar to applications that share credentials, but the credentials and password are stored on the device (oftentimes not securely) for continuous usage. These are not the passwords you use for email or social media accounts, but rather passwords that every device may have to connect. These include, but are certainly not limited to, the following:

- If WEP (hopefully not) or WPA2 is used for Wi-Fi, the shared key or passphrase may be the same for all devices to connect.

- Unmanaged credentials on a device that the help desk or an administrator may possess as a legitimate backdoor to gain administrative access.

- Tools like appliance-based vulnerability assessment scanners, network management solutions, and security solutions may share the same credentials and passwords across all deployments to connect or perform maintenance like auto-updates.

- Management of infrastructure devices, such as routers and switches using the same root password for either configuration management or synchronized network management functions.

- Devices that are natively capable of sending emails or Simple Network Management Protocol (SNMP) traps and store credentials locally for automated notifications.

Therefore, device passwords represent another vector for privileged attacks. The passwords, or certificates, are rarely changed and, once obtained by a threat actor, represent an easy and persistent method to penetrate an environment until they are detected, the services stopped, and all the device passwords changed. Also, these credentials are often initially configured during the setup of the network, frequently by a third-party vendor, and exposed to nonemployees, introducing yet another unnecessary risk.

To compound the problem, for insecure wireless networks using WPA2 or WEP, the likelihood of a passphrase leak increases over time. The more devices out there using it, the more people knowing it, the more likely someone with a rogue device can connect. This is even more of a hellish scenario when the wireless network is not properly segmented from production networks and sensitive data, and organizations blatantly post the SSID passphrase out in the open for anyone with physical access to see. The best recommendation for shared device passwords like WPA2 is a layered security approach to mitigate device threats:

- Segment all wireless networks from production access.

- Require all wireless devices have a certificate installed by IT to prove it is a managed device.

- Require centralized authentication against a directory store before granting access to a corporate wireless network. This should also include multi-factor authentication when appropriate.

And note, this is not necessarily true for properly segmented, monitored, and approved Guest wireless networks.

As for legitimate device backdoor accounts, a spreadsheet with laptop serial numbers and help desk backdoor passwords encrypted on a private share is much more secure than every laptop having the same password. This is especially true if the passwords have never been changed. Regardless, it is not a good security practice. If this is the only mechanism you have today to secure these accounts, keeping personally identifiable information out of the spreadsheet is also helpful, since the list would need to be cross-referenced to an owner to be eventually usable by a threat actor. Having all that information in an enterprise password manager is the recommended approach and best practice in lieu of any flat file technique. Table 3-1 illustrates this approach, but keep in mind, it is not recommended since all the passwords are exposed. In addition, outside of file security, the data would have to be cross-referenced to a user and/ or device to be usable by any threat actor since the actual hostname is not listed in the file, only the serial number.

Table 3-1. A Sample Obfuscate Spreadsheet of Serial Numbers and Password

Device Serial Number	Help Desk Password	Asset Tag
XDM7GT	1503VaBm@!	2036
PLOOHG3	9802PbWd^%	2020
LKJ678	PbUl7650!!	2049
LM7WQ4	RnSs1209)*	3069

Aliases

As a reader of this book, you are a human being. You are unique, have an identity, and have subtle differences from other humans, even if you have a twin. Today's biometric technology cannot necessarily distinguish you from someone else (i.e., think twins and facial recognition technology). When we translate the human aspect of our identities into the digital world, we can have more aliases, avatars, profiles, and, therefore, privileges. Information technology users can have multiple aliases, just like having more than one email address. This is different than accounts. Aliases are a representation of an account and its credentials using an alternative name. For example, John Titor may have an account named "jtitor," but his alias could be "TimeTraveler2036". We may have multiple aliases for home accounts, but we are less likely to have separate ones for work. Typically, account names in businesses can easily be translated back to an identity, and that is our alias. They are unique identifiers for who we are, but ultimately, they are just another description for the account and its potential role. And, surprisingly, they can exist for both human and nonhuman identities.

Aliases, and their associated accounts, can have a variety of privileges assigned to them. If we expand this concept a little further, they can be referenced as the actual usernames for our accounts. We may have an everyday account based on our name (Standard User). We may also have an administrative (or elevated privileges account) based on the same name with a prefix or suffix to indicate it is a privileged account. For example, my Standard User account could be "jtitor", and my administrative account is "jtitor admin". These are both aliases for my identity in the form of accounts and, again, should never share the same password.

This concept becomes exceptionally important when we work with multiple operating systems and directory services. We can easily encounter instances where these accounts do not inherently sync, have different criteria for complexity and naming conventions, and will not work on foreign applications or incompatible operating systems. This can leave us with multiple aliases for Unix, Linux, Windows, Mac, iOS, Android, social media, applications, and so on. I think you get the perspective.

From a threat actor's perspective, aliases are a hindrance to their goals, especially if all the alias schemas are different and the passwords are different too. For example, on Windows, John's account may be jtitor@corpdomain.com, but on Linux, his account may be "johntitor." Laterally moving from one resource to another is complicated since the threat actor needs to determine the proper cross-platform aliases to properly navigate through the environment. This is actually a good thing, but the problem lies with development and operations. The mapping of all the aliases (accounts) to the proper identities is potentially a nightmare, and having potentially hundreds or thousands of local, nonsynchronized accounts across multiple users could leave gaping holes in security from rogue or dormant accounts. It is the same reason security best practices prefer domain accounts over local accounts to manage systems.

They are easier to control, manage, log, audit, track, and maintain. Having every identity instantiated as a local, nonlinked account on every foreign operating system is worsened if the alias schema used to create them is different per resource. That is, John could have multiple permutations of his name created as accounts, depending on the resource. It is, therefore, best to keep the alias schema the same across all resources and, if possible, use technology to bridge authentication across platforms to consolidate directory stores. This minimizes the management overhead for accounts and the potential for sprawl in alias derivations.

From a privileged attack vector standpoint, the fewer the accounts and associated aliases, the better visibility into user activity. This is where directory services bridging comes into play. This capability allows one directory store, like Active Directory, to be the authentication store of authority for all supported platforms and applications. It can be leveraged for authentication and privileges using the same alias name (i.e., jtitor-admin) and the same password (or 2FA—two-factor authentication) everywhere. This means that one administrative alias works everywhere and authenticates against one directory store (the password is not stored locally in this model), and attestation reporting on an identity can occur anywhere and at any time. This is because all you need to do is query for the same alias name across all resources without having to deal with multiple derivations from nonstandard schemas. Without a directory bridge, with multiple aliases everywhere, each resource needs to store a password locally for authentication. That presents yet another attack vector for a threat actor to crack passwords. With a directory bridge, that risk is mitigated.

Minimizing the number of aliases per "human user" is strategically a best practice for any organization. It could then be easily inferred that minimizing the number of accounts per identity is also a good security practice too. Removing administrative accounts, and only keeping standard users, is even better and will be covered later.

As an illustration of how aliases can be used in a real-world environment, consider Figure 3-3. It illustrates how a batch process can be assigned any alias name such that it is not obviously associated with an administrative account.

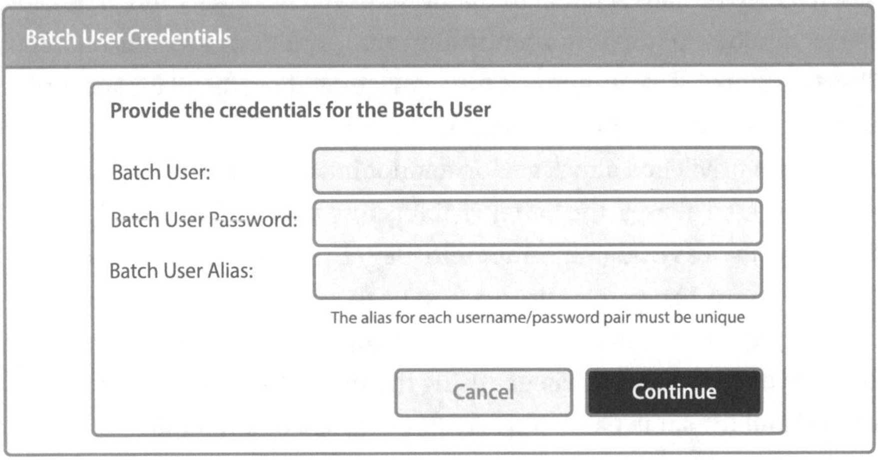

Figure 3-3. Assigning an Administrator Alias Name to a Batch User

Email Addresses as Account Usernames

Identity-based attack vectors represent the next biggest risk for consumers and businesses over the ensuing decade. One aspect of this risk is associated with an identity, or user, having a single account username leveraged for many different roles. In basic terms, if a person implements their account username using their email address for everything that they access, the risks are higher for an incident. Based on an attack using a single account, a threat actor can reuse that same account name based on an email address against other resources and apply a variety of techniques—such as brute force, spray attacks, and credential stuffing—to attempt to compromise the account (covered in Chapter 4). If the user has different email addresses for logging on to different types of resources, then a breach in one type of resource cannot necessarily be used against another. The threat actor has no email address or account username as a reference point to start from unless they can link all your email addresses back to your identity.

In business, these different accounts are generally associated with an identity governance solution and managed by business or information technology roles. For a consumer, people typically use one email account for all types of access with varying degrees of risk. This is where the problem lies. Consumers should adopt a model similar to businesses and have at least four email accounts for home use and at least two for business use when email addresses are being used as the account username. This is very similar to how businesses have multiple accounts to cover different types of access to applications based on risk and privileged sessions. Therefore, for every consumer, I recommend having at least four different email addresses for all of the resources they access on the Internet. The goal is to keep correspondence from different resources separate. And, to prevent usernames based on an email address from being used as credentials unnecessarily exposing a small, but important piece of personally identifiable information.

- The first email address should be associated with any type of sensitive accounts (in business, a privileged account). These can be banking or financial applications and should have a unique email address used for authentication, dedicated only for their access. In addition to logging on, this will help determine whether any correspondence sent to this address is legitimate. Any phishing emails that someone would receive in a different account can automatically be discounted as fake. You would have no accounts associated with another email address. For the highly security-conscious, it may be necessary to create an email account associated with each one of these sensitive systems, depending on the data contained within.

- The second email address should only be used for all personal correspondence (in business, a standard user account). This includes any type of emails that may be exchanged with family members, friends, or involved in other social activities. This email address should never be used for anything outside of sending or receiving email—that is, it should never be used as the logon (authentication) for any account on the Internet. Any rogue correspondence to this address will make it is easy to identify as spam targeting you.

- The third account should be for junk email or shopping (there is no corresponding business account, but loosely follows generic email addresses for a company like sales@domain.com or support@domain.com). For the sake of this section, we classify junk mail as a very broad term for websites that might frequently send you sales offers or nonmalicious spam. It should be for all of the applications and websites that send frequent coupons, event notifications, sales promotions, or other types of merchandise. It is not recommended to use this account for any other activities nor to use this email address for actually shopping on a website. Unless it is an eCommerce site you visit frequently (then it is a sensitive account since it has your credit card number), consider always shopping as a Guest patron to prevent the website from potentially storing your credentials, credit card number, and address.

This email address should be dedicated solely for spam or junk and should never be associated with any sensitive information.

- Finally, the fourth email address is relatively straightforward. It should be used for any correspondence associated with your employment or interactions with state, local, or federal government (this is analogous to domain or local administrators). This is a dedicated email account for which you share the address with your employer or other government entities so that they can correspond to you regarding healthcare, taxes, utility bills, or other official information. This email address should not be shared outside of these specific use cases, and any correspondence that deviates from its intended usage is definitely spam.

While having four email accounts may seem extreme for consumers, it helps separate the different use cases that you might perform for correspondence and sensitive authentication on the Web. Its roots (pun intended) are founded in privileged and standard user accounts present in businesses today. Modern applications can easily support multiple email addresses to separate correspondence, including Microsoft Outlook, Gmail on an Android, and Mail on an Apple device. Knowing what email should come into which category will help you avoid spam, phishing attacks, and other types of compromised credential attacks that could lead to your identity being compromised. Because if your personal identity is compromised, it is not hard for a threat actor to leverage you, and your assets, to compromise any shared resources (like bring your own device (BYOD)—Chapter 16) to gain access to your business. And, depending on your engagement with online resources, including social media or other types of high-risk applications like dating websites, you may choose to create even more email accounts to achieve further separation of roles.

This will continue to isolate any additional communications coming from high-risk sites and make it much easier for an end user to delete or disable an account if the website or correspondence are compromised or become a burden. Essentially, the rule of thumb to follow here is to not use one account (email address) for everything, just like at work. Your email account should not be the same for banking as well as dating sites, social media, and work.

Finally, if your Internet-based resources allow you to create a unique username for logging on in place of an email address, take advantage of this too. This is just an alias. This provides an additional layer of obfuscation, and the remaining threat is based on email correspondence and not having the same logon username for every web-based service. Essentially, keep all your account usernames separated, unique when possible, and monitor emails based on account name to help you safeguard against phishing attacks and modern identity-based attack vectors. And, it goes without saying (and I will say it over and over again in this book) that the passwords for each account should be unique, complex, and never reused or recycled!

Privileged access management is so much more than just password management, regardless of how credentials are implemented. We are now in an era of universal privilege management. Wherever and whenever privilege accounts exist (even ephemerally) and are being used, they must be tightly managed and monitored.

CHAPTER 4

Attack Vectors

An attack vector is a technique by which a threat actor, hacker, or attacker gains access to a system, application, or resource to perform malicious activity. This can include everything from installing malware, altering files or data, or even some form of persistent reconnaissance. Attack vectors enable threat actors to exploit system vulnerabilities, poor configurations, and introduce items like stolen credentials to compromise a system. Attack vectors can include human elements in the form of deception, social engineering, and even include physical traits like fake identification badges. Attack vectors can consist of malware, malicious emails, infected web pages, text messages, social engineering, and many other forms of deception. All of these methods involve intentionally coding software to create a programmatic attack vector (except social engineering) to leverage a resource for malicious intent.

Technology like firewalls and endpoint protection solutions were originally designed to block these attack vectors, but, in recent years, they have fallen short to the creativity and intent of threat actors. No single protection method is entirely attack-proof. A defensive strategy that is effective today may not be tomorrow, because threat actors are innovative, motivated, and pushing the limits of security in their pursuit to gain unauthorized access into systems and resources. To that end, the most common malicious payloads used for privileged attacks are malware designed to steal credentials or create a vehicle for a persistent presence to engage in lateral movement. As an analogy, if an attack vector is thought of as the barrel of a gun pointed at a target, its payload can be thought of

© Morey J. Haber 2020
M. J. Haber, *Privileged Attack Vectors*, https://doi.org/10.1007/978-1-4842-5914-6_4

as the bullet that pierces the target. This assumes, however, that someone or something is pointing the gun and that the attack is not random or opportunistic. Unfortunately, in today's world, we see these indiscriminate shootings too.

Password Hacking

Hacking of a password by a threat actor can be done using several techniques. Once successful, this can lead to administrator privileges if the account has been granted these rights in the first place. It's yet another reason to limit the number of administrator accounts in an environment to minimize the surface area for these attacks. If the account is an administrator, the threat actor can easily circumvent other security controls, perform lateral movement, and opportunistically attempt to crack other passwords for other privileged accounts on the same or remote systems. As a point of reference, password hacking should not be confused with the former discussions on password exposure, such as shared passwords and the insecure documentation of passwords. Password hacking is a threat action that involves attackers attempting to crack or determine a password using a variety of programmatic techniques and automation. These are covered in the following sections.

Guessing

One of the most popular techniques for password hacking is simply guessing the password. A random guess itself is rarely successful unless it is a common password or based on a dictionary word. Flat-out guessing is somewhat of an art, but knowing information about the target identity enhances the likelihood of a successful guess by a threat actor. This information can be gathered via social media, direct interaction, deceptive conversation, or even data gleaned and merged or aggregated from prior breaches. The most common variants for passwords that are susceptible to guessing include these common password schemas:

- The word "password" or basic derivations like "passw0rd" not found in typical password dictionaries.

- Derivations of the account owner's username, including initials. This may also include subtle variations, such as numbers and special characters.

- Reformatted or explicit birthdays for the user or their relatives, most commonly, offspring.

- Memorable places or events.

- Relatives' names and derivations with numbers or special characters when presented together.

- Pets, colors, foods, or other important items to the individual.

For a threat actor to succeed at password guessing, it is not necessary to use automation for repetitive guessing. This method may be more labor-intensive and has mixed success rates. Password guessing attacks also tend to leave evidence in event logs and result in auto-locking of an account after "n" attempts. For a threat actor, getting detailed information on the intended target usually involves advanced surveillance or inside knowledge. For the average person, it may just be a game of trial and error. In addition, if the account holder does not follow best practices and reuses passwords between resources, then the risks of password guessing and lateral movement increase dramatically. Imagine a person that uses only one or two base passwords everywhere for all of their digital presence. Unfortunately, this happens all the time.

Shoulder Surfing

Shoulder surfing enables a threat actor to gain knowledge of credentials through observation. This includes observing passwords, pins, and swipe patterns as they are being entered. This includes even observing a pen scribbling a password on a sticky note. The concept is simple, a threat actor is watching physically, or with an electronic device like a camera, for passwords and reusing them for a later attack. This is why, when using an ATM, it is always recommended to shield the entry of your PIN on a keypad to avoid a nearby threat actor from shoulder surfing your PIN.

Shoulder surfing represents one of the oldest privileged attack vectors and one of the easiest for anyone to leverage. For a threat actor, all they need to do is find a way to watch someone entering their secrets (password, PIN, etc.) on a data entry device.

Dictionary Attacks

Dictionary attacks are an automated technique (unlike password guessing) utilizing a list of passwords against a valid account to hack the password. The list itself is a dictionary of words (no definitions mind you) and basic password crackers use these lists of common single words like "baseball" to crack a password or hack an account. If the threat actor knows the resource they are trying to compromise, like password length and complexity requirements, the dictionary can be customized to target the resource more efficiently. Therefore, more advanced programs often use a dictionary on top of mixing in numbers or common symbols at the beginning or end of the attempt to mimic a real-world password with complexity requirements. An effective dictionary attack tool lets a threat actor do the following:

- Set complexity requirements for length, character requirements, and character set

- Allows for the manual addition of words, from names to other personally identifiable words

- Can include common misspellings of frequently used words

- Can operate with dictionaries in multiple languages

A weakness of dictionary attacks is that they rely on real words and derivations supplied by the user of the default dictionary. If the real password is fictitious, uses multiple languages, or uses more than one word or phrase, it will thwart a dictionary attack. There are just too many permutations for it to be successful.

Also, there are a variety of supplemental attacks based on dictionaries that are available to a threat actor. If the attacker knows the password-hashing algorithm used to encrypt passwords for a resource, rainbow tables can allow them to reverse engineer those hashes into passwords, if the password hash tables are exposed. Modern breaches have exposed vast troves of password hashes, but without a basis in the encryption algorithm, rainbow tables and similar techniques are nearly useless without some form of seed information.

Finally, the most common method to mitigate the threats of a dictionary attack is account lockout attempts. That is, after "n" times of wrong attempts, a user's account is automatically locked for a period of time, manually unlocked by an authority, like the help desk or via an automated password reset solution. However, in many environments, especially for nonhuman accounts, account lockout attempts can have undesirable effects to business runtime. This setting is, therefore, sometimes disabled, and, if logon failures are not being monitored in event logs, a dictionary attack is an effective attack vector for a threat actor. This is especially true if privileged accounts do not have this setting enabled as a mitigation strategy.

Brute Force

Brute force password attacks are the least efficient method for trying to hack a password. It is generally the last resort based on mathematics. By definition, brute force password attacks utilize a programmatic method to try all the possible combinations for a password. This method is quite efficient for passwords that are short in string (character) length and complexity, but can become infeasible, even for the fastest modern systems, with a password of eight characters or more. Therefore, if a password only has alphabetical characters, all in capitals or all in lowercase (not mixed), it would take 26^7 (8,031,810,176) guesses (you have a better chance of winning the lottery!). This also assumes that the threat attacker knows the length of the password. Other factors include numbers, case sensitivity, and other special characters in the localized language. The truth is, a brute force attack with the proper parameters will always find the password. The problem is the time required may make the brute force test itself a moot point by the time it is done. And, the time it takes to perform the attacks is not only based on the speed required to generate all the possible password permutations, but also the challenge and response time of a failure on the target system. That last lag time is what really matters when trying to brute force a password.

Pass-the-Hash

Pass-the-hash (PtH) is a hacking technique that allows an attacker to authenticate to a resource by using the underlying NT LAN Manager (NTLM) hash of a user's password, in lieu of using the account's actual password. After a threat actor obtains a valid username and hash for the password using a variety of techniques, like scraping a system's active memory, they then can use the credentials to authenticate to a remote server or service using LM or NTLM authentication. The attack exploits an implementation weakness in the authentication protocol, where the password hash remains static for every session until the password itself is actually changed. PtH can be performed against almost any server or service accepting LM or NTLM authentication, regardless of whether the resource is using Windows, Unix, Linux, or any other operating system. To that end, modern systems can defend against this type of attack in a variety of ways, but based on the weakness itself, changing the password frequently (after every interactive session) is a good defense to keep the hash different between the sessions. Password management solutions that can rotate passwords frequently or customize the security token are a good defense against this technique. Unfortunately, modern malware can contain techniques to scrape memory for hashes, making any active running user, application, service, or process a potential target. Once the hash is obtained, command and control or other automation allows for additional lateral movement or the exfiltration of data.

Security Questions

A common social technique used by financial institutions and merchants to verify a user against their account is to ask them security questions challenging them to respond to private and personal information. The sequestions are required by many organizations, when you set up a new account, as a form of two-factor authentication, and the correct answers are supplied during account creation. The end user is then prompted to respond to the security questions when logging on from a new resource, when you forget your password, or even when you reset your password. Some common security questions are these:

- The city in which you were born?

- Your high school mascot?

- Your first car?

- Your favorite food?

- Your mother's maiden name?

- What was your first pet's name?

- Who was your first kiss?

However, these security questions themselves present potentially far-reaching risks. Think about these scenarios:

- How many people would know the answer to any of these questions?

- Are the answers to these publicly available online via social media, biographies, or even school records?

- Have you played any social media games that may have revealed this information?

- Have the security questions, and possibly their answers, been stolen in a previous breach?

The relationship is clear. The more places and people that know your security question answers, the more likely they can be answered by someone else. In addition, if the information is public, then it is really not a legitimate security question at all.

When a resource requests that you complete and use security questions, my recommendation is to use the most obscure questions that no one besides yourself may know, and remember never to share information that is similar online or with another site that uses the same security questions.

The scenario is similar to password reuse and social engineering. Security questions are social facts about yourself and, unfortunately, can be used on multiple sites. If someone invokes "Forget Password" on one resource, already owns your email or text message platform, and your security phrase is the same on multiple sites, the threat actor can continue to own you through lateral movement between accounts associated with your identity. Making all your passwords different, using different accounts and emails for different types of resources (banks, merchants, friends, and spam), and never reusing the same security questions will help prevent an exploit based on your security questions and answers.

Finally, if the information in security questions cannot be mitigated from your public profile, or has already been potentially shared with malicious individuals, consider the following:

- Do not respond to the security questions in plain English. Consider using the philosophy of password complexity to obfuscate your answers. For example, if you were born in "Orlando," consider the answer to where you were born to be "0rl@nd0".

- Consider providing false information for the responses to security questions. In reality, no one checks your answers. Just like a password, consider obfuscating the results with a blatant lie. So, for example, for the question of where you were born, you could answer "TheMoon."

- If the same security question is required across multiple sites, like where were you born, consider using your password manager to store a unique response for each site. While this may sound paranoid, security questions are a form of passwords and keeping each one unique across every site may offer protection against reuse attacks. Therefore, in your password manager, you may have been born in "0rl@ndo" for one URL and "TheMoon" for another.

Credential Stuffing

Credential stuffing is a type of automated hacking technique that utilizes stolen credentials comprised of lists of usernames (or email addresses) and the corresponding passwords (typically previously stolen from other data breaches) to gain unauthorized access into a system or resource. The technique generally involves large-scale automation to submit login requests directed against a web application and to capture successful login attempts for future exploitation. Credential stuffing attacks do not attempt to brute force or guess any passwords, the threat actor simply automates authentication based on previously discovered credentials using standard web automation tools. The result can be millions of attempts to determine where a user potentially reused their credentials on another website or application. Credential stuffing attacks prey on password reuse and are only effective because so many users reuse the same credential combinations across multiple sites.

Password Spraying

Password spraying is a credential-based attack that attempts to access a large number of accounts by using a few common passwords. This is conceptually the opposite of a brute force password attack, which attempts to gain authorized access to a single account by pumping large quantities of passwords in over and over again. Brute force attempts, as discussed, can quickly result in the targeted account getting locked out. During a password-spray attack, the threat actor attempts a single commonly used password (such as "12345678" or "Passw0rd") against many accounts before moving on to attempt a second password. Essentially, the threat actor tries every user account in their list with the same password before resetting the list and trying the next password. This technique allows the threat actor to remain undetected, avoid account lockouts, and avoid hacking detection on a single account due to the time between attempts. If poor password hygiene has been used by any one user or on any one account—human or nonhuman—then the threat actor has succeeded in infiltrating the resource. The attack is compounded even further if any of these accounts are privileged.

In the real world, password-spray attacks typically are successful against cloud-based applications that are not monitored for failed logon attempts. The best mitigation for these attacks is to enforce password complexity and multi-factor authentication to every web-based resource. This is true for single sign-on (SSO) as well. SSO should never be implemented with only single-factor authentication.

Password Resets

How often do you *change* (not reset) your passwords? Every 30 or 90 days when prompted to at work? How about at home? How often do you rotate passwords for your bank account or social media? Probably not often enough, if ever. and surprisingly, that might be okay.

Without a password manager, keeping all of one's passwords unique, complex, and rotated frequently is a daunting task, even for the most seasoned security professional. One mental schema used involves using the month, year, initials, and a few special characters with each password change so the pattern can be memorized. If the pattern is unique, and not shared, the risk can be minimized, but it still allows for guessing since it is a repetitive pattern.

Unfortunately, there is a common risk in resetting (not to be confused with changing) passwords that makes them targets for threat actors. Resetting a password is the act of a forced change of the password by someone else, not a change initiated by the users themselves. These risks include:

- Pattern-based passwords (as described earlier) when reset

- Passwords that are reset via email or text message and kept by the end user

- Passwords reset by the help desk that are reused every time a password reset is requested

- Automated password resets that are blindly given due to account lockouts

- Passwords that are verbally communicated and can be heard aloud

Anytime a password is reset, there is a silent acknowledgment that the old password is at risk and needs to be changed. Perhaps it was forgotten, expired, or triggered a lockout due to numerous failed attempts. The reset, transmission, and storage of the new password are a risk until the password is changed again by the end user or, worse, not changed by the end user at all. The password itself resides in the "ether" and the security of which is unknown. A threat actor can request a password reset once an identity has been compromised and then create their own credentials for the account. Anytime a user requests a password reset, the following best practices should be implemented:

- The password should be truly random and meet the complexity requirements per business policy.

- The password should be changed by the end user after the first usage and require, if implemented, two-factor or multi-factor authentication to validate.

- Password reset requests should always come from a secure location. Public websites for businesses (not personal) should never have Forgot Password links.

- Password resets via email assume the end user still has access to email to access the new password. If the email password itself requires resetting, another vehicle needs to be established, the preferred method being verbally on the telephone.

- Do not use SMS text messages, because they are not secure for sending password reset information.

- If possible, password resets should be ephemeral. That is, the password reset should only be active for a predefined duration. If the end user has not accessed the account again within the predefined amount of time, an account lockout will occur.

While changing passwords frequently is a security best practice for privileged accounts, resetting passwords and transmitting them through unsecure medium is not. The risks of performing frequent resets, and for large numbers of users, represent a risk in themselves since the initial reset password has been communicated using potentially unsecure techniques. For the individual, a simple password reset can be the difference between a threat actor trying to own your account and a legitimate reason the password needs to be reset. Businesses must be able to distinguish the threat from the legitimate need. And, for standard end users without privileged access assigned to their account, the latest NIST[1] guidance does not recommend periodic password changes unless an indicator of compromise has been triggered.[2]

---

[1]Digital Identity Guidelines—https://pages.nist.gov/800-63-3/
[2]Breaking up with obsolete cybersecurity practices—www.beyondtrust.com/blog/entry/breaking-up-with-obsolete-cybersecurity-practices

SIM Jacking

SIM jacking is a type of account hijacking and account takeover that targets the SIM (subscriber identity module) in a mobile device. The SIM is typically a removable integrated circuit (but not always, some devices like iPhones and iPads can have them coded into nonremovable firmware) intended to securely store the phone number and identity of a device owner, regardless of connectivity status. The hijacking, SIM splitting, SIM swapping, or SIM jacking of the identification number is typically performed electronically without the removal of the SIM card. The account takeover itself can occur in a variety of methods from:

- Spoofed cellular access points and man-in-the-middle attacks

- Identity theft when purchasing a replacement device

- Weakness in two-factor authentication services that leverage voice or SMS text messages as a response

During the attack, a threat actor can capture your SIM number and recode another device with the same number to obtain nearly full access to your device (except physical). This allows access to phone calls, text messages, photos, and application data.

Since cellular mobile devices typically have a one-to-one relationship between the user (identity) and the device (asset), the privileges obtained by the threat actor are identical to the compromised user. This means they have full control, and if they root or jailbreak the device too, they can install remote software on the hijacked device as well. Therefore, once the threat actor has SIM jacked your device, they own you and everything you do on that mobile device, from personal photos all the way through access to work resources. This includes all your accounts and passwords you may use locally on your mobile device and potentially any credentials stored in a personal password manager, depending on attack vectors associated with its own implementation.

SIM jacking has grown into a considerable identity security crisis in the last few years and is a significant privileged attack vector. The best protection for this type of attack is to:

- Enable a password or PIN (depending on carrier) to protect your SIM from access

- Enable carrier protection to prevent stores and retailers from transferring a SIM from one device to another

- Disable roaming access to unknown cellular carriers

- Deploy a non-SMS text-based multi-factor authentication solution to protect all your applications and credentials from text-based attacks

Malware

The term malware is a portmanteau created by the contraction and combining of malicious and software. By definition, malware is any piece of computer software (including firmware, microcode, etc.) that was written with the intent of damaging devices, stealing data, and, generally, causing a resource to behave in ways not in accordance with its intended design or current state. Malware is often created by threat actors looking to:

- Make money, either by spreading the malware themselves or selling it to the highest bidder on the dark web

- Serve as a vehicle for protest and disruption, or to propagate real or "fake news"

- Serve as a proof of concept designed to test or exploit existing security controls

- Act as weapons of war between governments, terrorists, or other politically motivated groups

- Conduct corporate espionage

- Prove that it can be done, for personal amusement or for bragging rights

In general, there are eight different types and sources for malware:

1. **Bugs**: A type of error, flaw, vulnerability, or failure that produces an undesirable or unexpected result due to poor software coding or unexpected operational conditions. Bugs can exist in any type of software from local applications and websites. When bugs can be leveraged against an application and its data, they are called vulnerabilities, and the software used to leverage them are called exploits. It is important to note that a bug alone is not malware, but when leveraged it can be just as devasting.

2. **Worms**: Worms rely on bugs, vulnerabilities, and exploits to deliver a payload and spread duplicates of themselves to other resources. Initial infections are often hidden in attachments or file downloads, but once they execute, they can scan a network (or Internet) for other vulnerable systems to propagate. Based on their design, they consume vast amounts of bandwidth or operate in a slow, stealthy mode and, based on their intent, completely disable a network or web server. Ransomware that can self-propagate to infect multiple systems is a form of a worm.

3. **Virus**: A virus is any piece of malicious software that is loaded onto your website or computer without your knowledge. The intent of the virus may not be apparent from an initial infection and, in general, can reside on a resource until it is triggered to perform a malicious action.

4. **Bots**: Bots are malicious software programs created to perform a specific set of tasks with a known intent. Bots can be utilized by a threat actor to send spam or be used in a Distribution Denial of Service (DDoS) attack to bring down an entire website, network, or Internet-based service.

5. **Trojan**: A trojan piece of malware is based on Greek history and the city of Troy. Much like the mythical Trojan Horse, this malware disguises itself as a normal file or application and tricks the user into downloading, opening, or executing it. The payload can launch any other form of malware and continue to trick the user that their actions are actually interacting with a legitimate piece of software.

6. **Ransomware**: Ransomware (covered in Chapter 17) denies access to your files, typically through encryption, and demands a ransom (usually in the form of digital and cryptocurrencies) to release the threat actor's grip on your data. If the ransom is paid, and the threat actor is operating a real ransomware service, they will provide a method to decrypt your files and allow you to gain access to the resources (files) again. In some cases, payment is

made, and the threat actor has long abandoned their scheme, leaving the victim with infected systems and a financial loss that cannot be recovered.

7. **Adware**: Adware is a type of malware that automatically displays unwanted and potentially illegal advertisements to an end user. Clicking the ad could download malicious software, launch an exploit, or redirect you to a malicious website. The goal is to expose inappropriate services to the end user and trick them into performing additional steps to load more malware.

8. **Spyware**: Spyware is a type of malware that functions by spying on a user's activity. These functions can include monitoring the user's screen, capturing keystrokes, and even enabling the asset's camera and microphone for surveillance. This information is collected and transmitted through the Internet or stored locally for later retrieval by the threat actor. In today's world, next to ransomware, this is the most dangerous malware used by threat actors.

Each classification of malware has attack vectors that target the three pillars of cybersecurity, as illustrated in Table 4-1.

Table 4-1. *Malware Mapped to the Three Pillars of Cybersecurity and Types of Attack Vectors*

Malware	Privileged Attack Vector	Asset Attack Vector	Identity Attack Vector
Bugs	√	√	√
Worms	√	√	
Virus	√	√	√
Bots	√	√	
Trojan	√		√
Ransomware	√	√	√
Adware			√
Spyware			√

It is important to note, some malware requires user interaction to infect a resource, and some leverage weaknesses in the asset, or obtained privileges, to continue its nefarious mission. This is why some are categorized uniquely in each column and why there are three books in the attack vectors[3] series covering each of these methods. And, of these eight types, any one can be used as a malicious software delivery mechanism for other attack vectors. With this in mind, the vast majority of malware needs administrative privileges to execute on a host and to infect a system. This is yet another reason the removal and management of privileged access is more than just passwords stored in a vault, it is a universal view of privileged management everywhere.

---

[3]Morey J. Haber and Darran Rolls, *Identity Attack Vectors* (Apress, 2020); Morey J. Haber and Brad Hibbert, *Asset Attack Vectors* (Apress 2018).

Other Techniques

Consider that almost every word in this book, eight letters and longer, can be potentially used in a password hacking attack, if security best practices are not enforced. In fact, every word shorter than eight letters could be a password on a system that does not meet very basic password complexity requirements in length. Once we add simple derivations of these words to include upper- and lowercase, and substitution of specific letters for numbers, like 0 for o, we have a finite list of words that people would statistically choose for a password. An automated program can systematically check against an account to discover if the user has made a cardinal mistake by selecting a guessable password or, even worse, is using a default password. This is why, every year, we see multiple publications listing the most popular passwords used, and reused, by users. While these are basic assumptions for a password hacking, they are relevant for securing passwords and privileges using truly randomized and highly complex passwords found in privileged access management (PAM) solutions. Leveraging PAM solution means the only viable method for a threat actor to guess a password is by using brute force or memory-stealing hash technology, as with pass-the-hash attacks. Fortunately, these are only minor players as threat actors mostly attempt to steal passwords.

Password reuse, default passwords, and poorly secured passwords make up the bulk of all password-related breaches in modern businesses and government. It should be pointed out that there are a wide variety of other techniques to steal passwords that may leverage multiple techniques, from watering holes to golden ticket attacks. The list is more extensive than this book can accommodate. The main point in referencing them is that they are not the initial attack vector for stealing a password. Techniques like watering holes rely first on compromising a website to subsequently steal a user's login credentials. Social engineering may, or may not, play a factor. Golden ticket attacks are only experienced after the administrative rights of a domain controller are compromised. A threat actor had to compromise the domain administrator account first in order to create additional Kerberos certificates.

The key takeaway is that threat actors will always find another method to steal passwords. We will brand them with clever names and recommend best practices; but in the end, whatever the technique, they are ultimately after our privileged accounts.

CHAPTER 5

Passwordless Authentication

The concept of a human interface device (HID) has a deep history in keypads, keyboards, and even punch cards, to interface with computing technology. As output improved from fan folder paper to monitors, touchscreens, and other forms of motion-based interactive devices, the need to secure access when using a HID became clearly evident. In addition, privileged access to these devices was not only needed to protect the data and operations of the device, but also its configuration and other resources that could be leveraged from the interface. This includes even simple tasks, such as powering off the asset or inserting a DVD.

A Physical Discussion Around Passwordless Authentication

The question of privileged access to resources then becomes a question of physical security vs. electronic security. Take, for example, a keyboard. It typically has no physical protection to stop a potential threat actor from interacting with its keys. Rather, the keyboard relies on software to prevent resources from interacting with the applications hosted by the device. However, this was not always the case. Before Windows XP (August 2001), a simple Ctrl-Alt-Delete would reboot, or force the operating system to have terminal-based interaction with the end user, and potentially bypass

M. J. Haber, *Privileged Attack Vectors*, https://doi.org/10.1007/978-1-4842-5914-6_5

any security and privileged access to the resource. Software has been playing catch-up over physical privileged access for years.

And this is not an isolated or old-school case. Consider the facial recognition technology on your mobile device. Anyone can look at the device and the software, in conjunction with biometric sensors, to determine if you are authorized to access the device. If the technology is working as designed, access should be denied. However, should you have an identical twin, even Apple recognizes (pun intended) that their facial identification technology can be spoofed by identities that have a similar resemblance. As a simple matter of fact, even on a modern iPhone, I have family members that can unlock each other's phones with a simple glance. In my opinion, they do not look that similar, but the attribute-based technology in facial recognition computes that they are close enough to unlock the phone based on this HID technology.

Any form of access to human interface devices begins the journey for a threat actor when physical access is permitted, and a privileged attack becomes a combination of physical access to the device (including diagnostic interfaces and physically breaking into the internal electronics of the device), a password, biometrics, or a potential HID vulnerability. This all occurs before any lateral movement or advanced persistent threats (APTs) can form a beachhead. Therefore, any secure passwordless authentication strategy and technology must protect and be secure against physical threats first.

An Electronic Discussion Around Passwordless Authentication

Physical security alone is not the answer to a passwordless authentication strategy because it would limit usage altogether, not just who should have access or privileged access to the resource. The answer is surprisingly not obvious since devices like cellular phones are generally only used by individuals, and workstations are typically assigned to a single user, but hardwired telephones and other office devices have no physical restrictions or security around their usage. So, who should have access (especially privileged access) and how do you accomplish it without traditionally entered credentials using an HID? Answering this question merely with biometrics is inadequate. Biometrics, like fingerprints or facial recognition, is a single-factor authentication solution and, as we have already discussed, does not provide the confidence to allow for privileged access to sensitive resources. A threat actor can circumvent biometrics. What is needed is a form of multi-factor authentication that has exceptionally high confidence in the identity and that is truly passwordless.

To tackle this problem, let's first begin with your persona. What is your job title and what is your role(s) within an organization? Are you an executive, vice president, director, manager, contractor, or a sole contributor? How do you contribute to the success of your organization? What is your role? An auditor, information technology administrator, help desk engineer, salesperson, chief information security officer, or others? Your title and job role should implicitly determine what level of privileges you should potentially have and, therefore, the level of confidence needed for authentication. This statement is true for passwordless authentication, the use of credentials with or without multi-factor authentication, and applicable to any privileged access strategy you choose to adopt. It is included in this section because it is often overlooked for passwordless authentication models, yet always applicable.

The higher your professional title, the lower the privileges you should have access to within your organization. And, for the privileged access you do have, the privileges should be restricted, and not an administrator or root. In other words, in most organizations, a CEO, and, in fact, anyone in the C-Suite, should have neither privileged access nor unrestricted access to privileged credentials.

As you move down the organizational structure, privileged access should be assigned by role and follow the model of least privileged access. The least privilege model (discussed in detail later on in this book) entails assigning only those rights and privileges absolutely necessary for a role to perform its functions.

This should also hold true for midlevel management. Barring the ego of a direct report owner, privileged access should only exist and be viable against a resource by the team members that actually use it, and not anyone else, unless an emergency or break-glass scenario warrants it.

Moreover, these privileged user accounts should not be "always-on," meaning they should not have persistent privileged access. An always-on privileged access model, which remains the default practice for most organizations, significantly swells the risk surface, since the accounts always have privileges enabled and, thus, always pose a potential threat via misuse, whether intentional or inadvertent. The best practice is to adhere to a just-in-time privileged access model (also discussed later in this book) that secures the accounts, only activating them for use for the finite duration they are needed to perform an authorized activity. This is an ephemeral approach to privilege management and inherently limits privileged access, especially when confidence is based on a passwordless strategy.

This brings us back to the original discussion of electronic passwordless authentication. Only the roles needing privileges should get them. The privileges should not be exposed unless:

1. The workflow warrants the privileges be activated at that time

2. The confidence of the passwordless authentication model is high

3. The identity requesting access is correct and follows a multi-factor authentication approach to ensure that the user has not been spoofed

Figure 5-1 illustrates this model of privileges by title and confidence.

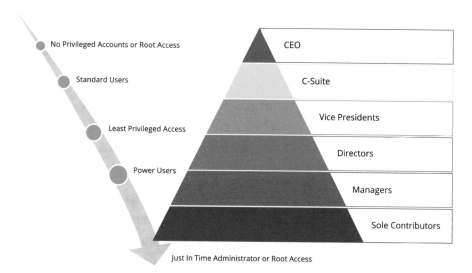

Figure 5-1. *Privileged Access in Relationship to a Company's Organizational Structure*

While there are always exceptions to this model, passwordless authentication models should also consider a second aspect of appropriate access: "Where can they be used? This is a problem for HIDs and leads us to consider role-based access and attribute-based access to authenticate a user properly. This is a context and confidence problem. For example, privileged accounts should not work on resources that are misaligned with the employee's role. Privileged accounts should definitely not work on resources owned by executives in the C-Suite. In addition, if passwordless authentication access attempts are inappropriately made from these resources, they should be flagged as potential indicators of compromise since they should not be used by upper management. This also includes all the relevant context data for access, including geolocation, source IP address, time of day, device requesting access, and so on. Passwordless authentication must go beyond just a Boolean acceptance of credentials in order to approve access.

Requirements for Passwordless Authentication

Finally, concerning passwordless authentication, consider the following for any solution and model you choose:

- When using an HID, all passwordless authentication should be monitored based on the method of input. That is, did it originate from another application or from an HID? And, what HID?

- The method used for privilege elevation is just as crucial as the passwordless authentication model itself since inappropriate usage rarely occurs via a threat actor typing on a keyboard, but rather from leveraging automation for malware, scripts, or another compromised application. Also, attacks almost always leverage some form of remote access.

- The physical security for passwordless authentication is just as important as the characteristics of electronic passwordless authentication.

- Any passwordless authentication model is only as good as the security of the underlining operating system, infrastructure, and supporting resources. A threat actor can circumvent any passwordless authentication model if the platform hosting it is itself vulnerable. Consider how it is maintained, updated, and hardened.

- Any passwordless authentication solution should integrate with role-based access and attribute-based access models. The technology should support, and work in conjunction with, multi-factor solutions—even if they are passwordless—to provide a high level of confidence for authentication.

- Passwordless technology needs to be context-aware to determine if the access is appropriate on authorized devices and by authorized individuals. It essentially needs to be HID-aware, especially for privileged access.

- Passwordless authentication technology should be identity- and role-aware. This is best suited when the technology can integrate with directory stores and identity governance solutions.

- Passwordless authentication relies on algorithms to provide a confidence rating for authentication. It is not a Boolean match like a username and password combination. For any organization looking into implementing passwordless authentication, they should request an explanation of the algorithms or patents behind a vendor's technology and any testing or proof for its accuracy. If the vendors say "no" or it is proprietary, select a different solution. You are basing user authentication on some form of mathematical model and you should have at least a basic understanding of how it works. This is especially true if it is needed in a court of law to defend or prosecute inappropriate access.

- Finally, the higher the privileges trusted with passwordless authentication, the higher the confidence needed to be in the technology itself. This explains the detail provided for roles, privileges, and job titles in the organization. Therefore, it is safe to assume that passwordless authentication may not be the best fit for everyone in the organization.

While this discussion and analysis may be new to some readers, passwordless authentication is definitely possible within many organizations struggling with privileged access management (PAM) initiatives. Any PAM solutions chosen to help you on your journey need to manage by role, job, HID, and context in order to secure passwordless authentication models for anyone, and anytime.

The Reality Around Passwordless Authentication

While there is a movement to remove passwords and traditional credentials from the authentication process, and many emerging solutions are claiming to do so, the unfortunate fact for any of these technologies is that they are still tied to the binary nature of all computing systems. You either have been authenticated or you have not; the outcome is always Boolean. While you can apply context-aware scenarios and sophisticated algorithms to limit access as we covered earlier, the user still has to be authenticated based on a confidence level. Their location may limit access, the device may be restricted to specific resources, but in the end, they still have been authenticated in a binary manner. The emerging technologies that layer upon existing solutions, such as biometrics, keyboard response time, and even multi-factor authentication, still need to translate to that same "yes" or "no" answer. For many of these technologies, new security concerns have been raised, and others may have inherent flaws in their approach. Figure 5-2 outlines the most popular of these technologies that currently drive passwordless authentication.

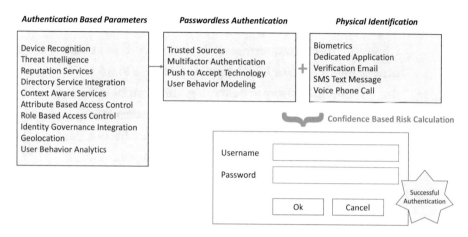

Figure 5-2. *Sample Passwordless Authentication Mechanisms*

- **Biometrics**: This technology has been deemed by many technologists as the Holy Grail to replace credentials. While it is true that biometrics should be unique per identity, it has been proven that fingerprints can be replicated, facial recognition bypassed (the twin and child factor for FaceID), and the databases storing biometric information stolen for future malicious activity.[1] Therefore, biometrics as an authentication mechanism alone is never a good idea for privileged access. It is a single-factor technology when used stand-alone. Biometrics should always be paired with multi-factor authentication technology before allowing privileged access.

---

[1]OPM Biometric Breach—www.wired.com/2015/09/opm-now-admits-5-6m-feds-fingerprints-stolen-hackers/

- **Keystroke Timing**: An emerging patented technology that provides authentication based on the rate keys are typed on a keyboard. Surprisingly, the results of this method are very good, but it has been shown to have "known" false positive authentication rates when the user is under duress. For example, if the user breaks their hand, or is only typing with one hand due to something they are carrying, these models falter in authenticating a user since the pattern and rates have never been documented for them before. The machine learning portion needs to be retrained for this situation. And using traditional credentials is unfortunately the only viable fallback mechanism (with multi-factor authentication for privileged access, of course).

- **Federated Services**: One of the more promising approaches uses a blended technology approach from single sign-on and multi-factor authentication. The approach requires you to authenticate once to a federated service using a traditional, trusted mechanism. This service may be based on traditional credentials and include other multi-factor technology normally hosted in the cloud. Once authenticated, your presence (geolocation, device, asset risk, time, and date, etc.) is used to authenticate against other services and applications. This can be seamless or rely on a two-factor code sent to a dedicated mobile application, SMS text (not as secure due to SIM swapping attacks), or another vehicle to authorize a new session. Social media accounts like Facebook and Google have been at the forefront of this technology, but outside of Microsoft Active Directory Federation Services, Microsoft Live, and Microsoft Hello, the adoption of these models has been slow and organizations have been hesitant to trust this approach unless a dedicated multi-factor vendor has also been installed.

At this time, passwordless solutions still rely on traditional credentials under the hood within the operating system, application, and authentication standards. They are just a new layer for authentication and currently cannot replace credentials completely. Please consider the following technology problems that must be resolved to go fully passwordless:

- As a backup when passwordless layers fail, credentials are the only viable backup. This still needs to be managed.

- Legacy technology (and every piece of technology created at the time this book was published) still requires credentials under the hood, whether this is an administrator account or service credentials. Passwordless solutions are just a new security layer on top and may not be compatible, especially for custom applications.

- A physical injury to the hand, eye, or face can cause biometrics to fail. Microsoft Hello, Samsung Galaxy Note, and Apple iPhones FaceID are the first generation to take these to consumers. However, their reliability, false positives, and potentially false negatives will also drive whether or not these ultimately prove acceptable passwordless solutions.

For a threat actor, passwordless solutions represent a real challenge to gain privileged access as compared to traditional credentials. However, just like recent tribulations in election hacking, sometimes it is better to go after the supplier of the technology than trying to hack the organization that has deployed it. If you can break the passwordless solution by stealing a biometric database, finding faults or vulnerabilities with the tool itself, or installing malware on a mobile device, the end results of a breach are virtually the same.

CHAPTER 6

Privilege Escalation

Once we have established an authenticated session of any type, whether the session is legitimate or hacked via any of the attacks previously discussed, a threat actor's typical goal is to elevate privileges and extract data. Figure 6-1 illustrates this based on the models we have been discussing. A standard user typically does not have rights to a database, sensitive files, or anything of value *en masse*. So, how does a threat actor navigate an environment and gain administrator or root privileges to exploit them as an attack vector? There are five primary methods:

- Credential exploitation
- Vulnerabilities and exploits
- Misconfigurations
- Malware
- Social engineering

In addition, some security solutions designed to protect against these threats, when not properly hardened or maintained, could lead to exploitation using any of the techniques listed here too.

© Morey J. Haber 2020
M. J. Haber, *Privileged Attack Vectors*, https://doi.org/10.1007/978-1-4842-5914-6_6

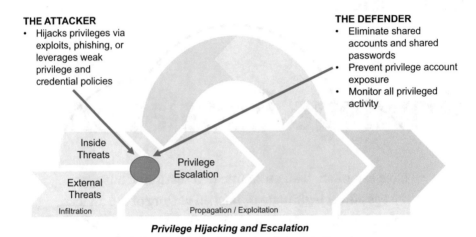

THE ATTACKER
- Hijacks privileges via exploits, phishing, or leverages weak privilege and credential policies

THE DEFENDER
- Eliminate shared accounts and shared passwords
- Prevent privilege account exposure
- Monitor all privileged activity

Inside Threats

External Threats

Infiltration

Privilege Escalation

Propagation / Exploitation

Privilege Hijacking and Escalation

Figure 6-1. *Privilege Hijacking and Escalation*

Credential Exploitation

We have already established that valid credentials will allow you to authenticate against a resource. This is how authentication works. However, once a username is known, obtaining the account's password becomes a hacking exercise. Often a threat actor will first target an administrator or executive since their credentials often have privileges to directly access sensitive data and systems, enabling the cybercriminal to move laterally while arousing little or no suspicion. For a threat actor, going undetected is key to the success of their mission. They need to start infiltration by gaining a foothold within the environment. Gaining this beachhead could be the result of anything from leveraging missing security patches all the way through social engineering. Once the initial infiltration has been successful, threat actors will typically perform surveillance and be patient, waiting for the right opportunity to continue their mission. Threat actors will customarily pursue the path of least resistance and will perform steps to clean up their tracks in order to remain undetected.

Whether this involves masking their source IP address or deleting logs based on the credentials they are using, any evidence about their presence can be an indicator of compromise. Once identified, this can be used to either stop their movement or allow the organization to ramp up forensics to monitor their intentions.

There are multiple philosophies on what to do once a breach is detected that are outside of the scope of this book. Regardless, when dealing with compromised credentials, everything privileged to that account is now fair game for the attacker. Resetting passwords is typically a priority and reimaging infected systems is a standard practice (especially if it involves servers). However, simply requesting the end user to change a password does not always resolve the incident because the method of obtaining the credentials in the first place may involve other attack vectors, like malware. Compromised credentials are the easiest privileged attack vector for a threat actor, and the accounts associated with them control almost every aspect of a modern information technology environment, from administrators to service accounts.

As previously discussed, the theft of credentials can be performed in a variety of ways, ranging from password reuse to memory-scraping malware. Stolen administrator credentials allow direct exploitation of resources. Standard user credentials could allow access to sensitive data based on a user's role and job title. Privileged escalation of credentials from a standard user to administrator can happen using any of the techniques described in the following texts. Therefore, credentials compromised for the most sensitive accounts (domain, database administrator, etc.) can be a "game-over" event for some companies, and those accounts should always be treated with care and properly identified during a risk assessment. These credentials are a prime attack vector for privilege escalation and their protection should be prioritized over the course of your PAM journey.

Vulnerabilities and Exploits

A vulnerability itself does not allow for a privileged attack vector to succeed. In fact, a vulnerability in and of itself just means that a risk exists and that any type of attack could succeed. Vulnerabilities are nothing more than mistakes. They are mistakes in the code, design, implementation, or configuration that allow malicious activity potentially to occur via an exploit. Thus, without an exploit, a vulnerability is just a potential problem and used in a risk assessment to gauge what *could* happen. Depending on the vulnerability, available exploit, and resources assessed with the flaw, the actual risk could be limited in scope, or it could signify an impending disaster. While this is a simplification of a real risk assessment, it provides the foundation for privileges as an attack vector. Not all vulnerabilities and exploits are equal, and depending on the privileges of the user or application executing in conjunction with the vulnerability, the escalation and effectiveness of the attack vector can change.

For example, an operating system vulnerability executed by a standard user vs. an administrator can have two completely different sets of risks once exploited. As a standard user, the exploit might not work at all, could be limited to just the user's privileges as a standard user, or it could have full administrative access to the host. In fact, as reported by BeyondTrust in 2019,[1] 81% of Microsoft vulnerabilities could be mitigated by being a standard user vs. an administrator. And, if the user is using a domain administrator account or other elevated privileges, the exploit could have permissions to the entire environment. This is something a threat actor targets as low-hanging fruit. Who is operating outside of security best practices and how can I leverage them to infiltrate the environment?

---

[1]BeyondTrust Microsoft Vulnerabilities Report for 2019—www.beyondtrust.com/assets/documents/Microsoft-Vulnerabilities-Report-2019.pdf

With this in mind, vulnerabilities come in all "shapes and sizes." They can involve the operating system, applications, web applications, infrastructure, and so on. They can also target the protocols, transports, and communications in between resources from wired networks, Wi-Fi, to tone-based radio frequencies. However, not all vulnerabilities have exploits. Some are proof of concepts, some are unreliable, and some are easily weaponized and even included in commercial penetration testing tools or free open source hacking tools. In addition, some vulnerabilities are sold on the dark web to perpetrate cybercrimes, and others are used exclusively by nation-states until they are patched or made public (intentionally or not). The point is that vulnerabilities can be in anything at any time. It is how they are leveraged that makes them important, and if the vulnerability itself leads to an exploit that can change privileges (privilege escalation from one user's permissions to another), the risk is a very real privileged attack vector. To date, less than 10% of all Microsoft vulnerabilities allow for privilege escalation, yet, these are the types of vulnerabilities that have been responsible for some of the worst exploits in recent years—from BlueKeep[2] to WannaCry[3] to NotPetya.

The security industry has multiple security standards to convey the risk, threat, and relevance of a vulnerability. The most common standards are the following:

- **Common Vulnerabilities and Exposures (CVE):**
  A standard for information security vulnerability names and descriptions.

---

[2]BlueKeep— https://portal.msrc.microsoft.com/en-US/security-guidance/advisory/CVE-2019-0708

[3]WannaCry—www.csoonline.com/article/3227906/what-is-wannacry-ransomware-how-does-it-infect-and-who-was-responsible.html

- **Common Vulnerability Scoring System (CVSS)**:
  A mathematical system for scoring the risk of
  information technology vulnerabilities.

- **The Extensible Configuration Checklist Description
  Format (XCCDF)**: A specification language for writing
  security checklists, benchmarks, and related kinds of
  documents.

- **Open Vulnerability Assessment Language (OVAL)**:
  An information security community effort to
  standardize how to assess and report upon the
  machine state of computer systems.

- **Common Configuration Enumeration (CCE)**:
  Provides unique identifiers to system configuration
  issues to facilitate fast and accurate correlation of
  configuration data across multiple information sources
  and tools.

- **Common Weakness Enumeration Specification (CWE)**:
  Provides a common language of discourse for
  discussing, finding, and dealing with the causes of
  software security vulnerabilities as they are found
  in code.

- **Common Platform Enumeration (CPE)**: A structured
  naming scheme for information technology systems,
  software, and packages.

- **Common Configuration Scoring System (CCSS)**:
  A set of measures of the severity of software security
  configuration issues. CCSS is a derivation of CVSS.

The results from all this information allow security professionals and management teams to discuss and prioritize the risks from vulnerabilities. The ones with privileged escalation exploits that can operate without any end-user intervention pose the highest risk. These are weaponized in the form of malware called "worms."

In the end, information technology teams must prevent any type of exploitation, especially ones that are simple for a threat actor to perform. With a common language and structure across vendors, companies, and governments, we can better define mitigation and remediation strategies. A critical risk for one company may not exist for another simply based on their environment. Standards like CVSS allow for that to be communicated correctly to all stakeholders and help define best practices for mitigation. Figure 6-2 illustrates perimeter exploitation typically associated with vulnerabilities as it relates to privileged attack vectors.

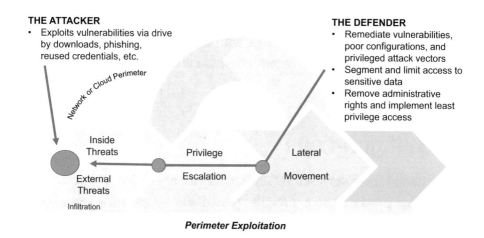

Perimeter Exploitation

Figure 6-2. *Perimeter Exploitation and Considerations*

As discussed, exploits require a vulnerability. Without a documentable flaw, an exploit cannot exist. We may just not understand the vulnerability when a new exploit appears in the wild. It can take some time for security professionals to reverse engineer an exploit to figure out what vulnerability was leveraged. This is typically a very technical forensics exercise performed by specialists in the industry. An exploit that can gain privileges, execute code, and go undetected is not only dependent on the vulnerability, but also on the privileges the exploit has when it executes. This is why vulnerability management, risk assessments, patch management, and privileged access management are so important. Exploits can only execute in the confines of the resource they compromise. If no vulnerability exists due to remediation, the exploit cannot execute. If the privileges of the user or application with the vulnerability are low (standard user), and no privilege escalation exploitation is possible, then the attack is limited in its capabilities or may not work at all. However, don't be fooled: exploitation, even at standard user privileges, can cause devastation in the form of ransomware or other vicious attacks. Fortunately, the vast majority can be contained, or otherwise mitigated just by lowering privileges and minimizing the surface area for a privileged attack. Exploits wreak the most havoc with the highest privileges, hence the recommendation to operate with the least amount of privileges as a mitigation strategy.

Misconfigurations

Configuration flaws are just another form of vulnerabilities. They are, nonetheless, flaws that do not require remediation—just mitigation. The difference between remediation and mitigation is key. Remediation implies the deployment of a software or firmware patch to correct the vulnerability. This is commonly referred to as patch management. Mitigation is simply a change at some level in the existing deployment that deflects (mitigates) the risk from being exploited. It can be a simple change within a file, group policy, updating certificates, or other type of setting. In the end, they are vulnerabilities based on weak configurations or improper hardening and can be easily exploited as a privileged attack vector.

The most common configuration problems exploited for privileges involve accounts that have poor default security practices. This could be blank or default passwords upon initial configuration for administrator or root accounts, or insecure access that is not locked down after an initial install due to a lack of expertise or an undocumented backdoor.

Regardless, configuration flaws just require a change to the resource. And, if the flaw is severe enough, a threat actor can have root privileges with little to no effort.

Malware

Malware, which includes viruses, spyware, worms, adware, ransomware, and so on, refers to any class of undesirable or unauthorized software designed to have malicious intent on a resource. The intent can range from surveillance, data leakage, disruption, command, and control to extortion. If you pick your favorite crime that can be translated to an information technology resource, malware can provide a vehicle to instrument cybercriminal activity for a threat actor. Malware, like any other program, can execute at any permission from standard user to administrator (root). Depending on its creation, intent, and privileges, the damage it can do can be anything from an annoyance to a game-over event. Malware can be installed on a resource via a vulnerability and exploit combination, or through legitimate installers, weaknesses in the supply chain, or even social via engineering, such as phishing. Regardless of the delivery mechanism, the motive is to get unauthorized code executing on a resource. Once running, it becomes a battle of detection by endpoint protection vendors and threat actors to keep executing, avoid detection, and remain persistent. This includes malware adapting itself to avoid detection as well as disabling defenses to continue proliferation. Malware itself, based on intent, can perform functions like pass-the-hash and keystroke logging. This allows for the stealing of passwords to perform attacks based on privileges by the malware itself or other attack vectors deployed by the threat actor. Malware is just a transport vehicle to continue the propagation of a sustained attack and, ultimately, needs permissions to obtain the target information sought by the attacker. It is such a broad category of malicious software–but when discussing privileges, the subset that scrapes memory, installs additional malicious software, or provides surveillance is the most relevant.

Social Engineering

If you grew up with siblings, you might have had the fortune of being the brunt of a practical joke—everything from smell my finger, open this box, through taste this. While the examples are rather crude, they are no different from the hacking capabilities we all experience via social engineering and the desire of a threat actor to gain privileges. The main motive from our relatives was to leverage our trust into doing something mischievous or embarrassing for the amusement (usually laughter) of our siblings. As harmless as it sounds, we hopefully learned for the next time.

Social engineering is no different. We have a blind trust in the email we receive, the phone call we answer, or even the letter we receive to believe someone is contacting us. If the message is crafted well enough, and potentially even spoofing someone we already trust, then the threat actor already gained the first step in deceiving us and potentially carrying out a ruse. If, in fact, we act on the fake correspondence from a work colleague, friend, company, or even a sweepstakes, we may just become a victim of social engineering.

Considering the modern threats in the cyber world, from ransomware to recording our voices on a phone call, the outcome can become much more severe than eating a dead worm presented as beef jerky by a sibling. At the risk of becoming paranoid about every email we receive and phone call we answer, we need to understand how social engineering works and how to identify it in the first place, without losing our sanity. This learned behavior is no different than figuring out whether your sibling has lied about a message from your parents or not. Sometimes you just need to verify the message before taking action and understand the risks from the outcome, should you engage.

From a social engineering perspective, threat actors attempt to capitalize on a few key human traits to meet their goals:

- **Trust**: The belief that the correspondence, of any type, is from a trustworthy source.

- **Gullibility**: The belief that the contents, as crazy or simple as they may be, are, in fact, real.

- **Sincerity**: The intent of the content is in your best interest to respond or open.

- **Suspicion**: The contents of the correspondence do not raise any concern by having misspellings and poor grammar, or by sounding like a robot corresponding on the phone.

- **Curiosity**: The attack technique has not been identified (as part of previous training), or the person remembers the attack vector, but does not react accordingly.

- **Laziness**: The correspondence initially looks good enough, but investigating the URLs and contents for malicious activity does not seem worth the effort.

If we consider each of these characteristics, we can appropriately train team members to be resistant to social engineering. The difficulty is overcoming human traits and not deviating from the education. To that end, please consider the following training parameters and potential self-awareness techniques to stop social engineering and privileged attacks:

- Team members should only trust requests for sensitive information from known and trusted team members. An email address alone in the "From" line is not sufficient to verify the request, nor is an email reply. The sender's account could be compromised. The best option is to learn from two-factor authentication techniques and pick up the phone or verify the email using another communications path. For example, call the party requesting the sensitive information and verify the request. If the request seems absurd, like requesting W-2 information or a wire transfer, confirm this is acceptable according to internal policies or other stakeholders, such as finance or human resources (it could be an insider attack). Simple verification of the request from an alleged trusted individual, like a superior, can go a long way to stopping social engineering. Also, all of this should occur before opening any attachments or clicking any links due to any existing vulnerabilities and exploits. If the email is malicious, the payload and exploit may have executed before you performed any verification.

- If the request is coming from an unknown source, but is moderately trusted—such as a bank or business you interact with—simple techniques can stop you from being gullible. First, check all the links in the email and make sure they actually point back to the proper domain. Just hovering over the link on most computers and email programs will reveal the contents. If the request is over the phone, never give out personal information. Remember, they called you. For example, the IRS will never contact you by phone; they only use USPS for official correspondence. Don't let yourself fall for the "sky is falling" metaphor.

- Teaching how to distinguish between genuine, legitimate correspondence and fraudulent correspondence is rather difficult. Social engineering can take on many forms—from accounts payable, love letters, and resumes, to human resources interventions. Just stating "if it seems too good to be true" or "nothing is ever free" only handles a very small subset of social engineering attempts. In addition, if peers receive the same correspondence, it only eliminates spear-phishing attempts as the probable attack vector. The best option is to consider if you should be receiving the request in the first place. Is this something you normally do or is it out of the ordinary to receive it? If it is an unusual request, default back to caution and verify trust, and therefore verify the intent, before proceeding. This is especially important with the inception of deepfake voice and photos that are nearly impossible to distinguish from real people and images.

- Suspicious correspondence is the easiest way to detect and deflect social engineering attempts. This requires a little detective-style investigation into the correspondence by looking for spelling mistakes, poor grammar, bad formatting, or robotic voices on the phone that could be deepfakes. This is expressly true if the request is from a source with whom you have never had an interaction in the past. This could be an offer of a free cruise, or from a bank at which you have no accounts. If there is any reason to be suspicious, it is best to err on the side of caution: do not open any attachments or files, click any links, or verbally reply—just delete the correspondence. If it is real, the responsible party will call back in due course.

- Curiosity is the worst offender, from a social engineering perspective. Nothing should happen to me since I *believe* I am fully protected by my computer and my company's information technology security resources, right? That's a false and dangerous assumption. Modern attacks can circumvent the best systems and application control solutions—even leveraging native OS commands to conduct their attacks. The best defense for a person's curiosity is purely self-restraint. Do not reply to "Can you hear me?" from a strange phone call; do not open attachments if any of the preceding criteria have been realized; and do not believe that nothing can happen to you (even for people using MacOS). The fact is, it can, and your curiosity should not be the cause. Being naïve will make you a victim.

Social engineering is a huge problem, and there is no technology that is 100% effective. Spam filters can strip out malicious emails, and endpoint protection solutions can find known or behavior-based malware, but nothing can totally stop the human problem of social engineering and potential insider threats. The best defense for social engineering is education and an understanding of how these attacks leverage our own traits to be successful. If we can understand our own flaws and react accordingly, we can minimize the threat actor's ability to compromise resources and gain privileges within the environment.

Multi-factor Authentication

While we have been focusing on passwords as the primary form of authentication with credentials, other authentication techniques should be used to strengthen the authentication model. This is especially true for privileged accounts. As a security best practice, and required by many regulatory authorities, multi-factor authentication (MFA) techniques are required to secure access instead of a traditional username and password credential combination only (single factor). MFA provides an additional layer that makes it more difficult (but not impossible) to hack and, thus, is always recommended when securing sensitive information.

The premise for MFA (two-factor is a subset category for authentication) is simple. In addition to a traditional username and password credential, an additional "passcode" or evidence is needed to validate the user. This is more than just a PIN code; it is best implemented when you have something physical to reference. The delivery and randomization of "proof" varies from technology to technology and from vendor to vendor. This proof typically takes on the form of knowledge (something the user knows that is unique to them), possession (something they physically have that's unique to them), and inherence (something they are in a given state).

The use of multiple authentication factors provides important additional protection around an identity. An unauthorized threat actor is most likely unable to supply all the factors required for correct access due to an additional authentication variable. During a session, if at least one of the components is in error, the user's identity is not verified with sufficient confidence (2 of 3 criteria match), then access to the resource being protected by multi-factor authentication is denied. The authentication factors of a multi-factor authentication model typically include the following:

- A physical device or software like a phone app or USB key that produces a secret passcode re-randomized on a regular frequency.

- A secret code known only to the end user, like a PIN that is typically mentally stored.

- A physical characteristic that can be digitally analyzed for uniqueness, like a fingerprint, typing speed, or voice. These are called biometric authentication technology.

MFA is an identity-specific layer for authentication. Once validated, the privileges assigned as a potential attack vector are not any different unless policies explicitly require multi-factor authentication in order to be assigned. For example, if credentials are compromised in a traditional username and password model, a threat actor could authenticate against any target that will accept them locally or remotely. For multi-factor, even though there is an additional variable required, including physical presence, once you are validated, lateral navigation is still possible from your initial location (barring any segmentation technology or policy). The difference is solely your starting point for authentication. Multi-factor must have all the security conditions met from an entry point, while traditional credentials do not. A hacker can leverage credentials within a network to jump from host to host while changing credentials as needed. Unless the multi-factor system itself is compromised, the hacker cannot target a multi-factor host for authentication unless they have compromised the multi-factor system itself, or have in possession an identity's complete multi-factor challenge and response. Hence, there always needs to be an initial entry point for starting a multi-factor session, and once in, using credentials is the easiest method for a threat actor to continue a privileged attack with additional lateral movement.

Local Vs. Centralized Privileges

In subsequent chapters, we will discuss the various approaches to strong and efficient privileged access management options that are available to organizations. As we discuss the privileged attack vector in-depth, it will become apparent that this goal may be best served by an identity governance solution that leverages a directory service foundation. However, as organizations consolidate and simplify identity infrastructures, they must be cautious. If not implemented or secured correctly, they can become a privilege's greatest weakness. If one privileged account is compromised, the risk of lateral movement (Figure 6-3) to other resources relying on and trusting this service for authentication may be possible.

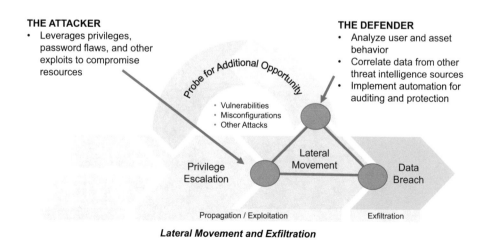

Lateral Movement and Exfiltration

Figure 6-3. *Lateral Movement and Exfiltration*

A strong, centralized IAM implementation permits authentication between layers from file systems, operating systems, users, applications, data, and even business partners. It is an age-old information technology dilemma to provide the best security, but allow for smooth and seamless business functions. Too much security, and nothing works. Too little security, and it can be an instrument for continued execution by a threat actor to operate anywhere within the environment.

In the end, the best considerations for privileges are granularity and centralization using an identity governance model. This allows finite controls for rights and a single place for management. For today's modern infrastructure, this is the best security practice we can implement today.

CHAPTER 7

Insider and External Threats

The threats facing an organization can either originate internally through trusted employees, contractors, or temporary workers or through external threat actors attacking and penetrating your resources. Realistically, once either breaches your environment, the attack is internal even though the source of the incident is external. To that end, we need to explore how the personas for both external and internal threat actors apply to your organization.

Insider Threats

By now, most security professionals are tired of hearing about insider threats. Years ago, these attacks occurred regularly, but did not have the same labels or stigma they have today. I am not saying they were acceptable back then either. We just need to be realistic about what an insider threat is and acknowledge that it has been going on in various forms for hundreds of years.

By definition, an insider threat is an internal persona behaving as a threat actor. Figure 7-1 is an illustration of this based on the privileged attack chain we have been discussing.

© Morey J. Haber 2020
M. J. Haber, *Privileged Attack Vectors*, https://doi.org/10.1007/978-1-4842-5914-6_7

THE ATTACKER
- Intentional malicious behavior
- Unintentional and acting as a
  conduit for a threat actor

Inside
Threats

Infiltration

Figure 7-1. *Insider Threats*

Regardless of the techniques they are using, insider threat actors are
not behaving in the best interest of the company. They're potentially
breaking the law, and likely exfiltrating information they do not have
permission to possess, or performing other damaging actions. An old-
school example of this type of threat is client lists. It's an insider threat
that's still relevant today, by the way. A salesperson, executive, or others
who are planning to leave an organization may have photocopied or
printed client lists and orders before leaving the organization to have
a competitive edge when they start with a new employer. The volume
of paper would probably have to be substantial to make an impact, but
leaving with confidential information on printed paper is still an insider
threat. Obviously, they were not leaving with file cabinets of material, but
today, with electronic media, and the Internet, that volume of data could
easily be egressed without anyone noticing. And, as a reminder, that file
cabinet of sensitive information can easily fit on a USB thumb drive in
a person's pocket. Therefore, we now have a label for this type of threat,

and insider threats are becoming more relevant. It still makes security professionals sick to their stomachs because the crime is old, but the methods and volume are now something to consider and require a new strategy to protect against.

Insider threats occur for a variety of reasons. This includes aspects of a human persona looking to hurt or gain an advantage against an organization. Regardless of their intent, it's the digital aspect of an insider threat that warrants the most attention. Human beings will do the most unusual things in the direst of situations, but if they are not permitted to, many of the risks of insider threats can be mitigated.

As we consider privileged attack vectors and insider threats, how does the following impact your business?

- How many people have access to sensitive information *en masse*?

- Who can export large quantities of information from a query or third-party system?

- Are all the active accounts valid?

- Are all accounts related to people that are still employed or third parties?

- How do you identify rogue or shadow IT accounts?

- How often do you change the passwords for sensitive accounts?

- Do you monitor privileged access to sensitive systems and data?

So, in fairness, answering those questions could be opening Pandora's box. Nonetheless, you should answer them if you care about insider threats. Here is why:

- Only administrators (not even executives) should have access to data *en masse*. This prevents an insider from dumping large quantities of information, or an executive's account being hacked and leveraged against the organization.

- No user should ever use an administrative account for day-to-day usage, like email. This includes administrators themselves, in case their accounts are compromised too. All users should have standard user permissions.

- All access to sensitive data should be for valid employees only. Former employees, contractors, and even auditors should not have access daily. These accounts should be removed or deleted per your organization's policy.

- Employees come and go. If the passwords are the same as people leave and new hires are onboarded, the risk to sensitive data increases since former employees technically still have known passwords to the company's sensitive information.

- Monitoring privileged activity is critical. This includes logs, session monitoring, screen recording, keystroke logging, and even application monitoring. Why? If an insider is accessing a sensitive system to steal information, session monitoring can document their access and identify how they extracted the information and when.

If you think that if you follow all of these steps to protect against insider threat you will be safe, you are mistaken. The preceding steps assume the threat actor is coming in from the front door to steal information or conduct malicious activity. Insider threats can also evolve from traditional vulnerabilities, weak configurations, malware, and exploits. A threat actor could install malicious data-capturing software, leverage a system's missing security patches, and access resources using backdoors to conduct similar types of data-gathering activity. Insider threats are about stealing information and disrupting the business, but depending on the sophistication of the threat actor, they can use tools that are traditionally associated with an external threat. Therefore, we need to realize insider threats pimarily come from two sides: excessive privileges (covered earlier) and poor security hygiene (vulnerability and configuration management). To that end, all organizations should also enforce these practices and perform these tasks to keep their systems protected:

- Ensure antivirus or endpoint protection solutions are installed, operating, and stay up-to-date.

- Allow Windows and third-party applications to auto-update or deploy a patch management solution to apply relevant security patches promptly.

- Utilize a vulnerability assessment or management solution to determine where risks exist in the environment and correct them in a timely manner.

- Implement an application control solution to ensure only authorized applications execute with the proper privileges to mitigate the risk of rogue, surveillance, or data collection utilities.

- Where possible, segment users from systems and resources to reduce "line of site" risks. That is, make sure your network is segmented, not flat.

While these seem very basic, the reality is that most businesses do not do a good job at even the most basic security. If they do, the risk of insider threats can be minimized by limiting administrative access and keeping information technology resources updated with the latest defenses and security patches. Insider threats are not going away. The goal is to stop the data leakage and be aware that an insider has multiple attack vectors to achieve their goals. As security professionals, we need to mitigate the risks at the source. A briefcase of paper is still an insider threat, but probably not as relevant as a USB stick with your entire database of client information. In the end, an insider still needs privileges to steal all this information.

External Threats

Many nursery rhymes have origins that date back hundreds of years. Their meanings have been attributed to political satires to simple educational lyrics that were easy for children to remember. The Humpty Dumpty nursery rhyme is arguably one of the most popular in the English language. The Humpty Dumpty lyrics have evolved from the 1800s when Humpty Dumpty was slang for a person's short stature and later evolved to mean a brandy and ale cocktail. Today's well-known Humpty Dumpty nursery rhyme has little resemblance to earlier versions except that it also involves a wall. Let's now try another interpretation. In relation to privileged attack vectors, Mr. Dumpty works in protecting a firewall, and if he falls off or fails to do his job, neither the information technology team nor executives may be able to put him back together again. Let's explore why this nursery rhyme has relevance in relation to external threats. Figure 7-2 is a reminder of its placement in the attack chain.

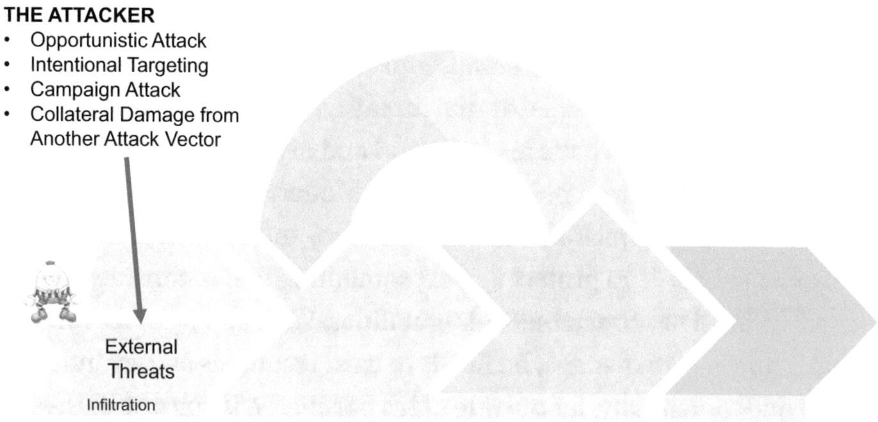

THE ATTACKER
- Opportunistic Attack
- Intentional Targeting
- Campaign Attack
- Collateral Damage from
  Another Attack Vector

External
Threats

Infiltration

Figure 7-2. *External Threats*

Not long ago, a firewall was the primary defense for every organization. Mr. Dumpty was responsible for its configuration, building rules, reviewing logs, and reviewing potential security threats. When something needed to be changed, it was his team's responsibility for getting it done, and done correctly. That still holds true for many organizations today. What has changed is how Mr. Dumpty now has to configure the firewall vs. what he did 10 years ago. He now has to consider mobile workers, business-to-business applications, and connections to the cloud. This is why we hear discussions around the "dissolving perimeter" and revelations on how perimeter defense is no longer truly effective. Mr. Dumpty is no longer sitting on a single firewall, he is walking a chain-link fence protecting the interior with multiple zones from attacks all along the exterior. I use the analogy of a chain-link fence since it is no longer a wall with a few ports open, but rather more of a filtered connection model allowing all sorts of communications in, but keeping a potential threat actor at bay. Regardless, it is no longer a single sturdy wall. It is thinner, harder to balance on, and there are many of them protecting a variety of external locations, all relevant to Mr. Dumpty's mission and job description.

So how can Mr. Dumpty fall? A firewall is not going to block social engineering attacks, phishing emails, ransomware, and web application vulnerabilities. These are all external threats. A firewall is designed to block traditional traffic patterns (inbound and outbound) and block IP addresses and ports from public exposure. Modern firewalls can also analyze traffic for suspicious content, malware, and even data leakage, but can do very little to protect against something that is considered trusted, or involves unpatched vulnerabilities. With all the zones Mr. Dumpty now has to manage, he needs to trust resources far beyond his control and, potentially, far outside of his perimeter. If any one of these is compromised, and lateral movement is possible, then not even a chain-link fence will help.

In the end, the goal is to protect against privileged attack vectors, that is, to protect against an external threat gaining credentialed access (standard or privileged) and to detect, and optionally block, lateral movement between desktops and servers within the same zone, or across zones. This is especially true when a user explicitly attempts a lateral connection via an unauthorized application or command. Mr. Dumpty's biggest fear is falling from unwanted traffic, communications, and data traveling through his firewall, or to the cloud, that could easily lead to a breach. If that happens, he could fall (metaphorically, lose his job). This is why protecting against lateral movement is so important. Today's implementations are no longer stone walls, they now allow traffic to flow almost everywhere between trusted zones. An outsider attacking any of these zones is an external threat and the threat actor's goal is to gain persistent privileged access.

While this section may have been written partly in jest, the point was to make it memorable. Where else would you find Humpty Dumpty in cybersecurity? External threats are the primary attack vector for privileged incidents. They represent the largest percentage of compromises in the industry. This is the biggest change in the universe for privilege management. The most common external threats include the following:

- **Compromised Credentials**: Stolen or guessable, default, reused, and so on

- **Remote Access**: Vendor, contractor, or remote employee using an insecure communications path

- **Excessive Privileges**: Accounts that should have little to no privileges inappropriately configured to have excessive privileges, and leveraged by a threat actor against a resource

- **Unpatched Vulnerabilities**: Missing security patches that have not been installed promptly and pose a risk from data leakage and privileged escalation attacks

- **Misconfigurations**: Incorrect installation or hardening of a resource from attacks based on a default or insecure installation

Hopefully, this list helps you see a pattern in our discussions and, as we explore further, a strategy to mitigating these threats within your organization.

CHAPTER 8

Threat Hunting

If you've ever played the game, "Where's Waldo?" you may already understand how this section relates to threat hunting. For those who have not heard of the game, the object is to find a picture of Waldo within a picture filled with other graphics and people. Spotting Waldo is difficult, and identifying him from the crowd is downright frustrating in some of the illustrations and illusions intentionally created by the artist. It is a game of patience, visual acuity, and a methodical review of graphics. To that end, a modern spoof on the game has graphics with nearly every person being Waldo. The objective is to find everyone that is not Waldo. This is a common analogy for false positives when performing threat hunting and the reason why this analogy is so important.

So, for new security professionals, what is threat hunting? Threat hunting is the cybersecurity act of processing information and process-oriented searching through networks, assets, and infrastructure for advanced threats that are evading existing security solutions and defenses. Firewalls, intrusion prevention solutions, and log management are all designed to detect and protect against threats—even if they are zero-day threats and have never been seen before. Threat hunting is the layer below this. What threats are actively running in my network that I am missing, and how I can find them? It assumes the basic premise that the environment has already been compromised and a threat exists within it. In the universe of privileged access, how can you determine if a privileged

© Morey J. Haber 2020
M. J. Haber, *Privileged Attack Vectors*, https://doi.org/10.1007/978-1-4842-5914-6_8

session is being executed by an authorized team member or has been compromised by a threat actor? Figure 8-1 illustrates the typical steps in the threat hunting process.

Figure 8-1. *Threat Hunting Process Steps*

The simple solution for most companies is to provide better inspection of the data already being collected. That includes diving deeper into log files, looking at denied logon access, and processing application events correlated from application control solutions. But that is not really what threat hunting is. Those steps are merely security best practices and adhering to the guidelines in many regulatory standards from PCI to NIST for log management and review.

Threat hunting can be an automated or manual process to find hidden threats. It assumes the threat is already there; you just need to find it. The process involves processing multiple sources of data simultaneously and correlating information with an inherent knowledge of the systems, mission, and infrastructure producing the information. While this may sound like a canned answer, it is not. Security information enterprise managers (SIEM) are designed to ingest this information, but only allow limited tagging of data by source and type to apply a business element. They fail, like many technologies, to apply the human element. To aid with this and provide data intuition, this process can be automated using behavioral analytics or machine learning. It raises the bar for identifying patterns as a repetitive process, but that is all that it does; it does not know the meaning of the patterns detected. For threat hunting to succeed, security professionals need to start with a hypothesis. This hypothesis assumes a threat and maps the patterns and manual review of data to the conclusion (a threat is actively occurring). To determine whether privileged access is being used by a threat actor or appropriately within an environment, consider these common hypotheses:

- **Analytics-Driven**: Patterns in behavior (or outlier events) can be assigned risk ratings and used to determine if a high-risk pattern is occurring.

- **Situational**: High-value targets are analyzed, including data, assets, and employees, for abnormalities and unusual requests.

- **Intelligence**: Correlation of threat patterns, intelligence, malware, sessions, and vulnerability information to draw a conclusion.

Therefore, for threat hunting to succeed, we need to meet the following requirements, or our data and hunt will be flawed:

- Crown jewels and sensitive (privileged) accounts are properly identified for data modeling. This includes monitoring of when they are used, who is using them, and what actions are being performed.

- Sources of information can be reliably correlated by CVE, IP address, and hostname. Changes due to DHCP, and even time synchronization (poor NTP implementation), can jade threat hunters. We need to trust the data almost implicitly.

- Consolidation tools, like an SIEM, are collecting all relevant data sources for pattern recognition. As a general rule of thumb, the more security data, the better. Extra data can always be filtered out, purged, or suppressed.

- Threats to the business, like a game-over breach event, are established and used to build a hypothesis. If a threat actor did "this," could my business ever recover, and what would be the cost?

- Tools for risk assessments, intrusion detection, and attack prevention are up-to-date and operating correctly. If these systems are faulty, your first lines of defense are in jeopardy.

- Documentation, such as network maps, descriptions of business processes, asset management, and so on, are critical. Threat hunting relies on the human element to correlate information to the business. Without being able to map a transaction to its electronic workflow, a hypothesis is blind as to how the threat occurred and is remaining persistent.

Threat hunting is much like "Where's Waldo?". You know the threat actor exists, you kind of know what he looks like, but it may be very difficult to find him.

While a threat hunter may not know what the threat actually is, it is a safe assumption that the threat actor(s) exist and is doing something wrong, or staging to do something malicious, in the future. If you can find that hidden threat, you can find Waldo. Think of the problem, puzzle, and game with clear objectives and leverage the tools you have to go beyond just a correlated black box report or an alert of an unauthorized login. Threat hunting requires you to dig in deep, use a magnifying glass, and rely on your senses to help find the threat. Having security best practices to begin with is an absolute requirement for success since everything you do for threat hunting depends on it. Also, skilled threat actors will leverage your existing security tools against you to remain hidden. This is yet another reason why best practices must be rock-solid before you embark on threat hunting. After all, if a threat actor is in your environment, and current solutions cannot find him, you need to question the privileges they are executing with in order to remain hidden. Those are definitely the privileges you should be actively monitoring every single day.

CHAPTER 9

Unstructured Data

Not so long ago, it was much easier to protect your data. Perimeter defenses were in place and meant something, and there were limited pathways to access your organization's data. Data came in from IT-approved, enterprise-controlled devices and applications. It lived on your servers and in storage arrays. It was protected by walling off the outsiders and trusting your insiders. But IT environments have changed in a big way. Now, data is increasingly collected from applications, users, devices, cloud services, and connected hardware, with dwindling amounts of it under enterprise control. New forms of doing business demand easy access from the *outside* world. With the emergence of the cloud, your data, users, and applications may not even be on the *inside* anymore. And "insiders" with access to your data increasingly include third parties who don't work for your organization at all. The approach to managing the granularity of access to this unstructured data at the file or application layer can be done with privileged access management.

Traditional computing models (Open Systems Interconnection model—OSI) allow access to all components on a server, in the cloud, and data based on a user's authentication. An authenticated user, depending on privileges, can access all the way down the stack to the file system (Figure 9-1). They cannot necessarily access the data in the file if it is encrypted, and that is where privileged access to unstructured data becomes relevant.

© Morey J. Haber 2020
M. J. Haber, *Privileged Attack Vectors*, https://doi.org/10.1007/978-1-4842-5914-6_9

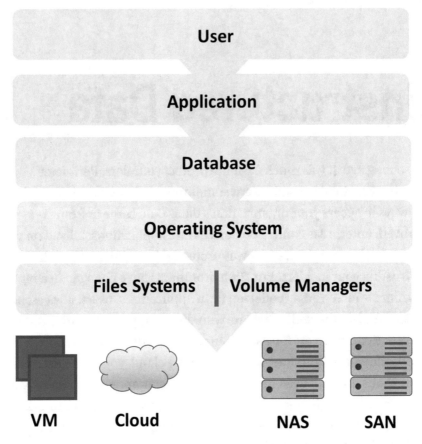

Figure 9-1. Unstructured Data—Stack Model

Encryption will protect the file's contents, but not the file itself. A threat actor stealing hundreds of encrypted files is harmless unless they have a method to decrypt the files. Password protection in the application associated with the file (like Microsoft Word or Excel) is insufficient to guard against modern hacking tools. Therefore, it is the keys to decrypt the file (or file system) that become the primary target for a threat actor.

With this in mind, restrictions and auditing are only governed by local access control lists and role-based access in applications, databases, and operating systems. An administrator can, therefore, have access to any file or volume by merely being an administrator. Users with permissions anywhere in between a standard user and administrator may need access to an application, but limited or no access to the file system that supports it. This is the basis for client-server architecture, or even a modern web application.

Unfortunately, for traditional operating system security controls across Unix, Linux, MacOS, and Windows, root or administrator allows access up and down the stack, and there is no native way to restrict access to it. Your organization may be able to remove user privileges, but as an administrator, you can always grant them back. Once an attacker has root or administrator privileges, it is truly game over, especially when it involves domain administrative rights. There is always a way to circumvent security controls when you are an administrator. Privileged access management (PAM) can control the user's access, but cannot necessarily control the file system and/or existing processes without taking ownership. This is especially true when the files are shared or stored in the cloud using a file storage solution like DropBox, iCloud, or OneDrive. File system and process control solutions can provide segmentation and encryption to files and directories (like DLP, DCAP, etc.), but cannot control the actual user being authenticated in the first place. Thus, if a threat actor is an administrator, there is probably a way to circumvent these technologies too and, with some effort, gain access to mechanisms protecting unstructured data files.

The solution to the problem utilizes privileged access management on the top of the stack to manage the operating system and applications and native File Integrity Monitoring (FIM) integrated with your PAM solution to strategically monitor and block threats vertically along the traditional layers of the ISO computing model. This implies managing privileges through all the layers—from user authentication to FIM policies that grant or deny access: even as root or administrator. This requires the solutions to work together so any tampering can be correlated between the layers to prevent a compromise. Unfortunately, this only applies to operating systems and file systems that you can control and not necessarily file storage solutions provided as SaaS or IaaS.

Therefore, when the concepts of unstructured data are applied to PAM and FIM, the following use cases can be satisfied:

- User access—from authentication to file access—is managed and monitored.

- Applications are run with least privilege to mitigate elevated privilege risks, without access to the supporting data structure.

- Databases and applications have passwords managed for automatic rotation and can restrict access, including any automation performed by scripts or tools.

- Operating system access is restricted to standard users, commands, tasks, and scripts, and features are elevated on a need-to-use basis with specific privileges.

- Individual files associated with commands and scripts are protected separately from tampering using FIM, but assigned or excluded to the same user privileges.

- User access in an attack chain can be monitored and mitigated along every horizontal plane in a traditional computing model. This is far deeper than just at the top using a traditional authentication model managing passwords per user access.

- Only trusted and authorized users have access to an asset and its supporting data using privilege and FIM technology.

- The removal of privileges from the user to the application, and from user to the file system, can be supported in a trusted computing environment across all major operating system platforms.

Protecting unstructured data is a natural extension of privileged access management. It applies the technical controls and policies for privileged use below the operating system to the file system and below access control lists. File Integrity Monitoring (FIM) solutions that integrate with privileged access management provide this vehicle and enable a holistic approach to monitoring any layer a threat actor may use for the exfiltration of information. This includes even blocking an elevated user from accessing files and directories based on FIM policies linked to their PAM profiles.

CHAPTER 10

Privilege Monitoring

The primary risk for any privileged access is the activity performed via that access. As a security professional you must ask the following questions: Was the activity appropriate? Did the user make a mistake? Or did a threat actor perform something potentially malicious using elevated credentials? Unless you are sitting over someone's shoulder and have the expertise to monitor the activity, there are plenty of gaps in the traditional security model to review this activity and verify every session, every command, and all the information downloaded or displayed on the screen. Reviewing all activity is a daunting task, but luckily, technology and automation exist to help address this challenge. Based on these use cases, let us explore the requirements for any privileged access monitoring performed within an environment.

Session Recording

Session recording is the act of logging all visible activity that may appear on an end user's screen during a session (Figure 10-1). It can be done in the form of video recording, text logging, or rapid screen captures based on screen changes. Typical session recording solutions ensure that recordings are securely stored, allow for indexing, and provide advanced capabilities

© Morey J. Haber 2020
M. J. Haber, *Privileged Attack Vectors*, https://doi.org/10.1007/978-1-4842-5914-6_10

for searching for details and understanding context by an auditor or via automation. Session recording can be implemented using a variety of technologies:

- An inline video capturing system that records monitor output before displaying on a screen. This technology typically also bundles OCR (optical character recognition) to scrape the screen for keywords and text in the display. This technology requires hardware on the video side of servers and is normally not viable for cloud or virtualized technologies.

- An end-user agent or browser plug-in that captures the screen or session based on activity. The results are cached or streamed to a central server for review and processing. This approach requires agent technology to be deployed and does not manage out-of-band connectivity that can circumvent recording technologies.

- A proxy technology that is protocol-aware to provide agentless screen recording of an active remote session. This approach supports segmentation and requires access to be routed through the proxy for a successful connection. All recordings are, therefore, recorded by the proxy, not stored on the end user's asset, and do not require hardware modifications, except for the introduction of the proxy itself.

Figure 10-1. *Session Recording Playback*

Regardless of the technological approach, the goal is the same: to review privileged session activity to sensitive data and systems. While this approach alone does not stop the activity of the threat actor, it documents their activity beyond the bounds of normal operations. The recording of privileged activity can be used for forensics and, when properly configured, can help identify a threat. This will be discussed further in the "Session Auditing" section later in this chapter.

In addition, if the session recording system is advanced enough, automation can enable more proactive responses to inappropriate behavior. For example, advanced rules can be configured to trigger onscreen output to perform mitigation activities, such as sending an alert, locking or terminating the session itself, or disabling the associated user account. While this functionally requires a mature and advanced setup, it steps up the game should a threat actor attempt to maintain a persistent presence by running specific commands or downloading information.

Finally, when discussing regulatory compliance with auditors, session recordings meet the basic requirements of documenting the privileged activity of appropriate use and privileged user attestation reports.

Keystroke Logging

While session recording documents the screen itself, graphical or text-based, it does not capture the end user's keystrokes from a keyboard: just the results if they show up on the screen. Shortcuts and keyboard commands, like copy (Ctrl-C), may not be captured at all. Based on the screen recording paradigms mentioned earlier, keystroke logging requires one of three methods as well to function and capture all user input:

- An inline physical device via USB or PS2 to capture keystrokes from a keyboard. These devices can store the information locally, or have a software or network component to upload the captured information. There is no physical solution for wireless keyboards that connect via Bluetooth or proprietary dongle.

- An end-user agent that captures keystrokes. This is a common approach, but needs to be whitelisted and not confused with malware that performs keystroke logging as well. This approach works with all wired and wireless keyboard technologies since the agent captures all input device data.

- Proxy technology that captures the difference between screen rendering and user input. This approach requires no physical hardware (outside of the proxy) and no local agent to capture explicit user keystrokes. Proxy technologies to capture keystrokes work with the virtual form of keyboard or textual input technology.

The primary purpose of keystroke logging is to stop a threat actor at the command level. Specific commands to add a user, retrieve a database, or install malware are relatively standard across operating systems, applications, and databases. If the privilege monitoring system is properly configured to monitor, alert, or terminate a session when these commands are issued, a breach can potentially be identified before valuable information is leaked. A threat actor must issue these commands to be successful in their attack. The commands themselves require privileged elevation via any of the methods we have previously discussed. Therefore, if we can identify and control authorized sessions successfully and flag for potentially malicious ones, we have another vehicle to mitigate privileges as an attack vector. See Figure 10-2.

Figure 10-2. *Command-Line Filtering and Command Searching*

Application Monitoring

Applications represent a unique challenge for privilege monitoring. Every application is essentially different, even if they share best practices for common menus, buttons, or depend on runtime engines from Oracle Java to Adobe Flash, and even native-compiled code. Session recording can capture mouse movement and screen recording, but reviewing the sessions for a specific button, client utility, or dialog screen banner is labor-intensive without additional technology. There is nothing in native session recording to capture application activity outside of a visual change since the primary input mechanisms are mouse clicks or using a touchscreen. Also, keystroke logging cannot capture mouse clicks outside of x axis and y axis coordinates unless it is aware of the application itself. Due to these problems, the only solutions that work for application monitoring are to have local code present in the form of an agent, dissolvable (temporary) agent, or advanced OCR (optical character recognition) technology. OCR, however, requires post-processing of the recording, may have trouble with fonts, cannot see file paths, and is not viable for real-time alerting. Therefore, the only viable method for application monitoring related to PAM is to use some form of agent technology.

Application monitoring agents, regardless of the delivery mechanism (persistent or dissolvable), monitor for API calls, mouse clicks, and screen changes based on user interaction. The application's title bar, button names, and menus are all exposed via Windows APIs, for example. When a user interacts, they can be captured and documented on a timeline with the session recording and keystrokes as well. This provides a complete audit trail for forensics or regulatory compliance attestations, and potential malicious activity. Think about our Where's Waldo example for threat hunting.

For a threat actor, the final vector for data manipulation is under security management. Tools that allow you to manipulate data and continue malicious activity graphically are monitored—even if they use the graphic user interface only for their attack. Buttons and dialogues are typically clearly labeled for data deletion, download, or querying for all programs. Therefore, similar automation techniques to keystroke logging can be used to look for keywords that contain indications of malicious activity. The results can alert security teams, or terminate the session using the same proxy or agent technologies.

Application monitoring is a vital part of thwarting a threat actor. Administrative tasks need privileges from the command line to a user interface, and monitoring the session ensures the actions performed are appropriate. In other words, as a user it interacts with a resource, session monitoring allows for sensitive user-interface components to be monitored for inappropriate activity. Figure 10-3 illustrates an example of explorer.exe being potentially inappropriately accessed by a user during an application session log.

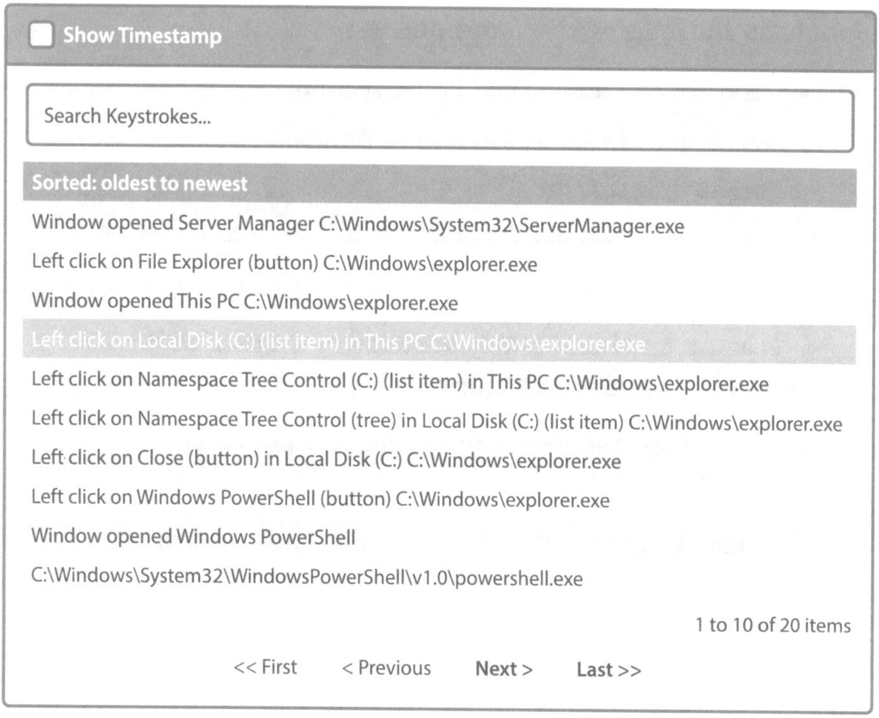

Figure 10-3. *Application Monitoring Using Agent Technology*

Session Auditing

Privileged session auditing is a critical reporting requirement for organizations looking to meet regulatory compliance initiatives (discussed in Chapter 20) and provides evidence in support of initiatives, like threat hunting. While most PAM solutions can perform session recording, it is the automated auditing capabilities that allow security teams to remain vigilant and zero in on sessions that have potentially malicious activity, vs. scouring through endless hours of real-time recorded sessions. While just recording the session meets the basics of regulatory compliance requirements stated earlier, truly implementing it in an efficient manner makes all the difference for sustainability.

To that end, when embarking on recording privileged sessions for auditing purposes, ensure that the solution captures the following information and indexes it for future queries:

- The account used to launch the session

- The source IP address or hostname of the originating session

- Timestamps for the duration of the session, from beginning to end

- Capturing of all keystrokes entered by the user, with corresponding timestamps

- Capturing of screen output seen by the user, even across multiple monitors, including timestamps

- Centralization of all captured session auditing data for playback, searching, and auditing with applicable security to protect against future malicious intent

- The ability to timestamp views of the session by an auditor and add notes to each reviewed session for future consideration

- Has an automated rule engine to interact with the session based on keywords, session attributes, or other activity to isolate malicious activity in real time and alert on any session recordings that need additional auditing

- Provide strong encryption for all recorded sessions to ensure there cannot be any tampering of the contents

- Archive capabilities to purge or move outdated sessions for backup, forensics, or legal preservation

- The ability to export graphical interface results to an OCR (optical character recognition) system for additional processing

- The ability to export all data in the form of events to analytics, artificial intelligence, and machine learning solutions for additional behavioral profiling

All of this information provides a complete audit of user activity and allows for a determination for any mistakes or potential wrongdoing.

These are not "nice to have" capabilities for any privileged monitoring solution, they are firm requirements to implement a low-friction solution and minimize the observer effect when recording a user's sessions.

Remote Access

Remote access is one of the hardest requirements to fulfill when performing privilege monitoring. By definition, privileged remote access eliminates the need for privileged users (vendors, contractors, or even remote employees) to remember or share credentials for the systems they need to access. Credentials can be stored locally in the remote access solution, integrated into a password manager, or manually entered by an end user. The latter defeats the entire purpose of a PAM-based remote access solution and negates the reason it is even included as a requirement.

To integrate privileged remote access with a credential storage solution, the password component must be able to seamlessly and securely inject valid credentials into any session without the end user's knowledge. In other words, it just works and provides a frictionless experience; the session just starts based on any role- or attribute-based security policy you have deployed.

Also, session auditing represents an additional challenge. Remote access is generally point-to-point. To perform session auditing, a flexible proxy or gateway is needed to route all remote session traffic to perform session recordings. This also must be a seamless user experience, or users will endeavor to circumvent the solution anyway they can.

Therefore, to help ensure secure remote access, consider the following requirements needed for privileged monitoring:

- Integrated or native password management capabilities

- Seamless capture of session recordings via a flexible network architecture needed for session auditing

- Support of multiple protocols from RDP, SSH, VNC, and HTTP(S)

- Secure capabilities to allow communications within a network as well as external connectivity based on personas and roles

- Flexible deployment model, on-premise or in the cloud, to support software as a service (SaaS), infrastructure as a service (IaaS), and platform as a service (PaaS) initiatives

- Remote access connectivity based on authorized users from common operating systems to mobile devices

- Support a complete workflow for ticketing solutions to multi-factor authentication to approve proper access

Remote access and privilege monitoring represent some unique challenges, but with a fully integrated PAM solution, these use cases can be implemented to make the entire user experience simple and rewarding.

CHAPTER 11

Privileged Access Management

Privileged access management (PAM) is often referred to as privileged account management (also PAM), privileged identity management (PIM), or privileged user management (PUM). The differences are subtle, and PAM (using access) is favored over the other in the analyst community. The discipline is considered a subset of the identity and access management (IAM) or identity and access governance (IAG) market, as defined by leading standards organizations and analysts.

PAM's primary goal is to keep your organization safe from accidental or deliberate misuse of privileged credentials and access, regardless of whether the system is being accessed remotely or a user is sitting directly in front of the keyboard and monitor. (Hopefully, you understand all of the risks which now have been clearly defined). Privileged access threats are particularly relevant if your organization is evolving and experiencing change due to growth, new markets, and other business expansion initiatives. The larger and more complex your environment's information technology systems become, the more privileged users you have. In the last several years, organizations have been experiencing an explosion of privileged user accounts and a new universe for privilege management. These new accounts include employees, contractors, vendors, auditors, and even automated users utilizing solutions on-premise, in the cloud, and in complex hybrid environments that may include multiple

© Morey J. Haber 2020
M. J. Haber, *Privileged Attack Vectors*, https://doi.org/10.1007/978-1-4842-5914-6_11

business-to-business connections. This does not diminish the need for small organizations to embrace PAM, but rather that security professionals have a more difficult time scoping the problem and conducting mitigation exercises at larger scales. Every business and every consumer is potentially at risk from privileges being used as an attack vector. This fact alone necessitates the need for PAM everywhere, even though only portions may be needed to mitigate relevant risks. Therefore, a successful strategy for privileges as an attack vector does not require all of PAM's disciplines to be implemented to mitigate the risk— only the ones that are relevant to your business. Generally speaking, the larger and more complex the business, the more PAM use cases you will need to implement.

A successful PAM strategy offers a secure workflow optimized to authorize and monitor all privileged users for all resources. This will provide your business with the following capabilities:

- Grant privileges to users only for resources on which they are authorized (least privilege).

- Grant secure privileged access from resources to resources brokered by an authorized third party (zero trust).

- Grant access only for those instances when appropriate and revoke access when the need expires (just-in-time administration).

- Eliminate the need for privileged users to have or need knowledge of system passwords (password management).

- Manage privileged remote access sessions for appropriate activity with credential management (secure remote access).

- Ensure all privileged activities can be associated with an account and, when accounts are shared, enforce mappings to an identity (certification reporting).

- Centrally and quickly manage access of all physical and virtual resources, on-premise or in the cloud, accommodating any set of heterogeneous resources that require privileged access (asset discovery).

- Create a sustainable audit trail for any privileged usage via session recordings, keystroke logging, and application monitoring (attestation reporting).

- Empower organizations to readily respond to breaches by logging privileged activity that provides indicators of compromise (reporting, analytics, and alerting).

When you consider these benefits of privileged access management, the threat actor's ability to gain privileged access and navigate undetected is greatly diminished. Mitigating the threats and risks is quantifiable when all activity can be logged, monitored, and audited. Otherwise, you have no idea when privileged sessions occur and what was performed within each session. Figure 11-1 illustrates a typical workflow for this entire process when using a privileged password management solution as a component of PAM.

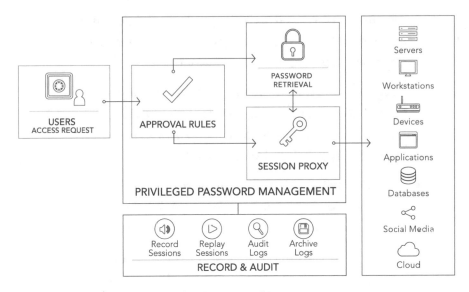

Figure 11-1. *PAM Access for Password Management*

Privileged Access Management Challenges

As we undertake the challenge of managing privileges, we must be aware of some of the intrinsic problems absent an efficient privileged access management strategy:

- **Lack of Visibility and Awareness**: Discovery and Documentation of all the privileged accounts and credentials across an enterprise pose a monolithic challenge, especially for those companies that rely on manual processes and homegrown scripts. Privileged accounts, many long forgotten, are sprawled across most organizations in legacy systems and one-off systems performing functions that are overlooked daily. Different teams may be separately managing (if managing at all) their own set of credentials, making it difficult to track all the passwords, let alone who has access to them and who uses them. A typical user may have access to hundreds of systems, possibly disposing them to take shortcuts in maintaining the credentials. Beyond this, as elaborated in the sections that follow, some types of credentials are virtually impossible to find, let alone bring under management, without third-party tools.

- **Lack of Privileged Credential Oversight and Auditability**: Even if IT successfully identifies all the privileged credentials strewn across the enterprise, this does not by default translate into knowing what specific activities are performed during a privileged session (i.e., the period during which elevated privileges are granted to an account, service, or process). Providing privileged access to a user or administrator should not amount to ceding *carte blanche* to use the credentials anytime nor for any activity. Moreover, regulatory controls like PCI and HIPAA require organizations not just to secure and protect data, but be capable of proving the effectiveness of those measures. So, for both compliance and security reasons, IT needs visibility into the activities performed during the privileged session. Ideally, IT should also have the ability to seize control over a session should inappropriate use of the credentials occur. But, with potentially hundreds of concurrent privileged sessions running across an enterprise, how does IT expeditiously detect and halt malicious activity? This is why automation is so important. While some applications and services (such as Active Directory) can track logon/logoff events and high-level application activity, only a privileged access management solution can enable you to determine if the activity was appropriate.

- **Sharing of Privileged Accounts for Convenience**: IT teams commonly share root, Windows Administrator, and many other privileged passwords so workloads and duties can be seamlessly shared as needed. However, with multiple people sharing credentials, it may be impossible to trace actions performed with an account to a single individual (identity), complicating auditing and accountability.

- **Hard-Coded and Embedded Credentials**: Privileged credentials are needed to facilitate authentication for app-to-app (A2A), application-to-database (A2D), and Development Operations (DevOps) communications and automation. Applications, systems, and Internet of Things (IoT) devices are commonly shipped, and often deployed, with embedded, default credentials that are easily guessable and pose a formidable risk until they are brought under management. These privileged credentials are frequently stored in plain text, perhaps within a script, code, or a file. Securing embedded passwords requires separating the password from the code so that when it's not in use, it's securely stored in a centralized secret store, as opposed to being constantly exposed as plain text in a file.

- **SSH Keys**: IT teams commonly rely on SSH keys to automate secure access to servers, bypassing the need to enter login credentials manually. SSH key sprawl presents a substantive risk for thousands of organizations, which may have upward of a million SSH keys. With this staggering quantity of keys, many of them may be long dormant and forgotten, but still viable backdoors for a threat actor to infiltrate critical servers. SSH keys are standard, and more prevalent, in Unix and Linux environments but are also used across Windows environments. Administrators leverage SSH keys to manage operating systems, networks, file transfers, data tunneling, and more. As with other privileged credentials, SSH keys are not necessarily tied to a single user; multiple people may share the private key and passphrase to a server, which holds the public key. As with other types of privileged credentials, when organizations rely on manual processes, there is a pronounced tendency to reuse a passphrase across many SSH keys or to reuse the same public SSH key in the form of a wildcard per domain. This means that one compromised key can then be harnessed to infiltrate multiple servers.

- **Privileged Credentials and the Cloud**: The challenges of visibility and auditability are generally exacerbated in cloud and virtualized environments. Cloud (SaaS, IaaS, and PaaS) and virtualization administrator consoles (as with AWS, Office 365, Azure, Salesforce, LinkedIn, etc.) provide a vast amount of superuser capabilities, enabling users to rapidly provision, configure, and delete servers and services at a massive scale. For example, cloud-based virtualization services allow for users to potentially spin up and manage thousands of virtual machines (each with its own set of privileges and privileged accounts) with just a few clicks. One predicament then arises around how to onboard and manage all of these newly created privileged accounts and credentials. On top of this, cloud platforms frequently lack the native capability to audit user activity with granularity needed to determine if the session was appropriate. And, even for those organizations that have implemented some degree of automation for their password management (either through in-house, or third-party solutions), if not architected with the cloud in mind, there's no guarantee a password management solution will be able to adequately manage cloud credentials outside of basic check-in and checkout processes, exposing the actual passwords to the end user.

- **Third-Party Vendor Accounts and Remote Access**: Finally, another quandary for organizations is how to extend privileged access and credential management best practices to third-party users, such as consultants or other vendors that may perform a variety of activities. How do you ensure that the authorization provided via remote access or to a third party is appropriately used? What communication tools do you provide to allow them to securely access only the resources you have deemed appropriate? How do you ensure that the third-party organization is not sharing credentials, or otherwise exercising poor password hygiene, such as by failing to terminate authorization credentials when an employee departs from the company? These are the compelling questions requiring remote access to be a part of your privileged access management strategy.

Password Management

Password management is a simple security function that helps a user store and organize passwords. Password storage solutions (commonly referred to as password managers, password safes, password vaults, or secret stores) store passwords encrypted and require the user to authenticate to the solution to retrieve stored secrets or begin a session. This assumes the solution is designed for direct business end-user password management and potentially supplemental personal usage. As with any solution, administrative credentials manage the configuration of the password manager, but they should not have access to the database or password keychain for retrieval of unauthorized credentials.

For a business environment to successfully implement a password management solution, these concepts need to be expanded to a different level. Solutions need to have role-based access to the storage and retrieval of shared passwords, automatically rotate the passwords, provide APIs for programmatic password access, and provide enterprise auditing, encryption, and logging capabilities for multiple users and applications across an entire enterprise. Also, the architecture cannot be monolithic— it must be able to accommodate network segmentation, firewalls, and even cloud resources securely to manage a modern environment. These features cover everything from session recordings to password attestation reporting. These capabilities are necessary to mitigate privileged threats, but also to demonstrate regulatory compliance, not just within one network zone, but across an entire infrastructure.

Password management solutions can also be implemented in a wide variety of formats based on an organization's needs. This can include software, appliances, virtual instances, or even hosting in the cloud. Regardless of the deployment philosophy, the goal is still the same: secure privileged account passwords, and most importantly, make sure the password manager itself does not become a liability to the business. For example, decrypting passwords and unrestricted access to the password manager's database itself, at any time, would be like finding the Rosetta stone for access to any resource managed by the business. Organizations are willing to trade off the risk of storing all their sensitive passwords in one highly secure, fault-tolerant location vs. the threats posed by unmanaged privileged access. Businesses just need to be aware of the Tier-1 critical system nature of a password manager and the policies and procedures necessary to facilitate its successful deployment. This includes making sure that cybersecurity hygiene basics like vulnerability, patch, and configuration management are operating perfectly and that high availability, disaster recovery, and break glass are periodically tested.

Least Privilege Management

The concept of least privilege has its foundation in mainframe security. Any user, when first instantiated, has absolutely no privileges to do anything. It is considered a fully closed security model. As a user needs to perform functions, privileges are added to their account to perform specific tasks. Hopefully, the privileges (permissions) are the bare minimum required to perform the specific task, and nothing more that could lead to privileged abuse.

Least privilege on every other platform operates the same way regardless of whether it's Unix, Linux, Windows, or MacOS. Unfortunately, the default model for Windows and MacOS is the opposite; default initial users are administrators. To facilitate least privilege, new or existing users are assigned basic (reduced) login rights, and the applications, tasks, and even operating system functions, are granted on an as-needed basis. The basic account assigned in this model is considered a Standard User. The basic user rights allow for interaction with the operating system, limited applications, but not the ability to perform any changes that could be a liability for the environment.

The problem with this model is that many tasks, applications, and configurations need higher permissions than a standard user. Traditionally, users have been granted a secondary account as an administrator to perform these tasks (dash admin accounts), but that introduces a privileged attack vector and risk. Every identity would have at least two accounts, one privileged and one not, and a threat actor can successfully move laterally between accounts operating on the same asset when used simultaneously by the same identity.

In a least privilege model, technology provides a solution. Via policy and rules, individual commands, applications, and operating system functions are granted the permissions they need to operate and nothing more. They have least-privilege rights. The users themselves are not granted the rights; this is critical in mitigating privilege risks that could breach the user's runtime. Only the application is elevated based on administrator-specified criteria. Thus, the application runs correctly, a user can interact with it, and excessive privileges are removed from the user to prevent a threat actor from leveraging them and executing lateral movement. The end goal is therefore achieved; the end user is never given privileged rights to perform their job functions.

Secure Remote Access

While we have touched on remote access in a variety of places, we really have not justified why it is a part of privileged access management. Let's consider our initial assumptions about threat actors. They are either internal or external. If you consider the fact that the majority of privileged attacks are external, they must be connecting to resources remotely. They are located somewhere else and are performing some form of remote session to gain access and to conduct their nefarious activities. Therefore, an external threat actor leverages some form of remote access to breach an environment. Logical, right? If you consider how many remote access sessions your organization needs to support vendors, contractors, auditors, professional services, managed service providers, and remote employees, then a threat actor has multiple attack vectors to hijack any one of them, or create a communication path of their own. Protecting the business is more important than anything else at this point. This contradicts Spock's quote in *Star Trek II: The Wrath of Khan*, "The needs of the many outweigh the needs of the few or the one." There is no justification for accepting an external threat of this nature over the security of the business.

With the preceding logic in mind, generic remote access needs to evolve to a state of secure remote access and:

- Provide the ability to securely connect to a resource internally or externally within an organization

- Encrypt all communications end-to-end for each session and each organization

- Provide strong authentication and integration into common directory stores and multi-factor authentication solutions

- Allow for privileged access point-to-point without the need for virtual private network (VPN) technology, client-based dedicated software, or protocol routing

- Support all major protocols for remote access: RDP, SSH, VNV, and HTTP(S)

- Support all major operating systems, including mobile devices as clients

- Integrate into password management and least privilege solutions to eliminate the need for credential exposure

- Provide complete privilege monitoring capabilities from session recording to keystroke logging and automated session auditing

While this list may expand based on your individual use cases, remote access does have one trait that must be called out specifically. Remote access is after all "remote." Any time you grant access, you may not have any control or management of the resource used to perform a remote connection. It may be an employee's home computer, a vendor's laptop, or even a mobile device owned by a contractor. Installing software on their device to make the connection may violate your licensing agreement, have compatibility issues with another organization's baseline configuration, or even open a routable network path from your organization to another company (VPN). It is, therefore, in the best interest of everyone to make sure remote access never requires (optional of course) any special dedicated software to facilitate the use cases listed previously. That is, keep remote access remote, and provide access within all the confines we have been addressing throughout this book.

Application-to-Application Privilege Automation

Application-to-application (A2A) privilege automation utilizes an application programming interface (API) to allow stored credentials to be managed automatically from an on-premise or cloud-based implementation between applications. If you are a commercial application developer or create custom applications for your business, the primary benefit allows applications to authenticate without an end user intervening, hard-coding credentials in a script, providing your own secret store for credentials, compiling secrets in code, or trying to obfuscate them in a file. Team members, like database administrators, never need administrator rights to access a database if the tools they use automatically retrieve stored credentials and apply them with little user interaction (low friction and no impact for the observer effect). Also, when applications are properly coded to the API, they can make additional database connections, communicate with other applications and instances, and perform their own functions without the risk of them maintaining their own credential storage.

Organizations and application developers will realize multiple benefits in using a password manager or secret safe API to secure credentials from a threat actor by implementing these use cases:

- **Secure Credential Management**: Instead of entering static credentials, developers call on a PAM API to retrieve the latest credentials for the user, application, infrastructure, cloud solution, or database to authenticate and then release the credentials at the end of the session. This triggers automatic, randomized cycling of the password. The end user is never exposed to the username or password. All authentication is performed silently behind the scenes with complete activity auditing, if desired. This is a foundational component for zero trust.

- **Simplified Developer Access**: Improve the agility and responsiveness of IT by never requiring the entry of a username and password for connectivity to custom applications. End users, like database administrators, never need administrator credentials to access a database if the tools retrieve stored credentials automatically. Management tools for services, remote access, and infrastructure automatically recognize the logged-on user and the asset they are on, and seamlessly request and pass credentials for the application. This is a foundational component for Just-in-Time privilege management.

- **Protection from Password Reuse Attacks**: Since credentials can be passed within the application itself, directly from the API, IT can secure runtime and avoid hacking techniques like pass-the-hash and keystroke logging, making this approach far more secure than traditional single sign-on (SSO) technology.

- **Vendor-Agnostic**: To enable developers to access the API and help secure their applications, PAM vendors offer samples and support for a wide variety of programming languages including C# (.NET), PowerShell, Ruby, Python, Java, and Bash shell and automation languages like Ansible, Puppet, and Chef.

The end result eliminates the need for static passwords and secures applications, whether in the cloud or on-premise, using passwords or keys that never see human exposure for their current runtime. Common API functions include these key features:

- The retrieval of the current password for an asset or application.

- Force the rotation of a password change.

- Register or decommission a resource for password management, including the technology owning the account (operating system, database, application, cloud resource, social media, etc.).

- Automate policy and criteria for password management, including retrieval.

- Access session monitoring details and events.

- Define groups of users and resources for simplified management and reporting.

Privileged SSH Keys

Enterprise IT environments often have dozens to thousands of Unix servers and only a handful of Unix admins to manage them. These admins typically rely on SSH keys to help them efficiently do their jobs. For what they offer in terms of convenient access, SSH keys can also pose security risks that are like those of shared accounts:

1. SSH keys are tied to accounts on a Unix server, not to an individual. What happens when you need to prove for an audit that a specific user accessed a server using SSH keys? This is where privilege monitoring helps solve the problem.

2. Replacing and managing SSH keys typically requires manual effort. As they're used on Unix servers, and there are typically a handful of Unix administrators, it can be easy to "set it and forget it." The significant operational risk here is obvious—the older the key, the more it is shared, the greater the chance of unauthorized access and a breach. Automating the inventorying and management of SSH keys helps mitigate these problems.

3. As a result of the risk stated in #2, managing and rotating SSH keys manually typically results in IT teams reusing the same passphrase for different SSH keys. Otherwise, you need a storage solution for all the passphrases themselves. As a result, IT teams are unwittingly putting their enterprise security at risk. If the passphrase falls into the wrong hands, a threat actor has a way to move laterally through your environment or potentially make their own keys.

Like passwords, organizations should automate the life cycle of SSH keys—from discovery to onboarding, rotating, distributing, managing, and finally destroying them. This is all another use case for privileged access management.

Directory Bridging

Applications and operating systems can have local, role-based access security models or integrate into directory services like Active Directory (AD) or LDAP. Unfortunately, many operating systems do not natively allow cross-directory authentication from *nix platforms to Microsoft Windows. This means that a user account on Windows cannot be used to authenticate against Unix and Linux, and that an alias account needs to be created to provide authentication.

When dealing with complex environments, this can lead to thousands of accounts, across thousands of systems, all potentially having slightly different aliases for the same user. This represents a management nightmare, a password headache, and an auditing disaster to link aliases with a single physical human user, a robotic identity, or even a shared account.

Directory bridging provides a solution for a non-Windows operating system to authenticate users based on accounts created in Active Directory. Therefore, the same account they use to log on to Windows can be used with the same password to authenticate against Unix, Linux, and MacOS. From a management perspective, you achieve the following benefits:

- A single account for all users, regardless of platform, with the same credentials or multi-factor requirements.

- Minimize the need for alias accounts, their management, and correlation of user accounts for activity monitoring.

- Simplified attestation reporting for any single user across all platforms since all the account names are now the same.

- Simplified account discovery and identity management for non-Windows platforms via Active Directory.

Directory bridging is such a basic function with so many benefits; it can help minimize insider threats to rogue account usage simply by eliminating all the additional accounts created for users on non-Windows systems. A threat actor would have few account backdoor options since all the aliases have been eliminated. This essentially forces a threat actor to have to attack accounts that are managed, potentially used daily, and no longer unique per resource (flying under the radar). When this is combined with data analytics, user behavior analysis, and good old-fashioned logging, finding malicious activity is much easier since all privileged accounts are associated with a single directory store.

Auditing and Reporting

Without the ability to audit changes, report on events and findings, and provide an actionable trail of activity, privileged access management projects only succeed in mitigating privileged attack vectors and their associated risks. While that is a huge accomplishment, it does nothing to help document regulatory compliance to auditors or identify intentional or unintentional mistakes that could lead to a data breach.

Therefore, to have a successful PAM deployment, consider components that help document the changes and processes along the way. These include the following:

- Provide a report for all rules, policies, and role-based access granted to an account for privileged access. This also includes documentation for any changes made to these resources.

- Utilize File Integrity Monitoring (FIM) across all your operating systems to identify unauthorized privileged changes to sensitive operating system files, critical applications, and unstructured data containing business-sensitive information.

- Provide certification reporting of all privileged session activity with complete details, including timestamps, keystroke logging, and application monitoring.

- Provide attestation reporting for all credential checkouts, check-ins, and rotation.

- Document all applications requesting and utilizing privileged elevation per asset, application, and user.

- Report on the health of managed credentials, including password age, managed accounts, and rotation schedule (including faults) for credentials and keys being managed.

Once these concepts are implemented, demonstrating privileged access management as a function of compliance becomes rather elementary. The output from reports, command filtering, privileged session review, and so on, all become collateral to support your standard operating procedures and, more importantly, provide, the security needed to stop privileges from being used as an attack vector.

Privileged Threat Analytics

While reducing permissions and embracing the concept of least privilege will minimize both the attack surface and potential impact of a breach, some employees and authorized third parties will, at some point, require elevated access to perform job functions. It is these users that pose a significant risk to organizations. These users have been authorized to perform sensitive tasks and to have access to delicate data repositories. The control and detailed auditing of these accounts fall outside of the scope of typical identity and access management and user provisioning solutions. So, how does one determine when an approved account is misusing their given privileges, or if these accounts have indeed been compromised? This is what we have been describing as appropriate or inappropriate behavior. For this, we need to start at the bottom and work our way up.

One of the strangest words in the English language is datum (not data from Star Trek, although that would make sense here). It is, by definition, the singular form of data, but is rarely used in conversation or written documentation. It generally refers to a single point of information or a fixed starting point of a scale or operation. When we review security or debugging information, we often refer to single entries in a log as "data" when it should be correctly referred to as "datum." While the term may be considered obsolete when it comes to security, there are many times we make critical decisions based on the datum and not data. This is where discussions on analytics, artificial intelligence (AI), machine learning (ML), and user behavior become essential. It would be a mistake to base a decision on user behavior strictly on datum. Analytics, AI, ML, and user behavior require data. For the sake of this discussion, however, we will focus on analytics.

Any analytics solution that makes a recommendation based on a single piece of information is more in tune with an event monitoring solution, or security information and event manager, than an analytics engine. For example, a single event based on user, time, date, and location is not analytics—it's datum. That information correlated with other event data, and processed via correlation, is not analytics either. That is just a correlation engine reviewing multiple events in a logical order. This technology has been around for decades.

If the events are unique, processed via cluster analysis, adaptive correlation engines, and so on, then we could potentially have analytics. It takes more than just a single event and event matching to create analytics based on variable event data. Being mindful of the analytics claim and data absorption model is key in understanding whether an analytics solution can really help you detect and resolve security anomalies.

An effective threat actor attempts to erase or eliminate any traces of their movement, surveillance, or actions within an organization. The primary point of privilege as an attack vector is to document any time the threat actor tries or has access to privileged accounts. This produces data of their activities based on unusual behavior and using data analytics provides an analytical automation engine to detect even the most skilled threat actors as they infiltrate an environment.

The trend is to implement advanced threat and behavior analytics to identify suspect behavior for sensitive accounts. However, many of these solutions require significant historical analysis, are not trusted given their "black box" approach, and only analyze high-level data elements, such as logs or data forwarded to a SIEM. Furthermore, these solutions are focused on identification, but not containment. This is an area in which integrated PAM capabilities can provide significant benefits. PAM is an inline solution that can grant or deny access for sensitive access. PAM is not restricted to rigid all or nothing access policies, but can rather dynamically adjust access policies and approval workflows to sensitive systems, applications, and data. This is an area that organizations and security professionals should continue to monitor as advancements will help automate the security within organizations.

CHAPTER 12

PAM Architecture

A successful privileged access management (PAM) architecture should secure privileges across every user, session, and asset. Traditionally, the first significant piece of a PAM solution that organizations look to implement is an automated credential management solution that provides secure access control, auditing, alerting, and recording for any privileged session. Other central pieces of PAM include least privilege management and remote access management. These three solutions should all be integrated and work together for your entire privilege universe.

Privileged credential management technology is designed to manage a local or domain shared administrator account, a user's personal administrative account, service accounts, application-specific accounts, network devices, database credentials, and automation accounts, regardless of being on-premise or in the cloud. By improving the accountability and control over privileged passwords, IT organizations can minimize privileged threats and achieve compliance objectives.

However, how this technology is deployed depends on the management of the use cases listed previously and the connectivity to resources on-premise, virtual, or in the cloud. In addition, environments need to consider high availability, disaster recovery, break glass, and time to recover once a fault occurs in the solution itself, or any component in the supporting infrastructure—from networks to Internet connectivity—that could cause an outage. These are all architectural considerations for a Tier-1, mission-critical application.

© Morey J. Haber 2020
M. J. Haber, *Privileged Attack Vectors*, https://doi.org/10.1007/978-1-4842-5914-6_12

Therefore, many different configurations need to be supported to scale from single site installations to multisite, geographically dispersed environments. If we consider a traditional on-premise deployment first, PAM architectures can be configured using the following paradigms:

- **Active/Active**: Sometimes called multiactive, this deployment type allows multiple nodes (distributed heads) to be active at one time. Each node is connected directly to the database.

  - *Advantages:*

    - Unlimited scalability, only inhibited by database performance and network bandwidth.

    - Redundancy of components for high availability.

    - Targeted password change events for specific locations and network zones.

  - *Disadvantages:*

    - Redundant external database configurations, such as Microsoft SQL Always On, can be costly and require dedicated staff for administration. And, open source database solutions may not be suitable for a Tier-1 application of this nature.

    - It is the responsibility of the customer to ensure that the database and supporting servers are securely hardened, monitored, and protected.

- **Active/Passive**: Two installations are required for active/passive. The internal databases are replicated, and a missing heartbeat sent from the primary to the secondary installation indicates if it should take over operations.

  - *Advantages:*

    - Easy to set up.

    - All high availability is incorporated within the solution.

  - *Disadvantages:*

    - An external load balancer is required for auto-switching users to the active appliance.

    - The failover process is not instantaneous and can take time to initiate.

    - Cold Spare versions can have databases that are out of sync or in a split-brain configuration if their age from initial backup is too large.

- **Third-Party Failover**: For deployments where only one installation is desired, virtualization technology can be used to keep the installation continuously available via replication, even if the physical server running the instance goes offline for any reason.

  - *Advantages:*

    - Cost-effective high availability with a single instance.

    - Provides high availability and continuous operation during host server outages.

- *Disadvantages:*

  - Relies on virtual replication technology to be licensed, set up, and configured correctly.

  - Does not provide redundancy in the event of a software failure.

Regardless of the selection for PAM availability and fault tolerance, the model needs to be adjusted depending on the deployment location, and it should consider if a hybrid model is required as well. Since these architectural variations address PAM as an on-premise deployment, clients additionally could deploy PAM in the cloud as an infrastructure as a service (IaaS), platform as a service (PaaS), or software as a service (SaaS) solution. These will be addressed later in this chapter since deployment architectures are different when hosting "as a Service" is involved. To that end, consider the PAM Maturity Model contained in Table 12-1. It will help you understand your journey in implementing PAM and which architecture and deployment model (cloud or on-premise) you may need to satisfy your desired goal and mission.

Table 12-1. *PAM Maturity Model*

The Privilege Maturity Model	Level 1 Absent	Level 2 Ad Hoc	Level 3 Standardized	Level 4 Managed	Level 5 Advanced
Shared Accounts	Limited controls to verify who is using which account and when No shared account password management Lack of accountability for access and activity	Manual controls and processes Audit trail is not reliable and may have missing or inconsistent information	Automated discovery, inventory, and onboarding Centralized password management with workflow approval and automated rotation Privileged account usage reporting and certifications	Passwordless session access and management Context-aware privileged access using RBAC, ABAC, and MFA	Identity integrated (IAM, SSO, AD Bridge, and AD Audit) Advanced coverage (cloud, SaaS, apps) HSM integration User behavior analytics

(continued)

Table 12-1. (*continued*)

The Privilege Maturity Model	Level 1 Absent	Level 2 Ad Hoc	Level 3 Standardized	Level 4 Managed	Level 5 Advanced
Application and Service Accounts	Unknown and unmanaged Stale accounts Potential for default or guessable passwords	Loosely documented Hard-coded and potentially exposed Rarely changed, if ever	Targeted application-to-application management Eliminated targeted hard-coded passwords API-driven retrieval	Centralized application-to-application management No hard-coded passwords	DevOps-integrated High volume and highly available Caching for redundancy and performance
Active Monitoring and Threat Detection	No monitoring	Distributed logs Lack of tracking individuals' use of shared accounts	Centralized audit controls Individual accountability over use of shared accounts Deep visibility over sessions and keystrokes	Advanced threat detection and UBA SIEM integration Automated keyword and activity indexing	Automated Privilege-Active Response (Deny, Disable, Quarantine, Alert) IAM integration Platform independence

Desktop Privilege Management	Unmanaged users have local administrative privileges or access	Remove or restrict some administrator rights Provide basic desktop tools for ad hoc elevation	Centralized Password Management Limited whitelist and blacklist proxy access Reputation services	Fine-grained access to privilege elevation Controlled remote access sessions File integrity monitoring (FIM) Controlled and monitored lateral movement	Context-aware access policy (user risk, asset risk, ITSM validation, MFA) IAM integration, with separation of duties by role Desktop asset and user policy independence
Server Privilege Management	Unmanaged users have root, local, domain administrative access	Siloed Open source (SUDO) management	Centralized Password Management Limited whitelist and blacklist application access Communications regulated by a proxy or jump server Platform-dependent	Fine-grained access by account, identity, and applications Privileged shell Controlled remote server sessions File integrity monitoring (FIM) Controlled and monitored lateral movement	Context-aware access policy (user risk, asset risk, ITSM validation, MFA) IAM integration, with separation of duties Server asset and user policy independence

(continued)

Table 12-1. (*continued*)

The Privilege Maturity Model	Level 1 Absent	Level 2 Ad Hoc	Level 3 Standardized	Level 4 Managed	Level 5 Advanced
Infrastructure and IoT Privilege Management	Unmanaged users have root access	Siloed management by department	Centralized Password Management	Fine-grained access based on context and user	Context-aware access policy (user risk, asset risk, ITSM validation, MFA)
	Credentials are potentially reused and guessable	Vendor-dependent security, hardening, and tools	Limited command level whitelist and blacklist	Monitored remote sessions	IAM integration, with separation of duties by role
			Bastion host for proxied access	Controlled and monitored lateral movement	

Secure Remote Access	Internet-exposed remote access protocols	Remote access is provided over secure tunneling technology like VPN or reverse proxies	Devices delegated for remote access are segmented and a bastion host is provided for remote access	A workflow is implemented with managed accounts to access internal resources	Just-in-time access is provisioned to users only when appropriate or needed
	No centralized account management model	Activity and sessions are not monitored	Activity is monitored based on context-aware principles	Activity and sessions are monitored for inappropriate behavior and lateral movement	Activity and sessions are monitored for inappropriate activity
					Direct resource communication is allowed without remote access protocol tunneling

On-Premise

On-premise deployments of privileged access management solutions operate within the confines of an organization's firewalled perimeter. They can be configured to manage resources externally as long as they are allowed to have outbound connectivity to the cloud from the data center or an authorized management node. Essentially, using any one of the paradigms previously discussed, software, appliance, or virtual appliances are deployed within the corporate data center to meet business objectives and some components are configured appropriately for external communications. Regardless of whether or not outbound communications are a requirement, the implementation can be air-gapped (no Internet access), but must have a logical network route to target systems, or through remote management nodes, to conduct password changes remotely, record sessions, capture events, or manage communication with agent-based technologies.

The final architecture is very similar to an on-premise email solution or antivirus system with centralized management. The primary difference is that the PAM manager needs to resolve hostnames and route to each managed object for password changes, and each node needs to be able to resolve the server and have a network route for any agent technology that may be a part of the PAM deployment for password changes, remote access sessions, or least privilege management.

If the network has stability issues with DNS, NTP, AD replication, routing, or performance, the integrity of any PAM deployment can be an issue. A well-architected and stable network is absolutely required since PAM relies on the infrastructure to onboard, manage, and change passwords efficiently with session monitoring and least privilege.

For a threat actor, a weak infrastructure is a perfect place to get lost in the noise. Errors from DNS, AD replication, as well as poorly managed logs can help conceal their identity, even with a PAM deployment. Think of Waldo if he can hide behind infrastructure errors that would normally not be present in a properly functioning environment. Errors should be the exception, and layering on security technology when the environment has poor cybersecurity hygiene will not make the infrastructure safer, just more complex.

Cloud

Cloud-based deployments of privileged access management can take on several different forms:

- Cloud-to-cloud for privilege management, including application-to-application (IaaS) in the form of secret storage

- Cloud-based privileged access management for all key functions: password management, session management, remote access, auditing, reporting, and least privilege (SaaS)

- Hosted privileged access solutions in support of hybrid deployment models (PaaS)

If this was a multiple-choice question, your strategic business initiatives might require more than one of these categories. It is highly uncommon for privileged access management to be used in only one silo of the business without any plans to expand the technology to all sensitive systems and privileged accounts. While initial deployments may start out small, the cloud may be needed later for management everywhere. This is critical when selecting PAM on-premise, in the cloud, or a hybrid approach. For hybrid approaches, they can be any combination of the three plus an on-premise implementation to link them all together. The size, complexity, and geographical dispersity of your organization will help drive which solution is right for you. And, as you begin to figure this out, be mindful of local and regional laws governing personal data privacy and the storage of secrets in the cloud. That alone may force one deployment model over another.

Infrastructure as a Service (IaaS)

Whether your organization chooses to operate within a single cloud provider, multiple vendors, or has to meet geographical requirements-based regulations, cloud environments need to authenticate applications and users like any other information technology implementation. Application-to-application (or cloud-to-cloud and any applicable combinations) privileged access management has unique requirements compared to an on-premise implementation:

- High-availability architectures may warrant additional cloud instances to provide high availability in case of a cloud or infrastructure outage that is out of the end user's control.

- Regulations may require separate, but duplicate, instances and filter data based on region or local laws.

- Environments may have public and private IP ranges to provide the required services and require special provisions to secure them.

- Environments may have internal IP and hostname collision domains due to poor network designs or acquisitions that cannot be properly resolved from the cloud.

- Vulnerability management due to public services takes a higher priority to mitigate threats vs. managing privileged access.

- API access requires special, extensive management for secure access and to limit exposure from authorized sources.

- Sensitive data in the cloud, such as passwords, require additional database security, such as HSM, to protect information. This may be a basic feature for a SaaS implementation, but not present in a PaaS implementation.

For organizations looking to perform PAM only in the cloud, there are multiple technology vehicles to implement a solution. The most common is to use black box technology based on PAM solutions hosted in cloud marketplaces (Amazon AWS, Microsoft Azure, Google Cloud, Oracle Cloud, or third-party managed service provider). These allow for hardened PAM deployments based on a variety of licensing models and cloud runtime costs. Some PAM vendors also offer solutions that can be instantiated as a software implementation in a cloud operating system template. These provide the most flexibility for a client, but security, hardening, and operating system configuration are the responsibility of the client, not the cloud provider or PAM vendor. The risks are higher for these types of implementations due to any internal lapses the environment may have in basic cybersecurity hygiene, but the benefit is that they can be highly customized to meet unique requirements.

Software as a Service (SaaS)

Privileged access management solutions deployed as SaaS can operate solely in the cloud and can require an on-premise management node to route password changes, perform remote access, deploy policies, and aggregate events. These implementations are entirely managed by the PAM vendor and share cloud resources with other PAM clients in the vendor's single-tenant or multitenant installation. While there are currently very few PAM solutions in the cloud using SaaS, the trend suggests businesses are gaining the confidence of storing passwords, policies, and management tools for PAM in the cloud. This trend is being led by individual vendors and managed service providers (MSPs) that are providing cost-effective services based on commercial PAM offerings, with little to no expertise needed by end users.

As with any SaaS solution, consider the following for managing passwords, remote sessions, and least privilege access from the cloud:

- Is the SaaS offering single tenant or multitenant? Changes in the offering may cause unexpected outages or affect your change control windows.

- Which regions does the SaaS solution support? Can they provide coverage for a worldwide deployment?

- How does the solution handle data privacy, and are they compliant with initiatives like GDPR?

- Is the SaaS vendor SOC, PCI, or ISO compliant? Do they offer a FedRAMP certified version for federal clients?

- What is their SLA for uptime and performance?

- What is their SLA for mitigating security threats, and do they publish the results from public penetration tests?

- What is their financial standing? Are they public or private?

- What is their high availability model if a crisis arises?

Respectfully, there are probably dozens of additional questions you should ask when licensing a Tier-1 solution from a vendor as a SaaS application. You are putting the lifeblood of your privileged accounts and remote sessions in the management of a third party and you need to be reasonably certain that their security is better than yours to prevent them from becoming the source of an incident.

Platform as a Service (PaaS)

Think of a platform as a service as a black box. It provides all the functions and features you need to perform a task, but without the maintenance headaches a software solution provides. It is different than SaaS because it is your platform to manipulate and customize, but similar in that upgrades and security patches can be deployed as a packaged solution for the entire platform vs. the operating system and applications as separate entities.

In many cases, PaaS is a lift and shift of on-premise software to the cloud with some enhancements to make it more of a black box than it was as an on-premise technology. Virtual appliances are a perfect example of this philosophy when applied to privileged access management. Vendors have taken their on-premise solutions and created a black box version that is available in the marketplaces of leading vendors like AWS, Azure, and Google to provide the same experience as on-premise, but without the need to deploy the solution yourself. Your on-premise platform for PAM is now available in your private cloud instance with just a few mouse clicks. Like anything, however, there are caveats that this deployment model uniquely possesses:

- While you maintain the platform, you do not control the hypervisor and its security. Make sure your cloud provider is actively staying vigilant with cloud security since this instance has the keys to your kingdom.

- Be mindful of the runtime costs for the platform. PAM solutions converted to PaaS need to be operational 100% of the time and may incur significant CPU and image size costs per month. In many cases, it may be more expensive than running a similar VM on your own hypervisor.

- PaaS PAM solutions typically do not take advantage of modern development concepts like containers and micro-segmentation. They are a monolithic shift from on-premise to the cloud. While they will function correctly, they are not optimized for cost, scalability, and fault tolerance. All need to be considered, just as with an on-premise architecture.

- Finally, be mindful of the gray area between PaaS, IaaS, and SaaS. Many solutions can operate across all three and it is up to the business to determine if the vendor's implementation actually meets the security and business objectives for their organization. Just because it is hosted in the cloud does not mean it is actually any one of the three. In the end, it could be a butchered implementation of all three.

These three types of PAM architecture will be discussed even further in Chapter 15.

CHAPTER 13

Break Glass

Break glass is an information technology term used to describe the solving of a catastrophic problem as if metaphorically smashing the glass of a fire alarm and instantly getting help. In the case of privileged password management solutions, it refers to retrieving sensitive credentials by a human identity when an emergency situation arises, and traditional access methods have failed. In other words, you need a special privileged credential to restore operations and there is no way to retrieve it due to some catastrophic event or outage. A break glass scenario, therefore, bypasses standard operating proceeds and access controls and should only be allowed during the most extreme situations. The method of getting these credentials can vary based on the outage and business ramifications of allowing a user out-of-band privileged access.

As a matter of process, a user performs a break glass checkout or reset of credentials when he or she needs immediate access, even if the user is not authorized to manage the system. This method is customarily used for the highest-level system accounts, such as root accounts for Unix and Linux, SYS or SA for a database, or administrator for Windows (local or domain). These highly privileged accounts are not usually assigned to specific identities, so instead, break glass restricts their access with various controls to limit retrieval. However, it is obvious that unrestricted user access to break glass credentials could create an unacceptable security risk if not implemented correctly.

© Morey J. Haber 2020
M. J. Haber, *Privileged Attack Vectors*, https://doi.org/10.1007/978-1-4842-5914-6_13

Break glass scenarios can be caused by network outage, application fault, or natural disaster that disrupts the normal availability of your privileged access management solution. Therefore, factors like a backup power source and network redundancy should be considered when designing your break glass policy and real-world implementation. Also, a threat actor may consider your break glass process a target since it does contain credentials that can be leveraged in an attack. To that end, access and monitoring of credentials used in break glass processes should also be considered in your design.

Break glass scenarios are usually required when information technology administrators are deploying critical infrastructure to secure system access. Here are three common break glass scenarios:

1. An emergency situation when direct access to a managed system is not possible and a break glass credential is retrieved as the enabler.

2. Getting access outside of the standard operating process because mission-critical systems are down, or a required approver is unavailable. The goal is service recovery in as short of time as possible.

3. Retrieving passwords or secrets from a physical safe or other offline backup on a physical device, such as USB drive, or other physically secured removable media.

Break Glass Process

When developing a break glass policy, there are a few important considerations and potential processes to implement:

- For authorized break glass users (new or existing), consider creating pre-staged emergency user accounts that are managed and distributed in a way that can make them quickly available. This should occur without administrative delay, but have the appropriate restrictions from a threat actor. The break glass accounts and distribution procedures should be documented and tested as part of any implementation and carefully managed to provide timely access when needed. These can be stored in a highly available password manager or a secure physical location and have physical counterparts stored on other media and in a highly secure environment (physical fireproof safe).

- To comply with auditing requirements, even if an approval is bypassed, the system should still fully log who has access and what actions were performed. Additionally, IT administrators should review the logs to ensure compliance with change management processes when a break glass process is used.

- Break glass processes that are implemented outside of the password management technology, such as a physical safe and storage of printed passwords, should be routinely updated and manually tested for effectiveness and change control. Only select users should have access to the combination or keys to the physical safe, and they should be treated like any other sensitive information within the organization.

Break Glass Using a Password Manager

Information technology (IT) organizations often utilize a password manager as a break glass solution to provide access to their environment when the established processes for logon or authentication fail. IT teams might typically authenticate against LDAP or AD, and then the user would execute sudo or a least privilege solution to gain managed administrative privileges. When this method fails, the break glass process would require IT to provide a password for an account within established parameters (timeframe, privileges, scope, etc.) to access the application or system.

During normal operation, users who need access to privileged passwords will access a password manager to retrieve a password or establish a session so that they can perform whatever tasks or operations are assigned to their roles. This requires that the password management solution have the rights to fully manage, rotate, and secure the current password for the target resource. Relying on end users to diligently remember, rotate, and securely document all their passwords is invariably less reliable and riskier, especially if any one of them is deemed available for break glass.

Therefore, when using a password manager, consider these break glass use cases:

1. The person who needs a managed password cannot log in to the solution.

    a. Repair user access to the password manager.

    b. Reset the managed credentials.

    c. Reset the password for the user accessing the solution.

2. Fault authenticating to the password management solution.

   a. Repair network connectivity for critical paths.

   b. Restore password management connectivity to critical authentication services.

   c. Repair authentication system.

   d. Store a printed-out copy of the passwords in a highly secure location.

3. The password management solution is not available.

   a. Repair network connectivity.

   b. Access solution through fault-tolerant node.

   c. Repair password management solution.

   d. Retrieve passwords through a password cache.

4. Managed passwords are invalid.

   a. Refresh the password by using the solution to generate a new one automatically.

   b. Use the password history feature of the password manager to determine the last valid password.

5. Catastrophic, but selective, connectivity anomaly.

   a. When critical services are not functioning, access may be required via iDRAC, management networks, or crash carts.

   b. When network connectivity does not allow access, lateral connectivity, not subject to segmentation, can provide break glass access.

6. Processes and workflow prevent access.

    a. No approver is available in the time period required.

    b. User access is restricted due to system ownership, such as employee role, contractor, or vendor.

    c. Time-of-day constraints or critical event requires immediate unrestricted access.

Session Management

For a non-break glass use case, the enterprise password management solution enforces connectivity through some form of session manager, proxy, or gateway to document activity and enforce segmentation. By design, there is no alternate way to connect to the target network and system without first accessing the session manager. Break glass has a requirement not to enforce this due to some form of outage. One option for achieving break glass access would be to drop security controls to restore availability. However, as with all risk-based decisions, it is important to review and document the risks and benefits and get organizational alignment. This is true for any access granted outside of normal operating procedures. As a potential alternative, management networks controlling Integrated Dell Remote Access Controller (iDRAC) access or terminal servers may provide a safer, alternate approach than reducing security controls in a break glass scenario, especially if the event is potentially security-related. Access to management networks can, therefore, be monitored independently to provide similar controls and security assurances. Access to a break glass scenario should include the following two ways to access the session manager in the event of an outage:

1. Controlling third-party access to managed systems.

    a. Open alternate access into the environment via backup connections.

    b. Disable session management access to the primary systems (not recommended).

2. Access session management in an alternate data center.

    a. Open network path around the session management device (not recommended).

    b. Access session management device in an alternate data center or disaster recovery environment.

    c. Operate session management independently for management networks to provide access.

Stale Passwords

There are many situations where a password stored in the password manager may be stale through no fault of the technology. Such cases could arise due to restoration of backup images, rollback of virtual snapshots, or even the deployment of a new instance or system based on a template. In these use cases, the break glass password manager has automated the rotation of passwords of human, service, or built-in accounts throughout the environment.

Consequently, no one knows the correct password, and the password is not written down for manual retrieval. During normal operation, password managers will randomize and change the passwords, update managed systems, and store and test the new password. This is why the conflict exists.

So, what do you do when this process fails? Here are some recommendations:

1. If the tool cannot change a single or small number of passwords:

    a. Repair connectivity or verify the configuration of the system to make password changes based on the uniqueness of the targets.

    b. Manually change the password using another account that has appropriate privileges. Most password management tools have an account assigned to perform such operational tasks, typically called the "functional account." This will be discussed further in Chapter 24.

2. If the tool cannot change any passwords:

    a. Repair network connectivity or system access.

    b. Verify functional accounts have proper privileges to manage passwords remotely.

    c. Verify supporting services from AD, NTP, DNS, and others are all working correctly.

3. If the password of a built-in account is not known:

    a. Randomize the password of the built-in account using the functional account.

    b. Repair system by booting to single-user mode and change password using a crash cart or similar via a known privileged account.

4. If the password of a service account is not known, so a service will no longer start:

   a. Randomize the password of the service using the functional account.

   b. Establish a privileged connection to the system using a stored credential and manually set the service account password before automating password management.

Application-to-Application Passwords

For application-to-application (A2A) use cases, IT administrators or developers have implemented a password manager to forgo hard-coded credentials, passwords, or keys in configuration files, scripts, or compiled applications. Instead, the application, script, or configuration file accesses the password manager via an application programming interface (API) to retrieve the current password. It then performs any tasks it needs to proceed with normal operation. The password manager via a remote operational node or the application itself can potentially cache the password for continuous use and release the password when it is complete. To do so, the environment must allow for password changes while applications are running, or schedule password changes to only be permitted during an authorized change control window that will not affect the application. IT administrators must know the process for rotating passwords and its potential impact on operations if performed out of cycle. Here are some recommended steps:

1. If automation jobs or applications develop a fault:

   a. Repair the password management solution.

   b. Enable fault tolerance for the API.

    c.   Add caching to the scripts, configuration, or application to be fault-tolerant for a network, connectivity, or password management outage.

    d.   Manually or automatically cycle the resources ensuring that all dependencies have been met for the retrieval of a credential (bounce the box or service).

    e.   Implement automatic retries for the application or job to refresh the cache with current credentials.

2. If automation jobs or applications require change control for password changes:

    a.   Schedule password changes during maintenance windows.

    b.   Develop applications that are fault-tolerant or can be resumed in the event of an API query failure for any reason.

Physical Storage

For any break glass plan, your environment should strongly consider a recovery policy that includes the ultimate break glass solution—retrieving physical copies of passwords. There are inherent risks with storing physical copies of privileged passwords. However, with the proper physical controls in place to securely store the credentials, physical storage of paper can serve as one of the best options in break glass scenarios.

Therefore, the following are recommendations for physical credential storage:

- Create a plain text copy of the credentials and automatically print them in a secure location or store them on reliable removable media. Regardless of the format type, ensure that final storage is highly secure.

- If your processes require, re-encrypt the digital media with an offline encryption package before writing to a USB drive or CD. Remember to back up the password for the offline encryption in a secure location as well. Typically, this should be another physical safe with a different combination. This creates a form of two-factor authentication to protect the offline versions.

- Fully document the process for creating and storing break glass passwords. Passwords should be rotated and tested periodically.

Finally, as with any disaster recovery process, the paper or removable media process must be implemented following any regulatory compliance mandates that oversee your organization.

Context-Aware

Break glass credentials that must be accessed outside the organization can be challenging to lock down. To get it right, you need to apply **context** to the access, and all the runtime parameters of the request must be evaluated to enforce appropriate access. This will help mitigate the risk from an external threat actor attempting to compromise these highly specialized credentials:

- *Who is trying to log on?*

- *What system are they trying to access?*

- *Where are they logging in from?*

- *What day of the week is it?*

- *What is the time of day?*

Applying context allows you to incorporate privileged access management best practices to better protect your organization from a breach. For example, if your break glass account is strictly for emergency use and never used for anything else, only make it available during off-work hours. If it is expected that the account would be accessed via a remote employee working from home, verify that the request is coming in via an authorized secure remote access solution. Therefore, always apply context to any break glass request.

Architecture

If any component of a break glass process or password management system itself becomes unavailable (natural disaster or outage), multiple levels of redundancy mitigate the risk of data loss or degradation of access capabilities. Flexible high-availability deployment architectures ensure that passwords remain available whether everything is installed in a single data center, across multiple geographic locations, or hosted in the cloud. This is traditionally the top priority of an architecture and defense before utilizing a break glass process. Physical copies of credentials should also be considered for disaster recovery locations, but the architecture for any PAM solution should consider relying on break glass only when absolutely needed.

Finally, for short-term outages (planned or uncontrollable) of the entire PAM infrastructure, passwords may be stored and retrieved via cloud PAM solutions. These would need to be configured to cache or replicate the information off-premise and secured against external threats, but this is a viable architectural deployment model to ensure maximum availability.

Break Glass Recovery

After a break glass event, the recovery to normal operations should consider a few security and operational events. While these may seem esoteric, the purpose of the break glass process is to provide access in a worst-case scenario. If restoration is provided too quickly, or change control and checks and balances not verified, the break glass process could be used against the organization in a future attack, or just lead to another similar event in the future. Therefore, consider the following before restoring normal services:

- What event occurred requiring the break glass process?

- Can this event be avoided in the future?

- Was the access to break glass credentials appropriate?

- Were there any resources in the break glass process that did not have coverage?

- Who was notified of the execution of the break glass process?

- Did the process introduce any additional risk (data loss, resource exposure, etc.)?

If these questions can be answered satisfactorily, services can be resolved to normal operations. After services are resumed, continue with the following queries:

- Was the restoration process of services accurate after a break glass event? If not, how can it be improved or fixed?

- Were all electronic credentials and passwords reset or rotated after the break glass event?

- Was all physical storage of credentials reinstated and codes to physical storage reset?

- Was all break glass session activity verified and audited for inappropriate activity?

- Were break glass credentials fully locked down again after the incident?

If break glass scenarios repeatedly occur, then the entire process should be evaluated to prevent their invocation in the first place. This could be anything from faulty hardware, network anomalies, to the unavailability of key personnel in a critical-need situation. The restoration of normal services should always include the complete postmortem of the break glass event.

Break glass scenarios should be considered for any sensitive privileged account, even in the event of the stakeholder's death. Using the technology to support itself and physical access as a backup ensures that the controls recommended do not become a liability to the organization and a gold mine for a threat actor.

CHAPTER 14

Industrial Control Systems (ICS) and Internet of Things (IoT)

Industrial Control Systems (ICS)

Critical infrastructure systems that span manufacturing, transportation, water supply, and energy all depend heavily on information systems for their monitoring and control. Historically, Industrial Control Systems (ICS) relied on physical separation (segmentation) as the primary means for security. However, modern control system architectures, management processes, and cost control measures have resulted in increased integration of corporate and ICS environments. While these interconnections increase operational visibility and flexible control, it can also increase risks that previously did not occur with isolated ICS.

© Morey J. Haber 2020
M. J. Haber, *Privileged Attack Vectors*, https://doi.org/10.1007/978-1-4842-5914-6_14

Through an interconnected network, the ICS system can be exposed to threat actors that have already exploited and compromised the Internet and corporate networking, or by insiders misusing their privileges. ICS-CERT[1] (Industrial Control Systems Cyber Emergency Response Team) provides ICS-CERT alerts[2] to assist owners and operators in monitoring these threats and provides actionable guidance to mitigate threats to ICS systems.

ICS-CERT encourages sound security practices using "defense-in-depth" principles, including, but not limited to, the following measures displayed in Table 14-1 mapped to PAM.

---

[1]https://ics-cert.us-cert.gov/
[2]https://ics-cert.us-cert.gov/alerts

Table 14-1. *ICS Risk Matrix Mapped to Privileged Access Management*

Risk Vector	ICS-CERT Recommendation	Privileged Access Management (PAM)
Secure Passwords	Remove, disable, or rename any default system accounts wherever possible.	Implementing a privileged password management solution that supports enterprise password management, password rotation, active session management, and session recording is an effective method to eliminate many of these common challenges.
Strong Password Management	Establish and implement policies requiring the use of strong passwords.	Implement an automated password and privileged session management solution offering secure access control, auditing, alerting, and recording for any privileged account. PAM strengthens the security of ICS and interconnected environments by:
Reduce Risks of Brute Force Attacks	Implement account lockout policies to reduce the risk from brute force attempts.	1. Ensuring no device has a default password 2. Guaranteeing each device has a unique, complex password 3. Automatically rotating passwords based on age and usage 4. Limiting administrative access and communications

(continued)

Table 14-1. (*continued*)

Risk Vector	ICS-CERT Recommendation	Privileged Access Management (PAM)
Minimize Network Exposure	This activity includes the implementation of firewalls and network segmentation. This can reduce the attack surface for bad actors and reduce the risks of lateral movement within a compromised environment.	Implement a PAM solution that can also be deployed as a secured enclave model to ensure all privileged accounts (employees, contractors, and third parties) do not have direct access to manage these devices. This model ensures that only approved devices and restricted network paths can be used to communicate with secured resources, which would include control system HMI computers (human-machine interfaces). Using this best practice model for securing sensitive servers and networking devices ensures that all administrative activities are proxied through the management server to ensure that each session is approved, tied to a specific individual, and is properly audited and that passwords are automatically rotated after each session is complete.

Secure Remote Access	This activity includes deployment and appropriately updating remote access solutions, such as VPN, if required.	ICS-CERT recognizes that remote access solutions such as a VPN are only as secure as the connected devices. Secure remote access via a PAM solution is a better approach since there is no protocol tunneling. PAM solutions can bulletproof your remote access infrastructure with complete control and audit access to privileged accounts,
Third-Party Vendors	Monitor the creation of administrator-level accounts by third-party vendors.	such as shared administrative accounts, application accounts, local administrative accounts, service accounts, database accounts, cloud and social media accounts, devices, and SSH keys. Enabling Secure Remote Management: 1. Vendors should access ICS resources using PAM and existing remote access facilities. 2. Vendors authenticate via PAM and request a session to managed resources, which can include a system running ICS control software. Note that this session be restricted to a specific device as well as to a specific control system application, further reducing the risks of compromise and lateral movement.

(continued)

Table 14-1. (*continued*)

Risk Vector	ICS-CERT Recommendation	Privileged Access Management (PAM)
		3. Vendor uses a native remote desktop tool (tool (MSTSC/PuTTY, etc.) or an RDP/SSH session, which is proxied through PAM for session monitoring.
		4. All vendor activities are logged and optionally recorded to comply with security and compliance policies.
Vulnerability Management	Apply patches in the ICS environment, when possible, to mitigate known vulnerabilities.	A vulnerability management process can proactively identify security exposures, analyze business impact, and plan to conduct remediation across network, Web, mobile, cloud, virtual, and IoT infrastructure.
		1. Discover network, Web, mobile, cloud, virtual, IoT infrastructure.
		2. Profile asset configuration and risk potential.
		3. Pinpoint vulnerabilities, malware, and attacks.
		4. Analyze threat potential, return on remediation, and more.
		5. Isolate high-risk assets through advanced threat analytics.
		6. Remediate vulnerabilities including default and weak passwords.
		7. Report on vulnerabilities, compliance, benchmarks, etc.
		8. Protect approved and shadow IT devices from attack.

Threat Detection	ICS-CERT recommends that organizations monitor for suspect activities and to report their findings to ICS-CERT for incident response support and correlation with other similar incidents.
	User behavior and risk analysis enable information technology and security professionals to identify the potential breaches and the indicators of compromise from specific incidents.
	Security information and event managers (SIEMs) and threat analytic solutions can set baselines for normal behavior, observe changes, and identify anomalies that signal critical threats via the following steps:
	1. Aggregate users and asset data to centrally baseline and track behavior.
	2. Correlate diverse asset, user, and threat activity to reveal critical risks.
	3. Measure normal behavior in asset and user changes to flag in-progress threats.
	4. Isolate users and assets exhibiting deviant behavior.
	5. Generate reports to inform and align security decisions.
	Any threat detection deployed by an organization must consider all the available security data and correlate the results. Threat detection should not rely on only one event and source.

While ICS represents a specific vertical targeted by PAM technology, the benefits for any implementation are easy to recognize:

- Discover all managed and unmanaged assets across your interconnected corporate and ICS infrastructure.

- Automatically discover and inventory privileged accounts used by third-party vendors.

- Provide central control by securely storing all credentials and SSH keys in a secure database.

- Reduce the risk of lost or stolen vendor credentials by systematically rotating passwords for all managed systems.

- Implement secure vendor enclaves to isolate ICS and vendor devices to reduce the risks of malware and attack.

- Verify that no default passwords exist on any managed system or device.

- Manage all managed devices automatically using smart rules and store a unique password per each device.

- Automatically rotate each device's password based on age or after each remote vendor session.

- Provide a complete workflow for device access, including an approval process for when remote vendor access is required.

- Record all or select remote sessions with playback to document and review what occurs when a device is accessed.

- Provide detailed reporting of all credentials used and requested when remote activity occurs.

Based on these recommendations, and the security guidance provided by ICS-CERT, ICS devices can be securely managed against privileged attack vectors.

Internet of Things (IoT)

The Internet of Things (IoT) introduces a unique set of threats based on privileges and asset attack vectors. By definition, IoT devices are single-purpose assets with embedded operating systems to perform a specific function. They possess unique characteristics, including the capability to interact with a physical environment, localized role-based access, and potentially a web server to provide the specified functionality. IoT devices include everything from network-based cameras, digital video recorders, thermostats, and lighting to digital personal assistants. The list of network-based IoT devices is growing every single day. In addition, these devices can be categorized for commercial use, like biometric door locks, to home use, like Bluetooth door lock keypads and thermostats. While these types of devices have existed for years, they have only recently been grouped and labeled IoT based on their mass adoption and, more importantly, their mass identification of security risks and privileged attack vectors. Therefore, as IoT devices become more commonplace, there is a need to ensure that they do not represent an unnecessary security risk to standard business operations. Unfortunately, it has already been proven that many of these devices are insecure by design, have unresolvable flaws, and can be leveraged to compromise an entire organization with something as simple as a default credential or faulty embedded operating system. These represent an easy target for a threat actor. Therefore, for any IoT deployment, consider these seven recommendations to mitigate privilege security risks:

1. **Segment Networks**

   Using basic capabilities in modern network routers and switches, all IoT devices should be networked using separate wireless networks and VLANs. All communications from IoT networks should be explicitly blocked from critical servers, databases, and workstations that should not communicate directly with the devices. This helps ensure that, even if an IoT device is compromised, it cannot directly be leveraged to steal critical information. If possible, all IoT network communications should be monitored to the Internet and other trusted networks to identify any anomalous behavior.

2. **Manage All Credentials**

   Almost all IoT devices ship with default passwords for initial configuration. We understand, based on previous chapters, how much of a risk these can be. End users should change all usernames and passwords on these devices to complex passwords and unique usernames and consider changing at least the passwords periodically. This is where a password management solution can assist in mitigating any threats and keep the passwords on every device unique to avoid password reuse.

3. **Limit Connectivity**

   Never place IoT devices of any type directly on the Internet with public IP addresses. It is just a matter of time before they will be compromised or subject to a DDoS attack. IoT devices are based on very simple networking technology and not robust enough to thwart all the potential IP traffic that contains malicious code on the net.

4. **Identify Shadow IT**

    Shadow IT is another buzzword for rogue devices and unsanctioned assets. Make sure any IoT devices placed on your network are approved and adhere to the security considerations outlined previously. Shadow IT based on IoT could easily violate many of your security policies and introduce a threat. Standard network discovery tools can find these rogue devices and help place them under proper management.

5. **Demand a Vulnerability Service-Level Agreement (SLA)**

    Request from the manufacturer a service-level agreement for patching critical vulnerabilities once they are identified. This will help you ensure IoT devices selected for your organization will stand up to regulatory scrutiny and patch compliance initiatives. Also, make sure these questions are asked during an RFP or procurement process to ensure the vendor has the proper maturity for managing risks.

6. **Remediate Security Flaws**

    Document a process and ensure all IoT devices can be patched promptly if a flaw is found, and without extensive disruption to the business. Some devices are very difficult to remediate and may have hidden

labor costs to manage one at a time. This includes
making sure that you maintain the latest firmware
on all IoT devices to mitigate any emerging threats
that could be leveraged against the devices.

7. **Role- and Attribute-Based Access**

Any security model present within these devices
is flexible enough to be integrated into an Active
Directory or a Radius server. As a longer-term goal,
all credentialed access to these devices should be
centrally managed and properly organized within
existing identity and access management solutions.
If it cannot be managed in this way, it may present
a new risk via rogue accounts and an easy target
for a threat actor due to the limited management
capabilities. Finally, if managed devices lack a role-
based access model, or if they are not feasible to
manage in this capacity due to operational reasons,
consider a least privilege solution for IoT and
network devices.

IoT devices are just another piece of technology that businesses are
enabling for convenience. They are not mature compared to their server
and desktop counterparts, and everything from default credentials to
backdoors presents a real privileged risk to an IoT environment. As
immature as IoT devices are, they should be treated as young children.
They need restrictions, governance, and should be monitored.

CHAPTER 15

The Cloud

The history of passwords dates back to the Roman military. Initially, they were carved into wood and soldiers passed them around via the active guard on duty. They were a shared resource. Today, the most common storage medium of a password is the human brain. We assign a password to a system or application, recall it when it needs to be used, and remember it each time we change it. Our brains are full of passwords and, often, we forget them, need to share them, and are forced to document them on Post-it notes and spreadsheets, and even communicate them via email or text message (a very poor security practice in itself). These insecure methods for sharing passwords have caused the press to report front page news articles on data breaches and compelled organizations to educate employees on the insecure methods for password storage and sharing. Humans should not be expected to verbally or typographically share a password, nor is it safe to communicate them using traditional business collaboration tools. Therefore, a better method to document passwords is needed that is highly secure, documents distributed access, and promotes sharing and collaboration with minimal risk—no matter where the access occurs, and from virtually any medium. The cloud is ideal for this situation when passwords need to be available outside of the organization, across multiple geographical locations, for small- to medium-sized businesses, and when on-premise technology is incapable or cost-prohibitive for meeting business objectives. Ergo, if the Romans

© Morey J. Haber 2020
M. J. Haber, *Privileged Attack Vectors*, https://doi.org/10.1007/978-1-4842-5914-6_15

had the cloud, Jupiter would have just updated everyone with the proper passwords and not left it to humans to scribe them on wood and accept the risk of physically passing them around.

Technology professionals have embraced the cloud for sharing, storing, and securing information outside of the organization. Depending on the sensitivity of the information, extra steps are needed to ensure that the information is protected against modern attack vectors, while still being usable for a variety of use cases. For password storage in the cloud, least privilege asset management, and secure privileged remote access, the cloud presents the newest method for achieving a universal privilege management model. However, by definition, the cloud can take on multiple forms as illustrated in Figure 15-1.

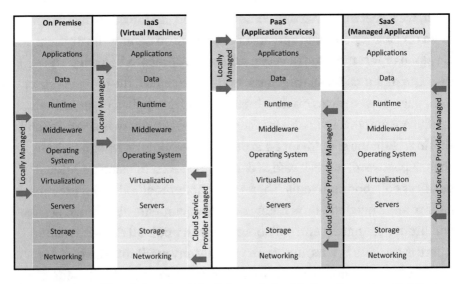

Figure 15-1. *Cloud Service Models and the Technology Available to Each One*

Therefore, consider these use cases that are satisfied by PAM in the cloud:

- **Mobile Workforce:** The ability for remote team members to access current passwords, obtain policies, modify rules, and securely connect to remote resources.

- **Distributed or Outsourced Information Technology Support:** The ability for outsourced, contracted, or remote information technology team members to access credentials and initiate secure remote sessions for resources they are responsible for, using context-aware methodologies.

- **Information Technology Collaboration:** Team members often need to share credentials (due to resource limitations) for assets and applications to perform a task or maintenance. A central repository for password storage allows collaboration without the risks of rogue password storage on documents.

- **Break Glass:** The technology-independent storage of passwords for key systems and applications in case of a crisis or break glass incident.

- **Cloud Models:** The organization has embarked on a cloud strategy and needs to secure the credentials for cloud resources. This includes everything from third-party SaaS applications to social media and cloud-based hypervisors.

With all of this in mind, there is a truth about XaaS (X referring to any type of cloud as a service offering) solutions that twists the definition of cloud-based technology. Is the solution being offered by the vendor a lift and shift of their traditional software solution offered in the cloud (normally a PaaS solution) or is it truly cloud-native (IaaS or SaaS), built from the ground up, to be optimized as a cloud solution? Now the twist. Do you actually care? If the price is right, the uptime is measurable against a service level agreement, and if the solution is secure, why do you care? Does it really matter if the solution is cloud-native and multitenant, or a reengineered version to work in the cloud as a single tenant? The answer is—it does matter, but not for the reasons you may be thinking. Moreover, being cloud-native may not be the right choice for your business after all despite all the marketing around multitenant PAM-based cloud solutions.

To understand the problem, let's establish a few definitions. The first is single tenant vs. multitenant. A single-tenant solution is the installation of an application that does not share backend or database resources with another operating instance. That is, the runtime and data are dedicated to a single company, department, or organization and a role-based access model is used to control permissions and isolate datasets. A multitenant solution shares common resources, including potentially a backend database, to provide a logical separation of data and permissions to isolate information, configurations, and runtime from other groups of users. It provides a method to scale the solution efficiently and, if properly implemented, prevents improper data bleed from one tenant to another while consuming shared resources. Traditional on-premise technologies are generally thought of as single-tenant solutions, while cloud-based solutions are generally thought of as multitenant solutions. That is not always true and, in many cases, not always good for your business. Here is why.

When you subscribe to an XaaS multitenant solution, the shared resources behind your subscription are utilized by multiple other organizations. Your company forgoes the following security best practices:

- **Change Control**: A multitenant XaaS vendor controls when your version is upgraded and patched. They will provide a maintenance window for the upgrade and you will be forced to accept the changes—even if it is not in a desirable timeframe for your business. If the upgrade introduces an undesirable change (bug or incompatibility), there is no way to roll back the changes since multiple organizations (businesses) are sharing the same multitenant shared resources.

- **Security**: With any multitenant solution, there is always a risk of data bleed with another organization or a vulnerability affecting one organization being used to expose data from another. This can even be true with a simple backend misconfiguration, or an insecure third-party add-on that risks the security of the multitenant model. In essence, this is out of your control.

- **Customization**: Outside of a few multitenant XaaS vendors that have designed customization directly into their platform, most multitenant solutions do not allow extensive customization to meet individual business requirements due to the number of shared resources they consume. While this may also be perceived as an advantage to avoid customized obsolesce, it can also cause distribution and unnecessary rework when APIs or features become deprecated as the service releases newer versions.

These are candidly a trade-off in lieu of maintaining the hardware, operating system, maintenance, and security patches for the solution compared to an on-premise instance. However, the same could be true of a single-tenant XaaS solution too. A single-tenant solution has a different set of concerns based on the same topics that are divergent to a multitenant solution:

- **Change Control**: In a single-tenant XaaS model, the end user can decide when to upgrade to a new version as well as whether they want to skip a version. The risk is waiting too long to upgrade and potentially operating with an end-of-support or end-of-life version. An XaaS-based single-tenant version needs to be managed within your current change control procedures and policy. This requires effort not normally associated with an XaaS solution—even if the upgrade is fully automated.

- **Security**: Your XaaS-based single tenant is your own. Any misconfigurations or missing security patches that need to be manually authorized can introduce unnecessary risk. Even though it is an XaaS-based solution, you still have the change control responsibilities of patching and maintenance, just like full versions, even though the vendor will fully automate their installation. Again, while this is probably fully automated, the organization will need to maintain this just like any other application for patch management. Since the solution is a single tenant, there is a very low risk of data bleed unless the hosting company is compromised.

- **Customization**: A single-tenant XaaS solution allows for the most possible customization since any changes will not affect any other tenants or organizations. However, there is a risk since compatibility with future versions might break when the version is upgraded. Luckily, since you can control the version, you may test customization before any upgrade and stay on an older version until you are ready.

So, what else is different between a single tenant and multitenant XaaS solution? If the cost to the end user is acceptable regardless of model, multitenant vs. single tenant is really just a trade-off between change control and acceptable security risk. If you always want to be on the latest version, either model is acceptable. You just have to manage the change control yourself. If you want to customize the XaaS solution, then it becomes the capabilities of the XaaS vendor that should be evaluated and not the tenancy model—and, finally, its security. All XaaS solutions should allow automatic security patching, but the difference defers back to your change control requirements. It is truly up to you to decide if change control, security, and customization are that important when choosing an XaaS solution for privileged access management.

Cloud Models

Growing use of cloud environments for processing, storage, and application hosting and development has opened new avenues for hackers and malicious insiders to access sensitive data and disrupt organizations. As cloud adoption continues to accelerate, organizations must secure access to these environments to mitigate security risks, while meeting the cost and efficiency demands of hosting more applications and services in the cloud.

Like any on-premise asset, unmanaged cloud environments can create a significant security gap that opens networks to security breaches, data loss, intellectual property theft, and regulatory compliance issues. The first step in getting control over cloud assets, or choosing a PAM solution in the cloud, is understanding the capabilities to operate within the cloud and ultimately manage from the cloud. Cloud-based deployments of privileged access management can take on several different forms:

- Cloud-to-cloud, application-to-application, or cloud-to-application for privileged management using an API primarily for implementation (IaaS). This is generally performed with a secret safe or a full password manager in the cloud.

- Cloud-based privileged management, asset-based least privilege management, and secure remote access for users (SaaS) and applications. This can be deployed as a single tenant or multitenant depending on the vendor.

- Cloud-based platform as a service to deploy your own solution based on an existing technology using your own virtual machines, or one provided in a cloud provider's marketplace for your private cloud instance (PaaS).

- Privileged access management for any resources by using any method in conjunction with an on-premise deployment (hybrid).

If this was a multiple-choice question, your strategic business initiatives might require more than one of these categories, thus a hybrid deployment. It is highly uncommon for privileged access management to be used in only one silo of the business without plans to expand the technology to all sensitive systems and privileged accounts. While initial deployments may start small, the cloud is also used for management everywhere. This is critical when selecting PAM on-premise, in the cloud, or a hybrid approach. Hybrid approaches can be a combination of IaaS, SaaS, PaaS, or on-premise, or a combination using remote management nodes to route and aggregate data securely.

Infrastructure as a Service (IaaS)

With regard to PAM, infrastructure as a service (IaaS) refers to the delivery of computing capacity for PAM use cases. In this model, another company operates the data center infrastructure and privileged access management is programmatically available via an API to integrate into other resources. For PAM to succeed as an IaaS solution, it needs to provide its own permissions model to provide delegated access to accounts and applications programmatically. These permissions are typically banded together in built-in or custom-defined roles that provide the required access. They can also be integrated into a cloud-based directory store or identity governance solution for centralized management. Given the power and possible business impact should these accounts be compromised, proper security and control of these permissions is paramount and must be included within the scope of an organization's multilayered security program. This includes the privileged access layer by rotating any keys or passwords used programmatically to secure them in the first place.

For organizations looking to perform PAM *only* in the cloud, there are multiple technology vehicles to implement a solution. The most common is to use black box container technology to store secrets in the cloud as an infrastructure component—essentially an API secret safe. This allows for a hardened PAM deployment catered specifically for cloud usage and using cost models that take advantage of cloud environments. This approach is typically used for SecDevOps and DevOps when implemented within the cloud. In addition, some PAM vendors also offer solutions that can be instantiated as a virtual machine based on a cloud operating system template. These provide the most flexibility for a client and are hardened and patched by the PAM vendor too. The risks are lower for these types of implementations, but may have a higher runtime cost if the infrastructure requires the virtual machine to be operating all of the time.

Software as a Service (SaaS)

Software as a service (SaaS) is a delivery model where a service is centrally hosted by the provider and licensed to customers on a subscription basis. Organizations and end users typically interact with these services via a web console or programming APIs. This allows you to consume a small part of an application without the cost and complexity of building servers and maintaining application software. Examples of corporate SaaS solutions include Salesforce, Workday, Concur, ServiceNow, Office 365, and even LinkedIn. In a SaaS model, an organization's core security responsibility is the application itself. This includes who can access the application, what authentication is required, and what access users should have. Each application may have its own access model with varying levels of granular provisioning available based on the vendor. Some SaaS applications have traditional business services and may have fine-grained permission models to provide flexibility and permissions to specific groups of users based on tasks or use cases. These applications may also have built-in governance features, such as separation of duties and fine-grained auditing to enable organizations to control and audit access to sensitive features and data. Other SaaS applications that have been traditionally consumer-focused, such as Facebook or Twitter, have minimal granularity in their permissioning models. In some cases, users share a common corporate account to manage the system on behalf of the company. While these SaaS applications may not have the same level of sensitive information, such as customer lists or financial data, these accounts do represent a significant risk to an organization. Issues could include inconvenience; for example, if the sole administrative user is on leave, updates would come to a grinding halt. Another issue could be a disruptive one, such as if a hacker uses a compromised account to post or tweet inappropriate material that could impact the company's reputation. In either case, proper management and control over these accounts should be considered when designing an overall security program. And, it is important to note that based on previous discussions, these SaaS applications can be single tenant, multitenant, or some hybrid implementation to overcome the business challenges and costs of hosting a cloud solution.

With this in mind, SaaS-based PAM solutions not only need to manage the privileged access to your cloud resources, but potentially manage your PAM requirements on-premise as well. PAM solutions deployed as a SaaS solution can operate solely in the cloud or require on-premise management nodes to route and aggregate policy and events and manage remote access sessions. These implementations are completely managed by the PAM vendor, hosted in the provider's cloud environment, and may operate using shared cloud resources with other companies. Only the business can determine whether or not the risks inherent with this shared model are acceptable, and whether or not the provider has implemented adequate controls to secure your privileged data from any potential leak or breach.

Ultimately, to service this type of cloud model, consider the following use cases that may be required for a successful SaaS deployment:

1. Secure agent-based technologies deployed on virtual machines or remote assets (laptops or other mobile user devices) running within the cloud or remotely connected to the Internet to meet PAM requirements.

2. Secure communications with on-premise management nodes to communicate with the cloud for remote sessions, password management, and managed least privilege endpoints.

3. Localized data obfuscation, filtering, or purging to maintain regulatory compliance.

4. Complete role- and attribute-based access for all data, reporting, and auditing.

Platform as a Service (PaaS)

Privileged access management, when delivered as a platform as a service (PaaS), provides an added level of abstraction to existing on-premise solutions. These cloud services provide a platform allowing customers to develop, run, and manage privileges based on technology they may already be familiar with on-premise. Examples of PaaS vendors that have shifted to on-premise solutions that are similar to their on-premise solutions include Oracle and Microsoft. In fairness, some may argue that PaaS does not strictly imply a lift and shift of on-premise technology to the cloud. For the sake of this conversation, I would loosely agree, but operating systems like Microsoft Windows, Red Hat Linux, and even your favorite database in the cloud originated from an on-premise solution and share similar capabilities. If they were built natively in the cloud and have no on-premise equivalent, I would argue it is a SaaS solution and not a PaaS. This is a semantic discussion worthy of a late night, beer, and a deeper discussion of whether the Death Star was a platform to destroy planets, or a space station as claimed by Tarkin. Regardless, PaaS-based PAM solutions are typically used to provide privileged management to an organization's critical applications and services and are rarely different (outside of cost) than moving your on-premise implementation of PAM into the cloud.

CHAPTER 16

Mobile Devices

Mobile devices represent a unique attack vector for a threat actor. They have accounts and credentials, but no role-based access, and there are generally only two permission types: user and root. In addition, root is generally not available to the end user, and there is only one account with a single owner and identity operating the device. These are simple facts regarding mobile device design. To aid in this discussion, a mobile device is defined as a handheld computer with a touchscreen interface and optional physical buttons that allows connectivity to the Internet or other computing devices via wireless protocols. These are typically smartphones and tablets and by definition, rarely include laptops or notebooks unless they are handheld in size.

For a successful attack to occur, a threat actor needs to compromise the operating system, gain access to the root account, and inappropriately leverage the device. This can be achieved through malware, jailbreak, or an exploit. The delivery of the malicious payload exceeds the scope of this book, but it can be anything from juice jacking to malicious software in a vendor's application store. The goal of the threat actor is to leverage the device to do the following:

- Egress information from the device considered personally identifiable or organizationally sensitive.

- Enable surveillance via GPS, camera, or audio.

© Morey J. Haber 2020
M. J. Haber, *Privileged Attack Vectors*, https://doi.org/10.1007/978-1-4842-5914-6_16

- Leverage the device using lateral movement to attack other corporate, home, public, or roaming assets.

- Establish a persistent presence for new or other advanced persistent attacks.

The threat actor's goal is the same regardless of whether it is a traditional corporate asset or other Internet of Things (IoT) device. Once privileged access is obtained, the offense by a threat actor is the same. However, the defense is completely different since there is no role-based access, access to root is restricted unless an exploit or jailbreak occurs, and protection in the form of antivirus is not permitted on some platforms (Apple iOS). Therefore, the best defense is to adapt to the models for security that are permitted:

- For businesses using mobile devices in a bring your own device (BYOD) or organizationally supplied model, utilize a mobile device manager (MDM) to provide application and data segmentation. This will allow the organization to enforce acceptable use policies and even block (uninstall) potentially malicious applications that could compromise the device. Also, most MDM solutions can also detect and block a jailbreak attempt, preventing root access.

- For non-Apple devices, there are a plethora of security solutions that can scan for malware, inappropriate permissions, and even poor configurations (like USB debugging) that could be used to compromise the device. Many of these agents are in the appropriate marketplace, but are also supplied by MDM solutions and traditional antivirus vendors. It is recommended they be utilized to identify risks and mitigate any platform-specific threats for that mobile device.

- When possible, mobile devices should never have direct access to the data center and sensitive systems. Their connections should always be proxied or routed through a jump host for remote access. Virtual desktops and remote applications are ideal for mobile device segmentation to restrict access, enforce multi-factor authentication, and prevent lateral movement. You may also use password management solutions to make the additional connections and session monitoring to capture that any potential roaming access is appropriate.

Mobile devices have provided the world with a vehicle to always stay connected. For a threat actor, they present a way to breach the perimeter of an organization, even when the asset is not in the office. Gaining privileged access to these devices is not as critical, and, as such, these devices just do not have the same robust security models as traditional information technology resources. However, leveraging a mobile device to gain a foothold may be good enough for an exploit or malware to do eventually inflict the same amount of damage as root.

So, how can a threat actor gain nonroot access needed to commit these crimes? It is easier than you think, and the security models for mobile devices are riddled with blatant flaws. Consider these potential scenarios:

- The installation of new software from a trusted marketplace can contain malware. Vendors can only provide so much screening for applications, and, repeatedly, malware has bypassed detection and been published. This is either intentional by the vendor or a consequence of a flaw in their supply chain that allowed the insertion of malware before the application was published.

- Some applications utilize their own auto-update or download mechanisms to retrieve supporting data or additional binaries. A successful man-in-the-middle (MitM) attack can intercept these updates and replace the contents with malicious code. While this may sound a little farfetched, simple DNS spoofing is all that is needed to redirect this traffic on a compromised Wi-Fi network.

- Biometrics have become the primary mechanism for authentication and authorization on mobile devices, and it even allows access to third-party application credentials. A compromise of biometrics not only provides device access, but it can also provide access to applications like banking or other applications dependent on two-factor authentication. Relying on biometrics for authentication is just a bad idea. Once a biometric data point is compromised, it is forever exposed and puts its owner at risk. Biometrics should only be applied as part of multi-factor since the base credentials can always be changed, while biometrics only proves your identity electronically. Unfortunately, many mobile device manufacturers are blurring this line and have ignored security best practices by making biometrics the only form of identification required to access a device during normal operations. This is gambling on the strength of their biometric security module, and time will tell whether the designs will be robust enough to stop modern threats. To date, they have not been.

- Mobile devices (outside of Qi charging) require a corded connection for battery recharging, typically on daily basis. Also, they have various bidirectional communication systems from NFC, Bluetooth, and Wi-Fi. The flaw is that there are minimal controls around remote exploitation of these communication paths. These include USB chargers (juice jacking) infected with malware to man-in-the-middle attacks that can compromise Wi-Fi communications. These are just security flaws due to the nature of mobile devices and represent a high risk with no real resolution outside of locking them down to known, trusted sources for charging. Basically, all mobile devices are at risk if plugged into a malicious charging source.

- For Android devices only, the operating system and hardware fragmentation represent unique security challenges per operating system version and device. The scope of the problems well exceeds the confines of this section, and, in many cases, a flaw on one Android device may not be present on another, nor may the manufacturer choose to remediate the flaw. For businesses, allowing Android devices via BYOD or corporate-purchased, minimum (or specific) versions and vendors should be considered (i.e., consider the US government ban on Huawei devices). Not all manufacturers maintain the same service level agreement (SLA) for supplying patches. Some manufacturers have been known to supply purposely built backdoors for their own devices for targeted updates and monitoring; neither of which may be acceptable to a business with sensitive operations.

Despite these flaws, there exist strategies and technologies to mitigate these risks. For example:

- Never use biometrics for both device access and sensitive applications on a mobile device. Implementing this policy is good practice to ensure the privileges of one system (biometric access) cannot be used against another (application). In fairness, this is a perfect example of password reuse via biometrics and a perfect reason to implement a multi-factor authentication to safeguard credentials and biometrics used on the device.

- Using MDM technology ensures that your organization can lock down BYOD devices to trusted networks and disable features like debugging mode that can make them susceptible to USB charging attacks (juice jacking).

- Decide on what you can support and what you cannot. BYOD does not mean every device an employee may own can be connected to the corporate network, even if your MDM can support it. Having a finite list of manufacturers, quantity of connected devices, and operating system versions will help mitigate risks, especially from outlier threats.

CHAPTER 17

Ransomware and Privileges

Let me get this out right off the bat: **no one solution is 100% effective in mitigating the risk of ransomware**. Some technologies are claiming to have tested hundreds of samples, and that their tool is perfect in stopping all types of attacks. I'm sorry, but that is a falsehood. Why? If any single vendor had a solution that could solve the problem completely, ransomware would not be such a problem.

At its core, ransomware is a form of malware that cybercriminals use to infect computers or cloud resources and then to encrypt files and data, making them inaccessible until the owner has paid a ransom. Of course, even paying the ransom is no guarantee that access will be restored by the perpetrators.

From catastrophic, lengthy downtime to economic devastation and even loss of life, today's ransomware is clearly beyond the scope of just being a nuisance. It has already been well documented that ransomware has even caused loss of life and reduced health outcomes. So, where are organizations getting it wrong? And what changes can you make to get it right when it comes to ransomware defenses?

All security professionals should be able to tell you that there's no silver bullet to defend against all varieties of ransomware. But there are strategic IT security practices, like privileged access management, that can help eliminate many types of ransomware outright and dramatically

© Morey J. Haber 2020
M. J. Haber, *Privileged Attack Vectors*, https://doi.org/10.1007/978-1-4842-5914-6_17

reduce the overall risk of suffering a devastating attack. For example, application control solutions, endpoint protection products, and least privilege solutions are effective in mitigating various types of ransomware, but none are 100% effective across all ransomware types. Modern ransomware can leverage privileges when available, does not always launch separate executables, does not always drop files on the file system, and sometimes targets obscure devices, like smart TVs. We have seen a spike in ransomware that uses Microsoft Office macros to propagate the threats, and even versions that use JScript embedded in a document to conduct malicious activity. We have also seen ransomware like WannaCry and NotPetya leverage exploits across modern and end-of-life operating systems to devastate organizations. The attack vectors are growing as ransomware continues to mature and escalate as this decade's (and last decade's) largest cybersecurity threat. Ransomware wasted no time in exploiting fears around Coronavirus (COVID-19) It's been quick to evolve and weaponized to hit us where it can do the most damage.

Unfortunately, the delivery of the ransomware payload is equally as horrific to identify as seeing a ransomware payment message. To understand how privileges affect ransomware, consider the sources in which ransomware may originate:

- An exploitable vulnerability in an application or website

- An errant, malicious executable executed by the asset

- A PowerShell script or batch file

- Embedded as an application macro or script in a file

- Compromised auto-update mechanisms per application or the entire operating system

- A phishing attack designed to socially engineer the user into high risk behaviors

What makes this a little more disturbing is that many attacks combine methods and use a command control server to hold encryption certificates, vs. locally based per infection that can be cured with a decryption solution. The privileges ransomware executes will help dictate how successful the malicious infiltration will be. And, modern ransomware may be just a Trojan Horse for other advanced threats designed to distract IT security teams. This is why ransomware is so difficult to stop, and no one technology is 100% effective.

As a defense, there are some actions you can perform with privileged access management to minimize the threats of ransomware. Unfortunately, nothing will ever replace training users not to select Run Macros when opening an unknown file. However, here are a few rules that are easy to implement that will block the vast majority of mistakes users can make, stop droppers from executing, and block vulnerable applications from being leveraged against your assets:

- **Implement Application Control**: Privileged access management solutions allow for application control and the ability to elevate applications based on rules. In addition, PAM solutions can operate in the opposite mode—they can block any unauthorized application from executing, regardless of the source, if it is not properly digitally signed, launched from an improper location, called inappropriately as a child process, or tries to execute a malicious child process of its own.

- **Secure Remote Access**: Remote access, particularly by third-party vendors, is often the weakest link in network security and can lead to a ransomware attack. Vendors authorized to access the network and applications might not adhere to the organization's same level of security protocols, or they may use virtual private networks (VPNs) to extend "secure" access to internal resources. If the vendor is infected, has malicious intent of their own, or is a carrier of ransomware, your organization could be the next victim. Therefore, the best way to mitigate the risk is to use remote access technology that does not use any protocol tunneling, VPN, nor rely on traditional remote access protocols that could be leveraged as an attack vector.

- **Secure Privileged Credentials**: Compromised credentials are a well-known ingredient of almost all IT security incidents and ransomware is no exception. To execute, ransomware wants privilege. Privilege is a critical path for ransomware's persistence. That's why it's critical to secure privileged credentials with an enterprise privileged password management solution that will consistently discover, onboard, manage, rotate, and audit these powerful credentials. Automated rotation of credentials and consistent enforcement of strong password policy protect your organization from password reuse attacks as well as infection by ransomware and lateral movement once ransomware has gained a foothold.

- **Enforce Least Privilege**: Ransomware can only run with the privileges of the user or the application that launches it. That is fundamentally its biggest weakness. The best defense starts by not granting it excessive privileges in the first place. Therefore, removing local admin privileges and applying least privilege access across all users, applications, resources, and systems won't prevent every ransomware attack, but it will stop the vast majority of them. It will also mitigate the impact of those ransomware payloads that make their way into an environment by closing down lateral pathways and reducing the ability to elevate privilege. Least privilege can even mitigate the impact of stolen credentials. If the credentials are for a user, endpoint, or application with limited or no privileges, the credentials can essentially not be used by the malware to infect another host unless it can scrape additional credentials or exploit a vulnerability that allows privileged escalation.

- **Apply Security Updates**: Of course, one of the most fundamental ways to reduce ransomware and other vulnerability-based exploits is simply staying up-to-date with patching and remediating of known, published vulnerabilities. This condenses the attack surface, reducing the potential footholds in your environment available to threat actors. To that end, very few ransomware attacks leverage zero-day vulnerabilities (MS Office Macros being the most prevalent). And, if a ransomware attack does happen to leverage a zero-day exploit, following all of the other strategies listed here will help reduce your attack surface to ransomware and, hopefully, blunt the impact of any attack should it make it into your environment.

- **Stopping Droppers**: Unfortunately, trusted applications can launch other applications to perform their intended functions. This includes browsers, email programs, and even PDF readers. The consistent part of this problem is that these executables almost always launch from temporary file directories. Using privileged access management to manage file integrity, administrators can track, alert, and block rogue dropper executables that appear in these directories or that do not meet minimum reputation requirements.

- **Leverage Application Reputation**: Privileged access management solutions typically have a reputation service engine or other technology to measure the risk of an application before its launch. This component allows for real-time assessment of an application's health with regards to malware, vulnerabilities, permissions, and privacy. To that end, policies can be established to deny (or notify of) the launch of risky applications that could be leveraged in a ransomware attack. This helps ensure service-level agreements are being met for cybersecurity hygiene and no system is left out that could pose an unacceptable risk.

Ransomware risk can be minimized using the same technology used for managing privileged accounts. While this approach is not 100% effective, it is a residual return on investment when organizations embrace this approach. Organizations can stop most ransomware from executing simply by not giving it the privileges it needs to execute in the first place.

CHAPTER 18

Remote Access

Driven in large part by the globalization of technology, focus on a healthier work-life balance, an increase in the number of millennials entering the workforce, and more recently, social distancing initiatives in response to the novel coronavirus, we are increasingly seeing companies across the globe offer their employees the option to work remotely. Not surprisingly, a recent survey from Bayt.com[1] found that 79% of professionals in the Middle East and North Africa (MENA) region would actually prefer to work for companies that offer a remote working option. Offering employees the opportunity to work remotely can actually work to the advantage of the organization. According to Gartner,[2] "by 2020, organizations that support a 'choose-your-own-work-style' culture will boost employee retention rates by more than 10%."

So, while there is no disputing the many benefits of remote working, it does add a layer of complexity that creates security challenges, especially for privileged access. As such, the onus is on an organization's IT team to ensure that their remote workers and vendors are empowered with the tools they need to be productive, without exposing the organization to excessive cyber risk. Figure 18-1 illustrates a basic remote access architecture that can meet these objectives.

---

[1] www.bayt.com/en/blog/26921/bayt-com-poll-preferred-work-arrangements-in-the-middle-east-and-north-africa/

[2] www.gartner.com/binaries/content/assets/events/keywords/digital-workplace/pcce13/cx18_research_note_summary_crafting-workspaces_1.pdf

M. J. Haber, *Privileged Attack Vectors*, https://doi.org/10.1007/978-1-4842-5914-6_18

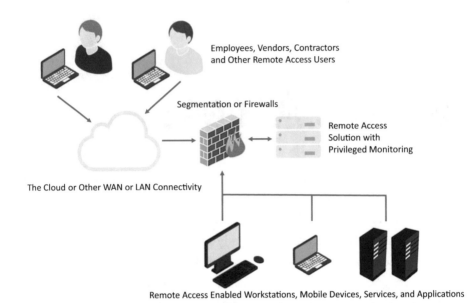

Employees, Vendors, Contractors
and Other Remote Access Users

Segmentation or Firewalls

Remote Access
Solution with
Privileged Monitoring

The Cloud or Other WAN or LAN Connectivity

Remote Access Enabled Workstations, Mobile Devices, Services, and Applications

Figure 18-1. *Remote Access Architecture*

For this to succeed and be secure, please consider the following attack risk surfaces:

Remote Access Connectivity: In most cases, remote employees connect to corporate resources directly via a VPN or via hosted cloud remote access solutions. These employees are often behind their own home routers that employ technology like Network Address Translator (NAT) to isolate the network. However, this poses a network routing challenge for traditional IT management and security solutions like VPN. For one, corporate cybersecurity solutions cannot push updates directly to remote employees, nor directly query their systems in real-time due to the lack of downstream network routes. As a consequence, the only way for these remote employees to get cybersecurity updates or submit data is to poll (initiate an outbound connection) into the corporate cybersecurity resources. This often requires a persistent outbound connection to determine state, regardless of using a VPN or cloud resources, and is susceptible to trivial network anomalies commonly found in home-based wireless networks or cellular technology.

Additionally, as a result of name resolution and limitations in routing, processes such as discovery and pushing of policy updates all become batch-driven, as opposed to near real-time. Even remote support technologies require an agent with a persistent connection to facilitate screen sharing since a routable connection inbound to SSH, VNC, RDP, and the like is not normally possible for remote employees. Thus, the number one hurdle to securing remote access for employees is around managing devices that are no longer routable, reachable, or resolvable from a traditional corporate network for analysis and support. This is entirely independent of the privileges the remote user may invoke while connected to the network.

Bring Your Own Device (BYOD): Remote employees' remote access clients can come in two forms:

- Corporate supplied IT resources

- Bring your own device (BYOD)

While corporate-issued devices and resources can be strongly hardened and controlled, personal devices are frequently shared and may not undergo the same level of security attention. Organizations may mandate Mobile Device Management (MDM is discussed in Chapter 16) tools on personal devices to aid in management, but user resistance may stymie adoption. For obvious reasons, corporate IT teams cannot harden employee-owned devices and govern the device operations as tightly as they could corporate-owned without the enforcement of MDM. The methodology your organization chooses to support BYOD is ultimately a balance between cost, risk, user acceptance, and usability for remote access. With threats like SIM jacking, it is nearly a must to consider an MDM solution for any personal mobile device that accesses corporate resources.

Cybersecurity Hygiene: Finally, there is the challenge of deploying basic cybersecurity controls like patch management and antivirus to remote access users. This assumes remote access is available to users via their home computers and laptops, not just mobile devices. Traditionally, these cybersecurity basics are performed using network scanners, agents, and services to execute various functions and require connectivity to on-premise servers. The good news is that cloud technologies have simplified the management of these security basics using SaaS and PaaS solutions. With the inability for cellular and other mobile technologies to maintain a persistent and routable connection, organizations must embrace the cloud for managing basic cybersecurity disciplines when remote access is a requirement. The cloud offers universal resources, outside of a traditional datacenter, to which remote devices can securely connect and take advantage of methodologies like geolocation and two-factor authentication. This ensures the source and health for any remote access can be managed and validated regardless of the device type. Also, the cloud can provide access without the flaws of VPN technology to ensure the health of a source device does not become a liability.

Remote Access Security: The best advice for IT teams that need to secure remote workforces (employees, vendors, managed service providers, and contractors) involves keeping an open mind and being accepting of new technologies, methodologies, and workflows to accomplish their goals. This includes new ways to perform secure remote access that does not require VPN, NAC, or traditional VDI bastion host technology. Team members need to think out of the box regarding connectivity and plan for the bandwidth revolution of 5G cellular technology. Large-scale data theft can transpire within minutes using the latest wireless technology and traditional remote access tools. It can happen via any remote session that has privileged access to sensitive corporate resources. With all the above taken into account, teams need to understand their business models, the roles remote users play, and the data and system risks they represent. Then, a defensive strategy can be built using modern remote access technology. Finally, with the proliferation of infrastructure components that have moved to web-based management interfaces in the cloud, information and security technology administrators are faced with new threats for managing credentials to administer these solutions remotely. It's a challenge to control, audit, and enforce proper authentication for privileged access to browser-based cloud resources without negatively affecting business productivity. Administrators, and even power users, need a way to effectively control and audit resources managed via cloud-based web consoles and treat them like a console that should only be accessed via a secure remote access solution, instead of directly from the Internet. This is why remote access and privileged access management go together hand-in-hand.

Vendor Remote Access

At any given time, vendors, contractors, building maintenance, managed service providers, and other organizations may have access to your network to fulfill contractual obligations, provide services, or resource maintenance. Many of these vendors and workers connect to your systems remotely to go about their daily business in supporting your organization. The problem is that many of the systems they interact with are also connected to your corporate network. Numerous high-profile breaches have demonstrated that vendor networks can be leveraged to gain access to customer environments.

Threat actors can steal credentials to gain access to vendor-controlled systems and then exploit vulnerabilities or poorly managed privileges to move throughout the organization, sometimes machine by machine. You are only as secure as your weakest link and the security of your environment may rest on the security practices, and controls, of a third party.

The big issue with adhering to policy and maintaining security across two companies is that often the credentials used by the remote vendor are not under the direct control of the customer. Two different networks with two different user directories, and perhaps two different security policies, make the job of security compliance a challenge. Even if you had a way to ensure security best practices were being followed, you still have no visibility into what activity is being performed on equipment that is connected to your network. This creates a unique set of new challenges when remote access is not being performed by an employee, but rather by some form of vendor. The following are some key best practices for ensuring secure vendor access:

- **Vendor Credential Management**: Vendors accessing an organization's resources remotely should have all credentials:

    a. Rotated regularly after any and all access, and completion of sessions. This can be done natively or via integration into a password management solution.

    b. Enforce a workflow to ensure the access was appropriate.

    c. Support multi-factor authentication to ensure credentials have not been shared or compromised.

    d. Provide ephemeral or just-in-time access.

- **Network Access**: Vendors requiring network access to manage resources should have:

    a. Access to only the applicable resources.

    b. Capabilities in place for detection and prevention of their lateral movement.

    c.   Support for connectivity without the need for a bastion host.

    d.   Support for connectivity without the need for protocol tunneling.

    e.   Routing of all sessions through a gateway or proxy to perform session monitoring.

    f.   Requirement for appropriate attribute-based proof that network access is from the proper source.

- **Privilege Monitoring**: Vendors requiring access should have all sessions monitored and audited with capabilities to review activity similar to shoulder surfing.

- **Application Control**: Vendors should be monitored for all application and command usage, including file access. In addition, vendors should only be granted specific least privilege access to the applications they require.

To alleviate all of these challenges for vendor remote access, privileged access management solutions should be fully integrated. Vendors typically need to access a third-party organization's resources with privileges and only this type of integration can securely provide the appropriate access.

Working from Home

The days of commuting to an office have evolved rapidly in the last 30 years to include telecommuting, remote employees, and flexible office hours. In early 2020, the changes have been life altering and realistically we may never go back to the office environments established B.C. (Before Corona). In addition, some countries have mandated for companies a few workdays at home to accommodate the overload at facilities, high volume of traffic, employee burnout, and even pollution. And, sometimes, finding the best employee may not even be possible within your geography, warranting the consideration of a purely remote employee. Generally, they work from home.

Information technology professionals are tasked with providing remote access for these employees and have implemented a variety of solutions, architectures, policies, and diverse technology over the last three decades to accommodate remote work. Some of the decisions by IT and security professionals are innovative, secure, and even cutting-edge, while others are downright cringeworthy and laden with potential risk.

One of the more common trends is to allow the installation of the organization's virtual private network (VPN) software on an employee's home computer for remote access. While some security professionals may think of this as an acceptable practice, this policy presents an unjustifiably high security risk. For example, consider the following:

Lower Malware Defense: Home users are typically local administrators for their personal computers. They rarely create secondary standard user accounts for daily usage. This makes them more susceptible to malware. The vast majority of malware needs administrative rights to infect a system, and home users typically do not place any restrictions on their own access simply for convenience. The older the home computer operating system, the worse the operating system is at defending against malware that requires administrative rights for system exploitation.

Multiple Users: If a personal computer is shared among multiple family members, even with multiple user profiles, there are very few mitigations to prevent an infection or poor judgment of one individual from infecting others. Also, techniques like fast user switching compound the problem by keeping other profiles in memory, making them susceptible to a variety of attacks based on other active profiles. A compromise of one user not related at all to the organization can be leveraged against an active VPN session connected to the organization.

Lack of Authority: Organizations do not have the authority to manage an individual's home computer. While network access control solutions can validate antivirus signature versions and other basic hardware characteristics, they cannot inventory a home computer to ensure it is hardened and maintained like a corporate asset. These gaps, even when connected to a bastion host, can allow data leakage from keystroke loggers and screen-capturing malware that can place data and the organization at risk.

Inability to Secure the Host: Corporate VPN solutions typically embed a certificate into a connection or user profile to validate the connection. This is independent of the authentication the user should provide via credentials and, hopefully, some form of two-factor authentication in order to make a connection. The security of the certificate and the credentials for authentication are only as secure as the security maintenance implemented for the asset. These are a prime target for a threat actor on a poorly maintained host to initiate their own connections or hijack sessions used by remote employees. If you cannot secure the host, how can you secure the connection software it is running?

Lack of Protective Resources: Lastly, home users typically only have antivirus on their computers. They usually do not have endpoint detection and response (EDR) or endpoint privilege management (EPM), nor do they have vulnerability or patch management solutions to ensure their assets are being properly secured and to elevate any threats for awareness. Home users typically operate as independent workstations with no monitoring from security professionals to respond when something goes awry.

Even with all of these elements, some organizations have accepted the risk of VPN software on resources not being maintained by the organization. They have developed highly secure virtual desktop infrastructure (VDI) environments and bastion hosts to proxy (or gateway) the connection to shield applications and sensitive data. They have created isolated networks and resources in the cloud to manage these connections and, in many cases, paid tens of thousands of dollars in licensing costs just to stand up resources in a defensive network strategy to mitigate these risks. In many cases, they are effective, but they are all geared to allowing the organization's VPN software on untrusted assets maintained by home users.

The initial decision to allow VPN software on home assets should be revisited, and businesses should consider other ways to allow remote access with lower risks. This is especially true when the remote employees require *any* form of privileged access:

- Issue corporate-owned assets that are hardened and managed to provide connectivity.

- License a third-party remote access solution that does not require a complex environment to provide connectivity and can perform the connection through a web browser without the need for VPN software, dedicated applications, virtual desktop environments, or protocol tunneling.

- If employees who need remote access have traditional desktop computers, consider replacing them with corporate-owned and managed laptops with docking stations. In the office, a laptop would operate as a regular desktop, including having large monitors, but when required at home, it could travel as a managed asset, minimizing the risk.

- And as a final thought (which may not be for every business, and will certainly not apply well in the era of the coronavirus), don't allow employees to work remotely. Companies like Yahoo[3] required

---

[3]Yahoo Working from Home Memo—www.businessinsider.com/yahoo-working-from-home-memo-2013-2

all employees to come into the office during its restructuring, and even certain governments require, by law, that employees cannot take work home after hours to prevent labor abuse. While controversial, this may result in less employee fatigue, happy work-life balance, and overall better security by keeping the perimeter better defined. Ironically, this is the exact opposite of zero trust.

There are so many factors to review when considering whether to allow home users VPN access from their personal computers. It is puzzling that so many environments allow this practice when, in many cases the cost of a tablet managed by the company can provide a more secure experience compared to the runtime costs of a bastion host and VDI environment. The choice is ultimately a business decision, but allowing VPN access to personal computers by remote workers is a technology practice that should never be deployed in the first place.

Secure Remote Access

To address all of these remote access concerns—from vendors to remote employees—rely on a next-generation secure remote access solution with privileged access management capabilities that provides connectivity based on the following criteria:

- Compatible with existing remote access protocols like RDP, VNC, SSH, and HTTP(S).

- Supports agent-based technology for remote access without the need for open listening ports.

- Supports a multitier architecture as management nodes to reach deep within an organization.

- Supports a deployment architecture that is on-premise, in a private cloud, or as a SaaS solution.

- Supports remote connectivity via x86, x64, or MacOS-dedicated client, mobile devices using dedicated apps, or via an HTML5 browser to avoid any protocol tunneling.

- Provides full session monitoring capabilities in accordance with privileged access management best practices.

- Provides strong authentication and workflow to determine whether or not the user requesting access is appropriate.

- Provides advanced capabilities to determine the inventory of the host and enumerate key settings.

- Protects against lateral movement and inappropriate application and command usage.

- Integrates or provides native password management capabilities that can be delegated to users to control appropriate privileged access.

- Provides remote access to any resource in any location from the cloud to on-premise and even supports remote employees. This solves the problem of having to secure cloud-based management consoles.

With these requirements in mind, connectivity, regardless of the source, can be secured for privileged remote access.

CHAPTER 19

Secured DevOps (SecDevOps)

DevOps is a blending of software development and operations, and a set of automated practices to condense release cycles across the life cycle of software development. SecDevOps (also referred to as SDevOps or DevSecOps) extends the methodology by integrating security best practices into the development, quality assurance, and deployment of software in this life cycle. DevOps automation tools use privileged credentials like any application-to-application solution, but security is, unfortunately, too often an afterthought. Consider the following DevOps security risks:

- Malicious insiders can leverage excessive privileges or shared secrets to compromise code.

- Vulnerabilities, misconfigurations, and other weaknesses in containers can open the door to security compromises.

- Insecure code, hard-coded passwords, and other privilege exposures can lead to external attacks.

- Scripts or vulnerabilities in CI (continuous integration) and CD (continuous deliver or continuous deployment) tools, such as Ansible, Chef, or Puppet, could deploy malware or sabotage code.

© Morey J. Haber 2020
M. J. Haber, *Privileged Attack Vectors*, https://doi.org/10.1007/978-1-4842-5914-6_19

- Automation to move and test code requires credentials
  to cross network zones—a compromise in the process
  can be leveraged for lateral movement by a threat actor.

While it is clear that security needs to be built into DevOps, how
do you do so without hampering speed, agility, and becoming a victim
of the observer effect? As organizations continue to adopt more Agile
development methodologies that require extensive integration and
automation across operational tools, they often find that it becomes
very difficult to effectively and securely manage the credentials required
to support these end-to-end processes. A typical DevOps process to
automate, QA, and deploy code builds may include the following:

- Operate with service accounts that run various services
  (TFS, Builds, SQL).

- Scheduled tasks and automation (custom scripts, Git
  and GitHub, Jenkins, Puppet, and others).

- Leverage third-party services (SMTP, cloud services,
  SSH, etc.) to provide status, notifications, and move
  software.

- Interact with certificates for SSL websites, automated
  code signing, and other processes that have security
  wrappers.

All these technologies that integrate and automate application
development and deployment into a more streamlined process require
credentials and have no identities since they are automated. In some
cases, these credentials may be stored and shared in scripts, code,
and configuration files. The risks of storing, sharing, and infrequently
changing credentials used to automate the DevOps processes make them
susceptible to hacking and misuse, especially if they are clear text. This
entire DevOps life cycle, secured with PAM, is illustrated in Figure 19-1.

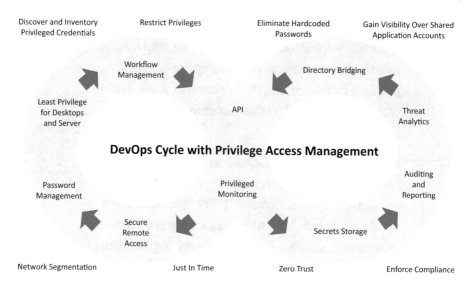

Figure 19-1. *Typical SecDevOps (DevOps) Life Cycle with Privileged Access Management*

To reduce these risks, organizations should look to expand their privileged access management initiatives and implement phases that include the following:

1. Eliminating hard-coded credentials in code (compiled), scripts, and service accounts. Most enterprise password management and secret storage vendors include service account and password APIs that can be implemented to address these items.

2. Implement a remote access solution with session monitoring to control when developers can access production servers. DevOps methodologies often require the pushing of code, compilation, and integration of postcompile workflows. The goal is to have developers safely and easily execute critical

workflows, but without having direct access to the systems themselves. Implementing a jump host based on remote access technology makes this possible by controlling the secure connection into your environment by administrators, automation jobs, or developers.

3. Implementing the concept of least privilege across the application environment. Do the developers, development tools, or development processes need to have administrator or root access to the systems and databases supporting the application environment? A process should be developed so they should not. Implementing least privilege would ensure that these developers and processes only have the privileges that they need to support their workflow in the end-to-end DevOps process. In addition, augmenting least privilege enforcement with session recording and keystroke logging would also help to identify compromised account activity and risks associated with privilege abuse and misuse.

4. Introduce application control into the DevOps process. This can be done by digital signature, source location, or other reputation services. The goal is to ensure that only authorized scripts and binaries are executed in the DevOps process and the malicious injection of malware will be denied execution due to the lack of reputational confidence for the program (whitelisting).

5. To reduce the complexity of creating and managing local accounts across non-Windows systems in a dynamic cloud environment, designers should investigate methods to consolidate and centralize accounts or dynamic secrets and manage them using a secure secret store. Storage, retrieval, and processing is then available via a secure API for DevOps automation.

Finally, organizations should examine solutions to proactively protect containers and microservices associated with enterprise applications. This becomes a high priority when implementing a new zero trust architecture with DevOps (covered in Chapter 22). And, as organizations transform their traditional applications to the cloud, they should consider how to mature the security basics by embracing SecDevOps over DevOps to make security an equal process in the workflow. Finally, embrace vulnerability scanning and configuration hardening assessments to continuously prove the workflow is secure and free from potential exploitation. This should literally be just another automated step in your SecDevOps process.

Moving all your development and applications to the cloud can be scary. Automating compilation, QA testing, and even deployment can be even scarier if there is no visibility or security in the process. Many of the controls that security professionals take for granted have alternative approaches when embracing DevOps and should not be ignored. The key to making this work for your organization is privileged access management and making it a foundation to protect the entire automation process!

CHAPTER 20

Regulatory Compliance

A threat actor does not care about the law, compliance, regulations, and security best practices. In fact, they are hopeful that your organization is lax on many of these specifications and frameworks to leverage them for malicious intent. While regulatory compliance is designed to provide legally binding guidelines for industries and governments, they do not provide the necessary means to stay secure. Compliance does not equal security. Regulatory compliance measures are enforced guidance toward good cybersecurity hygiene, but implementing them without good processes, people, training, and diligence will leave you susceptible to a breach. Therefore, when reviewing leading regulatory compliance initiatives, consider the following:

- How they apply to your organization based on laws, sensitive information, contracts, industry, and geography.

- What overlaps exist between them and what processes can satisfy multiple requirements?

- Be sure to adopt the strictest guidance for your initiatives. The strictest and most comprehensive requirement should always win since it will exceed any looser requirements.

© Morey J. Haber 2020
M. J. Haber, *Privileged Attack Vectors*, https://doi.org/10.1007/978-1-4842-5914-6_20

- Scoping is critical. Just applying the rules to sensitive systems is often not enough to provide good security. Consider the effort and cost of increasing the scope to mitigate risks through any connected system that could affect the legislatively required scope.

Keep in mind that any regulatory compliance requirements are the absolute minimum your organization should be doing. If you are not meeting the minimums, or have lapses in the requirements, you are the low-hanging fruit a threat actor is seeking, and slowest individual being pursued by the bear.

Payment Card Industry (PCI)

Initially developed in 2004 and currently on version 3.2 (PCI DSS-4.0, at the time of writing this book, is in draft form and in review with QSAs), the Payment Card Industry Data Security Standard (PCI DSS) is an information security standard for every organization that accepts credit cards such as Visa, MasterCard, American Express, and others. The PCI standard:

- Was created to increase controls around cardholder data to reduce credit card fraud

- Has become a de facto standard for protecting access to personally identifiable information (PII), especially in the retail industry

- Is mandated by the card issuers

- Is administered by the Payment Card Industry Security Standards Council (PCI SSC)

Organizations face several challenges when working to prove their compliance with PCI DSS. The largest organizations are challenged with assessments that are conducted annually by a Qualified Security

Assessor (QSA) who creates a Report on Compliance (ROC). And although compliance with PCI DSS is not required by federal law in the United States, the laws of some states either refer to PCI DSS directly or make equivalent provisions. If an organization has been breached and was not in compliance with PCI, the card issuers can impose significant financial penalties on the merchant. Since it is the responsibility of the merchant to achieve, demonstrate, and maintain their compliance at all times during the annual assessment, best practice for PCI DSS compliance is to continually improve processes to ensure ongoing compliance, rather than treating compliance as a point-in-time project. Naturally, this can create a tremendous resource drain on technology- and security-oriented teams.

As a part of this process, the primary mission is to protect cardholder data and the security of the transactions involved with this information. Privileged access management can assist with many of the requirements for PCI DSS compliance in various forms, from restricting access, to command-line filtering. Figure 20-1 provides a high-level diagram of PCI DSS requirements. Based on the requirements, it is easy to see how PAM can impact privileges everywhere.

PCI Data Security Standard - High Level Overview	
Build and Maintain a Secure Network and System	1. Install and maintain a firewall configuration to protect cardholder data 2. Do not use vendor-supplied defaults for system passwords and other security parameters
Protect Cardholder Data	3. Protect stored cardholder data 4. Encrypt transmission of cardholder data across open, public networks
Maintain a Vulnerability Management Program	5. Protect all systems against malware and regularly update anti-virus software or programs 6. Develop and maintain secure systems and applications
Implement Strong Access Control Measures	7. Restrict access to cardholder data by business need to know 8. Identify and authenticate access to system components 9. Restrict physical access to cardholder data
Regularly Monitor and Test Networks	10. Track and monitor all access to network resources and cardholder data 11. Regularly test security systems and processes
Maintain an Information Security Policy	12. Maintain a policy that addresses information security for all personnel

Figure 20-1. PCI DSS Requirements, High-Level Overview

HIPAA

Enacted by the US Congress in 1996, the Health Insurance Portability and Accountability Act (HIPAA) provides provisions to protect health insurance coverage for workers and their families when they change or lose their jobs. HIPAA requires the establishment of national standards for electronic healthcare transactions and national identifiers for providers, health insurance plans, and employers. HIPAA has become a de facto standard for protecting the privacy and security of personally identifiable information (PII) in the healthcare industry.

The Security Rule within HIPAA deals specifically with electronic protected health information (EPHI). It lays out three types of security safeguards required for compliance:

- **Administrative Safeguards**: Policies and procedures designed to clearly show how the entity will comply with the act

- **Physical Safeguards**: Controlling physical access to protect against inappropriate access to protected data

- **Technical Safeguards**: Controlling access to computer systems and enabling covered entities to protect communications containing PHI (protected health information) transmitted electronically over open networks from being intercepted by anyone other than the intended recipient

Based on these three safeguards, it is apparent that patient health information requires protection from a potential threat actor. While a single healthcare record is a viable target, especially when its a record for someone famous or of importance, bulk data is much more valuable on the dark web and for malicious data correlation. Accessing large quantities of data requires privileged access. A single doctor or healthcare provider should not have that level of privileges. Therefore, HIPAA requires privileged access management. Table 20-1 shows the sections in HIPAA solved by PAM (password management (PM), endpoint privilege management (EPM), and secure remote access (SRA)).

Table 20-1. *HIPAA Requirements That Can Be Addressed with PAM*

HIPAA STANDARD	REF	PM	EPM	SRA
Security Management Process	164.308(a)(1)	√	√	√
Assigned Security Responsibility	164.308(a)(2)	√	√	√
Workforce Security	164.308(a)(3)	√	√	√
Information Access Management	164.308(a)(4)	√	√	√
Security Incident Procedures	164.308(a)(6)	√		
Contingency Plans	164.308(a)(7)	√		
Business Associate Contracts and Other Arrangements	164.308(b)(1)	√		√
Facility Access Controls	164.310(a)(1)	√		√
Workstation Use	164.310(b)	√	√	√
Workstation Security	164.310(c)		√	√
Device and Media Controls	164.310(d)(1)		√	√
Access Control	164.312(a)(1)	√	√	√
Audit Controls	164.312(b)	√	√	√
Integrity	164.312(c)(1)	√	√	√
Person or Entity Authentication	164.312(d)	√	√	√
Transmission Security	164.312(e)(1)			√
Business Associate Contracts or Other Arrangements	164.314(a)(1)	√	√	√

SOX

In July 2002, the US Congress passed the Sarbanes-Oxley Act ("SOX"), which was primarily designed to restore investor confidence following well-publicized bankruptcies that brought chief executives, audit committees, and independent auditors under heavy scrutiny. The act applies to all publicly registered companies under the jurisdiction of the Securities and Exchange Commission (SEC). Financial data and documentation are at the heart of the compliance issue, and within the legislation, SOX Section 404: Assessment of Internal Controls defines vulnerability and privileged access management as a business requirement. This helps a business understand the flow of transactions, including IT aspects, to identify points at which a misstatement could arise, and evaluate controls designed to prevent or detect fraud. The latter places privileges as an attack vector and session monitoring clearly in focus for fraud detection and prevention.

GLBA

The Gramm-Leach-Bliley Act (GLBA) was enacted to ensure protection over customers' records and information. To satisfy the rules and provisions of GLBA, financial institutions are required to perform security risk assessments; develop and implement security solutions that effectively detect, prevent, and allow timely incident response; and perform auditing and monitoring of their security environment. Similar to SOX, a complete section covers risk management. The primary portions of Section 508 relevant to privileges as an attack vector include these:

- **Subtitle A**: Disclosure of Nonpublic Personal Information—Constructing a thorough [risk management] on each department handling the nonpublic information

- **Subtitle B**: Fraudulent Access to Financial Information—Social engineering occurs when someone tries to gain access to personal nonpublic information without proper authority

NIST

NIST Special Publication 800-53, Security and Privacy Controls for Federal Information Systems and Organizations, was developed by a joint task force composed of representatives from NIST, the Department of Defense, the Intelligence Community, and the Committee on National Security Systems. This interagency partnership formed in 2009.

This guide delivers a *holistic* approach to information security and risk management by providing organizations with a comprehensive set of security controls essential to fundamentally strengthen their information systems, as well as the environments in which they operate. The resulting systems are more resilient in the face of threats and cyberattacks. NIST SP 800-53 outlines a "Build It Right" strategy combined with various security controls for continuous monitoring and strives to provide the senior leaders of organizations information in near real-time to support making risk-based decisions related to their critical missions.

Controlling and monitoring privileged access is extremely important for mitigating the risks posed by insider threats, preventing data breaches, and meeting compliance requirements. With that being said, security and IT leaders should walk a fine line between protecting the organization's critical data to ensure business continuity and enable users and administrators to be productive.

The NIST publication recognizes this dilemma and formalizes separation of duties, change control, and privileged session auditing. This clearly defines how an organization should manage access and when. Unfortunately, the size and scope of actual PAM mappings to

NIST 800-53 is enormous. If your organization has NIST requirements, please consider external consultants (or in-house expertise if you have the resources) to map your business requirements to contracts and actual deliverables. The scope may even include your supply chain and be completely outside of your control, except for contractually-based audits.

ISO

The International Organization for Standardization (ISO) has established guidelines and general principles for initiating, implementing, maintaining, and improving information security management in an organization. The objectives outlined in ISO 27002:2013(E) provide general guidance on the commonly accepted goals of information security management.

The control objectives and controls in ISO 27002 are intended to be implemented to meet the requirements identified by a risk assessment. ISO 27002 can serve as a practical guideline for developing organizational security standards and effective security management practices, and to help build confidence in interorganizational activities.

For organizations that have adopted ISO 27002, it is important that all existing and new security solutions map into this framework. The standard contains 14 security control clauses, collectively containing a total of 35 main security categories and 114 controls. Whether an organization's objective is to achieve legislative compliance or to adopt security best practices, these controls apply to most organizations and in most environments. These clauses directly translate to privileged access management and privileged session monitoring. Table 20-2 shows the categories and controls influenced by ISO 27002 and PAM (password management (PM), endpoint privilege management (EPM), and secure remote access (SRA)).

Table 20-2. *PAM Mappings for ISO 27002:2013(E)*

6 ORGANIZATION OF INFORMATION SECURITY	PM	EPM	SRA
6.1 INTERNAL ORGANIZATION			
6.1.1 Information security roles and responsibilities	√	√	√
6.1.2 Segregation of duties	√	√	√
6.1.5 Information security in project management	√	√	√
6.2 MOBILE DEVICES AND TELEWORKING			
6.2.2 Teleworking	√	√	√
8 ASSET MANAGEMENT			
8.1 RESPONSIBILITY FOR ASSETS			
8.1.3 Acceptable use of assets	√	√	
8.2 INFORMATION CLASSIFICATION			
8.2.3 Handling of assets		√	
9 ACCESS CONTROL			
9.1 BUSINESS REQUIREMENT OF ACCESS CONTROL			
9.1.1 Access control policy	√	√	√
9.1.2 Access to networks and network services	√	√	√
9.2 USER ACCESS MANAGEMENT			
9.2.1 User registration and deregistration	√		√
9.2.2 User access provisioning	√	√	√
9.2.3 Management of privilege access rights	√	√	√
9.2.4 Management of secret authentication information of users	√		√
9.2.5 Review of user access rights	√	√	√

(continued)

Table 20-2. *(continued)*

6 ORGANIZATION OF INFORMATION SECURITY	PM	EPM	SRA
9.3 USER RESPONSIBILITIES			
9.3.1 Use of secret authentication information	√		√
9.4 SYSTEM AND APPLICATION ACCESS CONTROL			
9.4.1 Information access restriction	√	√	√
9.4.2 Secure logon procedures	√	√	√
9.4.3 Password management system	√	√	√
9.4.4 Use of privileged utility programs	√	√	√
9.4.5 Access control program source code	√		
10 CRYPTOGRAPHY			
10.1 CRYPTOGRAPHIC CONTROLS			
10.1.2 Key management	√		
12 OPERATIONS SECURITY			
12.1 OPERATIONAL PROCEDURES AND RESPONSIBILITIES			
12.1.2 Change management	√	√	√
12.4 LOGGING AND MONITORING			
12.4.1 Event logging	√	√	√
12.4.2 Protection of log information	√	√	
12.4.3 Administrator and operator logs	√	√	
12.5 CONTROL OF OPERATIONAL SOFTWARE			
12.5.1 Installation of software on operational systems	√	√	√
12.7 INFORMATION SYSTEMS AUDIT CONSIDERATIONS			
12.7.1 Information systems audit controls	√	√	√

(continued)

Table 20-2. (*continued*)

6 ORGANIZATION OF INFORMATION SECURITY	PM	EPM	SRA
13 COMMUNICATIONS SECURITY			
13.1 NETWORK SECURITY MANAGEMENT			
13.1.1 Network controls	√		√
13.1.2 Security of network services	√		√
13.1.3 Segregation in networks	√	√	√
14 SYSTEM ACQUISITION, DEVELOPMENT, AND MAINTENANCE			
14.2 SECURITY IN DEVELOPMENT AND SUPPORT PROCESSES			
14.2.1 Secure development policy	√	√	√
14.2.6 Secure development environment	√	√	√
14.3 TEST DATA			
14.3.1 Protection of test data	√	√	√
16 INFORMATION SECURITY INCIDENT MANAGEMENT			
16.1 MANAGEMENT OF INFORMATION SECURITY INCIDENTS AND IMPROVEMENTS			
16.1.2 Reporting information security events	√	√	√
16.1.3 Reporting information security weaknesses	√	√	√
16.1.7 Collection of evidence	√	√	√
17 INFORMATION SECURITY ASPECTS OF BUSINESS CONTINUITY MANAGEMENT			
17.1 INFORMATION SECURITY CONTINUITY			
17.1.2 Implementing information security continuity	√	√	√
17.1.3 Verify, review, and evaluate information security continuity	√	√	√

(*continued*)

Table 20-2. (*continued*)

6 ORGANIZATION OF INFORMATION SECURITY	PM	EPM	SRA
18 COMPLIANCE			
18.1 COMPLIANCE WITH LEGAL AND CONTRACTUAL REQUIREMENTS			
18.1.2 Intellectual property rights	√	√	√
18.1.3 Protection of records	√	√	√
18.2 INFORMATION SECURITY REVIEWS			
18.2.1 Independent review of information security	√	√	√
18.2.2 Compliance with security policies and standards	√	√	√
18.2.3 Technical compliance review	√	√	√

Security best practices have been adopted in almost every regulation and framework. ISO 27002 is no different when monitoring and managing privileges, and sessions form a fundamental part of managing the privileged attack vector and thwarting threat actors. Mapping these controls to your privileged access management deployment will help close off many of the attack vectors that we have discussed.

GDPR

The General Data Protection Regulation (GDPR) is one of the most important movements in the area of data protection in recent years. It was passed into European Union (EU) law on April 28, 2016, and became enforceable on May 25, 2018. Over several hundred million dollars in fines have already been levied for GDPR violations since the law went into effect.

In summary, the GDPR defines controls around how organizations store and process the personal data of EU citizens, irrespective of where the organization is based, owned, or operating. Anyone storing or processing the personal data of an EU citizen must comply with the GDPR or face significant fines in the event of a failed audit or data breach. Those fines can be up to 4% of the organization's global turnover, or €10m, whichever is greater. With this level of impact, it is vital that all organizations understand their obligations under the GDPR and take appropriate measures to ensure they are compliant by demonstrating that the proper controls are in place to protect information.

GDPR was designed to simplify requirements and not introduce a massive new burden on organizations. In fact, GDPR consolidates the 28 distinct implementations of the previous Data Protection Directive (95/46/EC) into one regulation for consistency, standardized version control, and reporting. To that end, the GDPR provides guidance relating to the protection of natural persons with regard to the processing of personal data and requirements relating to the free movement of personal data, including PII. It protects fundamental rights and freedoms of natural persons (human identity in GDPR terminology) and, in particular, their right to the protection of personal information. It also allows for unrestricted movement of personal data within the EU and the requirement that the collection of this data to be deleted or removed upon request of the user, protecting their digital identity. The regulation defines scope in two ways:

- Material Scope: How data is processed

- Territorial Scope: Where data is processed

In material terms, GDPR applies to the processing of personal data wholly or partly by automated (electronically) means and to processing other than by automated means, that is, as part of a paper or manual filing system. Processing related to the prevention, investigation, detection, or prosecution of criminal offenses, execution of penalties, and safeguarding public security is excluded from the GDPR. This is an important differentiation since law enforcement and their investigations are not participatory entities and may have exclusions when collecting personal data from organizations normally governed by GDPR.

In territorial terms, GDPR applies to the processing of personal data for data subjects who are in the European Union (EU)—in particular, when related to the offering of goods and services (irrespective of whether payment is required) and monitoring of their personal behavior. The regulation also applies to the processing of data by a controller wherever Member State law applies, through public international law.

Therefore, the million-dollar question is surprisingly simple—when is your organization required to comply with GDPR? There are several key areas to consider:

- **Consent of the Data Subject**: Any freely given, specific, informed, and unambiguous indication of the data subject's wishes by which he or she, by a statement or by a clear affirmative action, signifies agreement to the processing of personal data relating to him or her. Beyond the pure collection and processing of personal data, the GDPR also lays out specific requirements around the consent of the data subject for both the collection and processing of their data. This consent requires affirmation by the data subject to show consent to each form of processing the collected data will undergo; consent can no longer be given in a blanket manner, that is, covering multiple processes. Consent can also be withdrawn at any time by the data subject. For more detailed information, see Article 7 of the GDPR.

- **Personal Data Breach**: A breach of security leading to the accidental or unlawful destruction, loss, alteration, unauthorized disclosure of, or access to, personal data transmitted, stored, or otherwise processed. The regulation provides a much stronger response to personal data breaches than previous directives and regional legislations. It requires that the controller notify the supervisory authority of any personal data breach no later than 72 hours after having become aware of the breach. If the notification cannot be given within 72 hours, the controller will be required to provide the reasons for the delay. If the controller can demonstrate that the breach is unlikely to result in a risk to the rights and freedoms of the natural persons whose data has been breached, the need for notification within the timeframe is removed, but notification must still be made.

- **Accountability**: The GDPR also defines clear accountability for the controller over the management of personal data. The controller must ensure that data is processed lawfully, fairly, and transparently; that data is only collected for specified, explicit, and legitimate purposes and adequate, relevant, and limited to only what's necessary for the consented processing. The controller is also responsible for ensuring the personal data is accurate and, where necessary, kept up-to-date. The data should also be kept for no longer than is necessary for the purposes for which the personal data is processed. Also, the data must be processed in a manner that ensures appropriate security of the personal data, for example, not allowing it to be subject to a personal data breach. As a controller, you have responsibility for, and must be able to demonstrate, compliance with the defined regulation. As is clear from this, you must have control over who has access to personal data, when they accessed the data, and what was done with the data. Also, as far as possible, it's also vital to ensure that there are no opportunities for unauthorized access to the personal data. This is where privileged access management becomes a critical component of your GDPR strategy.

As a discipline, privileged access management (PAM) offers a number of solutions that can help organizations achieve GDPR compliance:

- A privileged password management solution can help control who has access to operating systems, applications, databases, infrastructure, and cloud resources and provide attestation reporting on complete session activity to avoid inappropriate activity and access at a controller.

- Server least privilege management solutions can manage privileged access to commands and applications, eliminating the need for root access and sudo.

- Endpoint least privilege management solutions can anonymize data collected around user and administrative activity, ensuring data cannot be linked to individuals within a single data store.

- Remote access solutions can regulate and authorize access at a controller to sensitive data stores to prevent unauthorized access that might lead to a breach.

CCPA

The California Consumer Privacy Act (CCPA) has been quoted as the beginning of America's GDPR-type data privacy laws. Similar to the GDPR, the CCPA requires organizations to focus first on consumer data in 2020 and then personal data shared between businesses in 2021. It requires organizations to provide transparency in how they are collecting, sharing, and using personal information based on an individual's request. And remember, a privileged account typically can access this data en masse, making it relevant, from an incident or breach perspective, to secure.

Based on the GDPR requirements covered earlier, it should not be a difficult extension for an organization to cover CCPA unless their business has no overseas activity in Europe. Then the ramifications can be costly to implement. Therefore, to assist global organizations, a comparison between GDPR and CCPA has been created in Table 20-3. It is important to note that internal policies, processes, and systems will still need to be updated to address differences between the two laws.

Table 20-3. *A Comparison of GDPR to CCPA*

Governance	GDPR	CCPA
Scope	All personal data collected for European Union citizens	All California residents whose personal data is collected after January 2020 and for business-to-business data, starting January 2021
Right to Access	An individual has the right to review all European Union personal data processed for an individual	An individual has the right to access personal data in scope collected for the last 12 months with restrictions imposed on whether the data was stored, sold, or transferred between organizations

(continued)

Table 20-3. (*continued*)

Governance	GDPR	CCPA
Right to Portability	Data must be able to import and export in a user-friendly format. This is similar to US HIPAA regulations	All individual access requests must be exportable in a user-friendly format, but there is no requirement for importing data
Right to Remediate	An individual reserves the right to correct and verify any personnel European Union data that has been collected	CCPA lacks a corrective actions provision for personal data
Right to Halt Processing	An individual has the right to withdraw consent or stop processing, within an entity, of personally collected data	An individual has the right to "opt-out" of selling personal data and businesses must provide an opt-out link or procedure on their website or through a similar data collection vehicle
Right to Stop Automation	An individual has the right to enforce a human decision in an automated process that may have a legal effect for the inquiring party	CCPA has no provisions to stop automated decision-making
Right to Stop Information Sharing	An individual has the right to request the halting of third-party data transfers based on a specific category of data	An individual has the right to "opt-out" of selling their personal information to third parties

(*continued*)

Table 20-3. (*continued*)

Governance	GDPR	CCPA
Right to Information Erasure	A European Union citizen can request the right to erase personal data if specific conditions are met	An individual has the right to erase personally collected data only under specific conditions
Individual Damages	No limits to pursue damages based on actions	Each consumer breach is limited to a minimum of $100 and a maximum of $750 per data breach event
Enforcement Penalties	Global annual revenue is capped at 4%	Regulator penalties are limited to $2500 for unintentional violations and $7500 for intentional violations

ASD

The Australian Signals Directorate (ASD) has developed a list of strategies to mitigate targeted cyber intrusions. The recommended mitigation strategies were developed in 2014 through ASD's extensive experience in operational cybersecurity, including responding to serious cyber intrusions and performing vulnerability assessments and penetration testing for Australian Government Agencies.

In 2017, the ASD expanded the Top 4 recommendations to contain the Essential Eight. The dynamic nature of cybersecurity required a course correction to address the latest threats, like ransomware. Businesses and governments are accustomed to broad stroke changes occurring every few years, but rarely are recommendations made that are very precise to manage specific threats. The Essential Eight are the following:

Australian Signals Directorate Top 4 (Original from 2014)

1. Application whitelisting of permitted/trusted programs, to prevent the execution of malicious or unapproved programs, including executables, scripts, and installers.

2. Patch applications—for example, Java, PDF viewer, Flash, web browsers, and Microsoft Office. Patch/mitigate systems with "extreme risk" vulnerabilities within 2 days. Use the latest version of applications.

3. Patch operating system vulnerabilities. Patch/mitigate systems with "extreme risk" vulnerabilities within 2 days. Use the latest suitable operating system version. Avoid Microsoft Windows XP.

4. Restrict administrative privileges to operating systems and applications based on user duties. Such users should use a separate unprivileged account for email and web browsing.

Essential Eight (Amended in 2017)

5. Disable untrusted Microsoft Office Macros, so malware cannot run unauthorized routines.

6. Block web browser access to Adobe Flash, web advertisements, and untrusted Java code on the Internet. If possible, uninstall all browser plug-ins that are not required.

7. Apply multi-factor authentication for all systems when possible to make it harder for an adversary to access a system and information.

8.   Perform daily backup of important data securely
     and offline to ensure even if data is compromised,
     protected versions are available for recovery.

Based on a threat actor's methods to gain privileges, these
recommendations are completely in line with the threats solved by
privileged access management. The privileged attack vector mitigation
is included in the Top 4 and Essential Eight (5–7) and represents a
refined strategy to stop threats worldwide. Number eight is a backup
discipline and is not a privileged attack vector. It can, however, be used for
remediation for attacks like ransomware.

MAS

The Monetary Authority of Singapore (MAS) was founded in 1971 to
oversee various monetary functions associated with financial and banking
institutions. Throughout the years, their guidelines have been revised to
manage emerging technologies and the evolving threat landscape. In June
2013, the MAS created a new set of guidelines for Internet Banking and
Technology Risk Management (IBTRM). This addendum mandated certain
requirements for Technology Risk Management (TRM) and contained a set of
guidelines as well (TRM Guidelines), along with errata notices (TRM Notices).

The TRM Guidelines are statements of industry best practices to
which financial institutions are expected to adhere. The guidance is not
legally binding, but is used by MAS in risk assessment audits of financial
institutions.

Privilege as an attack vector considers four of these MAS TRM sections
relevant when protecting privileges from a threat actor:

- Section 4: Technology Risk Framework

- Section 6: Acquisition and Development of Information
  Systems

- Section 9: Operational Infrastructure Security Management

- Section 11: Access Control

SWIFT

The Society for Worldwide Interbank Financial Telecommunications (SWIFT) Customer Security Controls Framework 1.0, published on March 31, 2017, describes a set of mandatory and advisory security controls for participating SWIFT financial organizations. The framework is divided into three objectives:

- Secure Your Environment

  - Restrict Internet Access

  - Protect Critical Systems from General IT Environment (Lateral Movement)

  - Reduce Attack Surface and Vulnerabilities

  - Physically Secure the Environment

- Know and Limit Access

  - Prevent Compromise of Credentials

  - Manage Identities and Segregate Privileges (PAM)

- Detect and Respond

  - Detect Anomalous Activity to Systems or Transaction Records

  - Plan for Incident Response and Information Sharing

SWIFT requires that users self-attest compliance against the mandatory security controls (it is optional for the advisory controls). PAM provides coverage for the following mandatory controls:

1.1 Operating System Privileged Account Control

2.1 Internal Data Flow Security

2.2 Security Updates

2.3 System Hardening

2.6 Operator Session Confidentiality and Integrity

2.8 Critical Activity Outsourcing

4.1 Password Policy

4.2 Multi-Factor Authentication

5.1 Logical Access Control

5.4 Physical and Logical Password Storage

6.2 Software Integrity

6.4 Logging and Monitoring

Organizations can address their compliance and security requirements as defined in the SWIFT Customer Security Controls Framework by implementing PAM solutions. Please note, if your organization currently adheres to the NIST Cybersecurity Framework, ISO 27002, or PCI DSS, SWIFT provides mappings to other frameworks to expedite compliance verification and to help avoid duplication of efforts in attestation reporting.

MITRE ATT&CK

While technically not a regulatory compliance framework, the MITRE ATT&CK[1] knowledge base is designed to help third parties discover, prioritize, categorize, and recommend strategies for threat remediation. It is a practical structure based on real-world attacks that are categorized by operating system, privileges, method, and technical details for classes of attack vectors. Not surprisingly, the vast majority of attacks can be mitigated by privileged access management solutions, especially when password management, endpoint least privileged management, and remote access capabilities are used in concert. Organizations are using the knowledge base as a guide to prove their risk mitigation strategies actually meet compliance objectives for risk reduction.

Based on Mitre's Enterprise Tactics,[2] privileged access management solutions can either detect, prevent, or respond to the following attack vectors:

- **Initial Access** (TA0001): Represents the vectors adversaries use to gain an initial foothold within a network.

- **Execution** (TA0002): Represents techniques that result in execution of adversary-controlled code on a local or remote system. This tactic is often used in conjunction with initial access as the means of executing code once access is obtained, and lateral movement to expand access to remote systems on a network.

---

[1]MITRE ATT&CK—https://attack.mitre.org/
[2]MITRE ATT&CK Enterprise Tactics—https://attack.mitre.org/tactics/ enterprise/

- **Persistence** (TA0003): Any access, action, or configuration change to a system that gives an adversary a persistent presence on that system. Adversaries will often need to maintain access to systems through interruptions such as system restarts, loss of credentials, or other failures that would require a remote access tool to restart or alternate backdoor for them to regain access.

- **Privilege Escalation** (TA0004): The result of actions that allows an adversary to obtain a higher level of permissions on a system or network. Certain tools or actions require a higher level of privilege to work and are likely necessary at many points throughout an operation. Adversaries can enter a system with unprivileged access and must take advantage of a system weakness to obtain local administrator or SYSTEM/root-level privileges. A user account with administrator-like access can also be used. User accounts with permissions to access specific systems or perform specific functions necessary for adversaries to achieve their objective may also be considered an escalation of privilege.

- **Defense Evasion** (TA0005): Consists of techniques an adversary may use to evade detection or avoid other defenses. Sometimes these actions are the same as or variations of techniques in other categories that have the added benefit of subverting a particular defense or mitigation. Defense evasion may be considered a set of attributes the adversary applies to all other phases of the operation.

- **Credential Access** (TA0006): Represents techniques resulting in access to or control over system, domain, or service credentials that are used within an enterprise environment. Adversaries will likely attempt to obtain legitimate credentials from users or administrator accounts (local system administrator or domain users with administrator access) to use within the network. This allows the adversary to assume the identity of the account, with all of that account's permissions on the system and network, and makes it harder for defenders to detect the adversary. With sufficient access within a network, an adversary can create accounts for later use within the environment.

- **Discovery** (TA0007): Consists of techniques that allow the adversary to gain knowledge about the system and internal network. When adversaries gain access to a new system, they must orient themselves to what they now have control of and what benefits operating from that system give to their current objective or overall goals during the intrusion. The operating system provides many native tools that aid in this post-compromise information-gathering phase.

- **Lateral Movement** (TA0008): Consists of techniques that enable an adversary to access and control remote systems on a network and could, but does not necessarily, include execution of tools on remote systems. The lateral movement techniques could allow an adversary to gather information from a system without needing additional tools, such as a remote access tool.

- **Collection** (TA0009): Consists of techniques used to identify and gather information, such as sensitive files, from a target network prior to exfiltration. This category also covers locations on a system or network where the adversary may look for information to exfiltrate.

- **Exfiltration** (TA0010): Refers to techniques and attributes that result or aid in the adversary removing files and information from a target network. This category also covers locations on a system or network where the adversary may look for information to exfiltrate.

- **Command and Control** (TA0011): Represents how adversaries communicate with systems under their control within a target network. There are many ways an adversary can establish command and control with various levels of covertness, depending on system configuration and network topology. Due to the wide degree of variation available to the adversary at the network level, only the most common factors were used to describe the differences in command and control. There are still a great many specific techniques within the documented methods, largely due to how easy it is to define new protocols and use existing, legitimate protocols and network services for communication.

- **Impact** (TA0040): The adversary is trying to manipulate, interrupt, or destroy your systems and data. Impact consists of techniques that adversaries use to disrupt availability or compromise integrity by manipulating business and operational processes. Techniques used for impact can include destroying or tampering with data. In some cases, business processes can look fine, but may have been altered to benefit the adversaries' goals. These techniques might be used by adversaries to follow through on their end goal or to provide cover for a confidentiality breach.

While each Enterprise Tactic is comprised of multiple Technique IDs,[3] the detection, privileges, and mitigation detail provide a blueprint for using a tool, solution, policy, or configuration change to thwart each item as an attack vector. This alone is why many organizations embrace the MITRE ATT&CK framework, because it provides real-world guidance vs. theoretical aspirations like many legally binding regulatory compliance frameworks. And, if you manage to implement privilege security controls based on these real-world threats, it demonstrates compliance for many other regulatory initiatives.

---

[3]Technical ID for Enterprise Tactics—https://attack.mitre.org/tactics/TA0001/

CHAPTER 21

Just in Time

The utilization of always-on privileged accounts has been the default mode for administrative access for the last 40 years. However, always-on access, or persistent administrative credentials (referred to by most analysts as "standing privileges") represent a massive risk surface as it means the privileged access, rights, and permissions are always on and ready to be exercised—for both legitimate and illicit purposes. And, this risk surface is rapidly exploding alongside the growing use of virtual, cloud, IoT, and DevOps environments in our ever-expanding privilege universe. Of course, cyber threat actors are well aware of what is essentially the overprovisioning of privileges via the always-on and persistent model.

As we have discussed, traditional perimeter-based security technologies only can protect privileged accounts within their boundaries. Privileged accounts are now truly everywhere across your organization. Each one of them is potentially another privileged attack vector, and some of them are accessible directly on the Internet. This is where just-in-time (JIT) privileged access management (PAM) can help.

© Morey J. Haber 2020
M. J. Haber, *Privileged Attack Vectors*, https://doi.org/10.1007/978-1-4842-5914-6_21

Just-in-Time (JIT) Privileged Access Management

Just-in-time (JIT) privileged access management (PAM) is a strategy that aligns real-time requests for usage of privileged accounts directly with entitlements, workflow, and appropriate access policies. Companies can use this strategy to secure privileged accounts from continuous, persistent, and always-on access by enforcing restrictions based on behavioral and contextual parameters. This forces accounts to operate with ephemeral (time-based) properties. As much as possible, organizations should try to reach a state of "zero standing privileges."

To take a step back for a moment, let us ensure we have a solid definition for a privileged account again. A privileged account is one that is granted privileges and permissions above that of a standard user. This could be a superuser account with elevated privileges (somewhere between standard user and administrator) or the highest level of user privileges, such as administrator (in Windows environments) or root (in Unix/Linux environments).

JIT PAM sharply limits the amount of time an account possesses elevated privileges and access rights to drastically reduce the risk surface for when the account is available. This is essentially the window of vulnerability during which time a threat actor can exploit account privileges. In addition, JIT access helps enforce the principle of least principle to ensure that privileged activities can be performed in alignment of acceptable use policies, while forbidding privileged activities that fall outside of the right context and authorized time period. As an example, please reference Figure 21-1.

Figure 21-1. *Just in Time Applied to Sample Accounts and the Windows of Privileged Exposure*

During a week, an always-on privileged account is available 168 hours. With an always-on privileged account model, accounts are accessible all the time, even if they are under password management. The risk surface exists even if the threat actor does not know the password. With a JIT PAM model, individual privileged accounts are only used for just the time to complete the task or activity. Assuming separation of privileges and separation of duties have been implemented, each unique privileged account should only be active for a small fraction of the workweek to accomplish these goals. As illustrated above, when this reduction in the privilege account status is managed, the risk reduction potential is huge. As an example, Privileged Account A needs to perform tasks that take a little less than 5 hours in one week. The threat window is only 2.9% compared to the entire week. This example can be applied to accounts B and C too. Therefore, the quantifiable time exposure represented as risk is significantly less when using a JIT PAM approach to managing privileged accounts.

Just-in-Time Privilege Management Strategy

A just-in-time approach to privilege management does require organizations to establish criteria for just-in-time privileged access and accept that the accounts that fall within this policy are not available outside of potentially break glass scenarios.

While similar concepts for JIT existing across other use cases (e.g., manufacturing) are well established, applying the model for a security and operations solution does present some technical considerations during an implementation. An initial consideration is around the just-in-time account(s) delegated for privileged access.

The goal of a JIT privileged account is to assign or create the necessary account "on the fly" based on an approved task or mission, apply the appropriate privileges, and subsequently reverse the process once the task is complete or the window or context for authorized access is expired.

The modeling required to take an account and apply the appropriate privileges can be implemented using the following JIT techniques:

- **JIT Account Creation and Deletion**: The creation and deletion of an appropriate privileged account to meet mission objectives. The account should have traits to link it back to the requesting identity or service performing the operation for logging and forensics.

- **JIT Group Membership**: The automatic addition and removal of an account into a privileged administrative group for the duration of the mission. The account should only be added to an elevated group when the appropriate criteria are met. Group membership should be revoked immediately upon completion of the mission.

- **JIT Privileges**: The account has individual privileges, permissions, or entitlements added to perform a mission once all criteria are met, but only for a limited duration. These rights need to be revoked once the mission is complete and should include certification that no other privileges were inappropriately altered.

- **JIT Impersonation**: The account is linked to a preexisting administrative account(s), and when a specific application or task is performed, the function is elevated using those credentials. This is commonly done using automation or scripting with Windows "RunAs" or *nix sudo. Typically, the end user is unaware of the impersonation account for this type of operation, and the process may overlap with always-on privileged account delegation.

- **JIT-Disabled Administrative Accounts**: Disabled administrator accounts are present in a system with all the permissions, privileges, and entitlements to perform a function. They are enabled to perform a specific mission and then subsequently disabled again once operational criteria have been satisfied. This concept is no different than having always-on administrative accounts, with the exception that native enablement functionality is leveraged to control JIT access.

- **JIT Tokenization**: The application or resource has its privileged token modified before injection into the operating system kernel. This form of least privilege is commonly used on endpoints to elevate the privileges and priority of an application, without elevating privileges for the end user.

For any of these privileged account elevation methods to work according to the principles of just-in-time privileged access management, the following criteria should be considered as triggers. (These should also include attribute-based variables such as time and date for change control windows, as well as suspension or termination criteria if indicators of compromise are detected.)

- **Entitlements**: When privileged access management (PAM) is integrated with identity and access management (IAM) solutions, entitlements between solutions can be synchronized for privileged access. To that end, JIT access can be assigned directly via PAM solutions or, alternatively, programmatically through IAM entitlements. While the IAM entitlement workflow is a longer technology process for synchronization and has a lag time, it does provide a vehicle for account certifications based on privileges that are void when linking with PAM solutions to control access.

- **Workflow**: The concept of workflow approval is commonly associated with call centers, help desks, and other IT service management solutions. A request is made for access and, using a defined workflow of approvers, access is either granted or denied. Once the workflow satisfies an approval, a JIT account can be enabled. This typically corresponds to the user, asset, application, time/date, and associated ticket in a change control or help desk solution. Privileged session monitoring is typically enabled by PAM solutions in this scenario to verify that all corresponding actions were appropriate.

- **Context-Aware**: Context-aware access is based on criteria like source IP address, geolocation, group membership, host operating system, applications installed or operating in memory, documented vulnerabilities, and so on. Based on any logical combination of these traits, JIT account access can be granted or revoked to satisfy business requirements and mitigate risk.

- **Two-Factor (2FA) or Multi-Factor Authentication (MFA)**: A common method for authorizing privileged access to always-on or JIT privileged accounts is 2FA or MFA. While this does not distinguish between the two access techniques, it does provide additional risk mitigation by validating that the identity has proper access to a privileged account. It can, however, be used as a JIT trigger for an account using any of the techniques listed earlier.

Simply put, JIT triggers are just that, conditions for an account to be placed or created in a state for privileged access. They can be used stand-alone or logically grouped with other triggers to instantiate privileged account access or revoke it. The two key takeaways for teams to consider are what policies govern a JIT account for proper privileged access, and what conditions should be met for its revocation?

These policies should consider:

- Time and date windows for access and change control

- Commands or applications that may indicate a security compromise

- Detection of access to sensitive information

- Termination of the primary session

- Existence of corresponding collateral in a ticketing solution

- Inappropriate modification of resources, including installing software or modifying files

- Inappropriate attempts at lateral movement

- The manipulation, creation, or deletion of user accounts or datasets

While this is by no means an exhaustive list of all attribute-based variables, it can help filter the criteria for a JIT account to be made available or terminated based on corresponding triggers. Figure 21-2 illustrates this entire workflow.

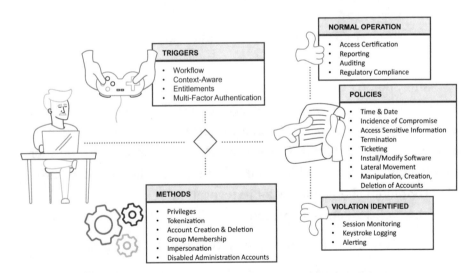

Figure 21-2. *Workflow for a Just-in-Time Privileged Access Request and Session*

Implementing Just-in-Time Privileged Access Management

While JIT privileged access management (PAM) is a relatively new concept, perhaps it is here just in time to meet the challenges of always-on, persistent, or standing privileged access to a sprawling universe of privileged accounts.

In order to be successful with JIT PAM, consider enabling privileged accounts only when needed for authentication and control when and where they can be used. This involves expanding the security model to deny all privileged activity until the appropriate business criteria are satisfied based on their usage. This entails not only restricting account access like traditional PAM, but the actual privileges, permissions, and entitlements that the account can use in real-time. For many organizations, this is the next, most impactful step they can take toward protecting their valuable IT estate. And, from an auditor's perspective, this works toward eliminating any findings that state you have too many privileged accounts.

Therefore, in order to successfully implement JIT PAM, consider the following use cases in your design:

- When are privileges needed for runtime, like service accounts, and when are they needed for a specific session or application usage based on a task? Task-based usage is ideal for JIT PAM.

- Any batch-driven, trigger-based, or scheduled tasks that are infrequently executed are worthy for JIT PAM consideration.

- The design and implementation of any new resource or applications should use the lowest necessary privileges from the start. Requiring, designing, and coding for the exclusive use of administrative privileges should be avoided.

- End users should never enter secondary administrative privileged credentials to invoke a JIT PAM workflow. A valid Trigger and Method should always be invoked, and not single-factor authentication.

- The discovery of always-on privileged accounts should be identified per asset and resource during normal inventory discovery and assessment processes.

- Accounts used for JIT workflows should not be shared in order to properly certify usage and demonstrate compliance to an identity.

- Account creation and deletion as a JIT method must fully document the requesting identity and account to properly provide certification for privileged usage.

- Any attempt to use an account used in a JIT workflow that is not in an elevated state can be considered a possible indicator of compromise since its attempted usage is outside of established workflows.

- If possible, design your JIT PAM workflows to integrate with your IAM (identity and access management) workflows for better visibility into your entire entity governance model.

CHAPTER 22

Zero Trust

By definition, a zero trust security model advocates the creation of zones and segmentation to control sensitive IT resources. This also entails the deployment of technology to monitor and manage data between zones and, more importantly, authentication within a zone(s), whether by users, applications, or other resources. In addition, the model redefines the architecture of a trusted network inside a defined perimeter. This can be on-premise or in the cloud. This is relevant today since technologies and processes like the cloud, DevOps, edge computing, and IoT have either blurred, or dissolved altogether, the idea of a traditional perimeter. Therefore, the concept of a trust zone is important to manage any resources operating and communicating together.

Zones in and of themselves can be delegated using micro-segmentation down to the host or data layer to enforce a zero trust model. This implies that a resource, like a server, or even a database, can have multiple zones to support the data collection and monitoring needed to achieve zero trust. Zero trust essentially establishes a model of trust, verification, and continuous reevaluation of trust for further access to prevent any unauthorized lateral movement.

While zero trust has become a trendy catchword in IT, in practice, this model is very specific about how things should be designed and operated and may not work for everyone. In practice, it is best suited for new deployments that can be designed from the ground up. The conversion of legacy deployments and network architectures in accordance with zero trust is generally impractical and unrealistic.

© Morey J. Haber 2020
M. J. Haber, *Privileged Attack Vectors*, https://doi.org/10.1007/978-1-4842-5914-6_22

Success with a Zero Trust Model

The analyst firm, Forrester,[1] has outlined a road map for a successful zero trust implementation. In summary, it can be summarized in five steps with some adaption to make each step achievable in a real-world environment:

1. **Identify Your Sensitive Data at Rest and in Motion**:

    a. Perform data discovery and classification. Ensure sensitive data is properly classified.

    b. Segment and zone the network based on data classification.

2. **Map the Acceptable Routes for Sensitive Data Access and Egress**:

    a. Classify all resources involved in the electronic exchange of sensitive data. Ensure they are compliant for security best practices like end of life and patch management.

    b. Evaluate the workflow of data and redesign, if necessary, who and what has access to sensitive data.

    c. Verify that existing workflows (like PCI architectures) for data are not only governed by the network but also who and what has network access via authorized routes.

---

[1]Forrester—www.forrester.com/report/Five+Steps+To+A+Zero+Trust+Network/-/E-RES120510

3. **Architect Zero Trust Microperimeters**:

   a. Define microperimeters, zones, and segmentation around sensitive data. Attempt to make them as small and self-contained as possible.

   b. Enforce segmentation using physical and virtual security controls.

   c. Establish access based on these controls and the microperimeter designs.

   d. Automate rule and access policy baselines and consider just-in-time access for all account types.

   e. Audit and log all access and change control.

4. **Monitor the Zero Trust Environment, in Detail, with Security Analytics**:

   a. Leverage and identify security analytics solutions already existing within the organization.

   b. Determine the logical architecture and best placement for your security analytics tools.

   c. If a new solution is needed, identify a vendor that is moving in the same security direction as your organization and that can provide analytics for your other security solutions.

5. **Embrace Security Automation and Adaptive Response**:

   a. Translate business processes into technology automation and remember not everything should be automated.

    b. Document, assess, and test security operation center policies and procedures for effectiveness and response.

    c. Correlate policies and procedures with security analytics automation and determine what can be lifted from manual processes.

    d. Verify the security and implementation of automation within your environment and current solutions.

Next, consider the zero trust architectural model defined by NIST 800-207.[2] It clearly states that the goal of zero trust is to focus security on a small group of resources (zones) in lieu of wide network perimeters or environments with large quantities of resources interacting "freely." It is a strategy where there is no implicit trust granted to systems based on their physical or network location (local area network, wide area networks, and the cloud), but rather access is granted by a trusted source for either a user or application. That is where privileged access management comes in. Consider the enhanced NIST core zero trust architecture presented in Figure 22-1.

---

[2]NIST 800-207—https://csrc.nist.gov/News/2019/zero-trust-architecture-draft-sp-800-207

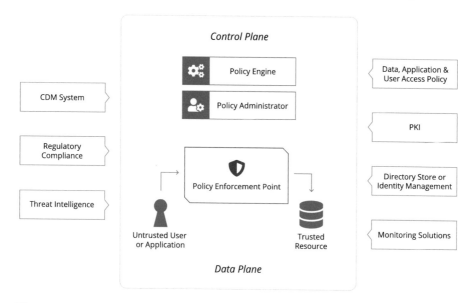

Figure 22-1. *NIST Enhanced Core Zero Trust Architecture*

The key components of the control plane and data plane are typically found in privileged access management solutions:

- The *Policy Engine* is responsible for the decision to grant access to a resource. It uses as much data as it can based on roles, attributes, and threat intelligence to determine if access should be granted.

- The *Policy Administrator* is responsible for establishing the connection between a client and a resource. It provides the negotiation between the resources to "state" that the connection is allowed.

- The *Policy Enforcement Point* is responsible for enabling, monitoring, and terminating the connection between the untrusted resource (user or application) and trusted enterprise resource.

If we map this to PAM, we find:

- The *Policy Engine* can be found in the management capabilities of an enterprise password manager, the rules and policies governing least privilege within endpoint privilege management solutions, and the role- and attribute-based access models found in a secure remote access solution.

- The *Policy Administrator* can be found in the session management capabilities of an enterprise password manager and a secure remote access solution.

- The *Policy Enforcement Point* can be found in enterprise password managers that have session management and privileged monitoring capabilities, and in secure remote access solutions.

And, all of this is dependent on secure credentials that follow the model of least privilege, just-in-time access, and single-use authentication. If your applications can be designed to match this model for user and application access regardless of the network, you can achieve a true zero trust architecture. Any partial implementation of this is a great step in secure computing, but represents only a hybrid approach. This is something most organizations have implemented since a pure approach is not always technically feasible.

Obstacles for Zero Trust

Zero trust has been developed in response to industry trends that include remote users and cloud-based assets that are not located within a traditional enterprise perimeter. It focuses on protecting resources, not logical network segments, as network segmentation is no longer seen as the prime component to the security posture of the resource. This, in itself, begins the discussion of why zero trust may not be for everyone and may not be compatible with existing systems leveraging PAM. Many times, a hybrid approach is needed that borrows some characteristics from zero trust, but which does not constitute a true zero trust architecture. Therefore, the following obstacles are the most common considering Forrester's and NIST's models:

- **Technical Debt**: If your organization develops its own software for consumption, and the applications are more than a few years old, you have technical debt. Redesigning, recoding, and redeploying internal applications can be costly and potentially disruptive. There needs to be a serious business need to undertake these types of initiatives. Adding security parameters to existing applications to make them zero trust-aware is not always feasible. Odds are your existing applications have no facilities today to accommodate the authentication and connection models in the specification, nor are coded to operate in small groups as specified by NIST. Therefore, depending on the architecture of your custom application, it will dictate whether or not you can adopt zero trust for those processes and potentially determine the effort and cost required if they are not compatible. This is especially true in instances when applications are not microperimeter-compatible, use large quantities of resources that are network-dependent, or where they lack application programming-level interfaces to support the required automation.

- **Legacy Systems**: Legacy applications, infrastructure, and operating systems are most certainly not zero trust-aware. They have no concept of least privilege or lateral movement, and they do not possess authentication models that dynamically allow for modifications based on contextual usage. Any zero trust implementation requires a layered or wrapper approach to enable these systems. However, a layered approach entails enveloping all resources regardless of their location with the concepts of zero trust. This defeats the premise of zero trust because you have just created a bubble with even more resources that need to be managed than the original implementation you are trying to protect. You cannot necessarily monitor the behavior within a noncompatible application as well because it has now been shielded from what was traditionally normal interaction. You can, however, screen scrape, keystroke log, and monitor logs and network traffic to look for potentially malicious behavior, but your reaction is limited to this new bubble. You can only limit the external interaction of the legacy application to the user or other resources, but not the runtime itself. This limits the coverage of zero trust, and based on the characteristics of the legacy application, organizations may find that even monitoring network traffic is infeasible due to heavy encryption requirements, including TLS 1.3.

- **Peer-to-Peer Technologies**: If you think your organization does not use peer-to-peer (P2P) networking technology, you are probably unaware of the default settings in Windows 10. Starting in 2015, Windows 10 enabled a peer-to-peer technology to share Windows updates among peer systems to save Internet bandwidth. While some organizations turn this off, others are not even aware it exists. This represents a risk of privileged lateral movement between systems that is fundamentally uncontrolled. While no vulnerabilities and exploits have materialized for this feature, it does present communications that violate the zero trust model. There should be no unauthorized lateral movement—even within a specified microperimeter. In addition, if you use protocols like Zigbee or other mesh network technology for IoT, you will find that they operate completely counter to zero trust. They require peer-to-peer communications to operate, and the trust model is based strictly on keys or passwords, with no dynamic models for authentication modifications. Therefore, if you decide to embrace zero trust, please investigate if your organization has P2P or mesh network technologies, even for wireless networks. These present a huge stumbling block to embracing the access and microperimeter controls required for zero trust.

- **Digital Transformation**: Even for organizations that are in a position to build a new data center, implement a role-based access model, and embrace zero trust 100%, the digital transformation considerations can make the theory difficult to embrace. The digital transformation driven by cloud, DevOps, and IoT does not inherently support the zero trust model as it requires additional technology to segment and enforce the concept. For large deployments, this can be cost-prohibitive and may even impact the ability for the solutions to interact correctly with multiuser access. If you doubt this, consider simply the storage requirements and license costs to log every event for dynamic access on all resources within the scope of the project. While some may disagree that the cloud does embrace segmentation and zero trust models, it all depends on how you use the cloud. A straight migration of your raised floor to the cloud does not embrace zero trust. If you develop a new application in the cloud as a service, then it certainly can embrace zero trust. However, just moving to the cloud alone as a part of your digital transformation does not mean you inherently get the prescribed zero trust model benefits. Lift and shift does not equal zero trust; it must be designed in from the beginning to take advantage of privileged access management.

Considering Zero Trust?

Realistically, the only successful zero trust implementations that have gone from marketing to reality are ones that have had zero trust designed in from day one. Typically, this is not something everyone can do unless they are embarking on a brand new initiative. To put it simply, if your organization has not yet embraced the concepts of password management, least privilege, and secure privileged remote access, or still maintains shared accounts for access, zero trust is a distant goal and not something you can embrace first. It is a matter of privileged access management maturity along your journey. Finally, while some PAM vendors market "zero trust" solutions, they are really selling a solution to begin the journey of zero trust. They are not actually offering a self-contained zero trust solution to solve the entire problem, but rather a product that fits a niche in the model. This is a "buyer beware" problem.

CHAPTER 23

Sample Privileged Access Management Use Cases

A threat actor thrives on the weakness of processes and the inability of an organization to establish best practices. Privileged access management can stymie a threat actor, even if other security best practices are not being fully followed. Consider these top three problems almost every organization faces:

1. **Employees and Other Insiders Have Unnecessary Access**: Employees, vendors, and other insiders are often given excessive access to systems and data— and that access can go unmonitored.

2. **Credentials Are Shared and Unmanaged**: Passwords are created and shared, but aren't audited, monitored, or managed with discipline or accountability.

3. **Information Technology (IT) Assets Communicate Unchecked**: Desktops, laptops, servers, and applications communicate and open paths to sensitive assets and data.

© Morey J. Haber 2020
M. J. Haber, *Privileged Attack Vectors*, https://doi.org/10.1007/978-1-4842-5914-6_23

Even with security best practices, these three deficiencies can often materialize in almost every enclave or implementation. Consider the use cases in Table 23-1 to address these problems in the form of challenges, needs, solutions, and benefits.

Table 23-1. *PAM Use Cases*

Challenge	Need	Solution	Benefit
Tasks Require Administrative Credentials			
Applications require privileged credentials to operate correctly. Security policies do not provide administrative or root credentials to users to complete their assigned tasks.	Users need to execute applications that require privileges above Standard User.	Implement a least privilege solution to change the privileges of the application, or seamlessly apply privileged credentials to the application.	Users can perform their intended tasks, and security policies are maintained by not providing privileged credentials.
Local Credentials Have Stale Passwords			
Local accounts have passwords that are reused, well known, or have never been changed on servers, desktops, laptops, and tablets.	Security best practices and regulatory compliance require privileged password management and that reused, well-known, or nonmanaged passwords are mitigated.	Using a password management solution or agent technology, provides a method to identify credentials used for user logins and services, and place them under management.	Ensures security best practices for credential management and ensures even mobile devices can be managed against password reuse and stale password problems.

(continued)

Table 23-1. (*continued*)

Challenge	Need	Solution	Benefit
Correlation and Consolidation of Account Aliases			
Organizations have too many local and directory service aliases for the same identity, making reconciliation difficult.	Organizations and regulations require reliable identification of a user's activity. With disjointed aliases, this mapping is difficult to maintain.	Utilize a directory bridging technology across all Unix, Linux, and MacOS environments to centralize authentication via Active Directory.	Ensures that an identity's Active Directory account is the same authoritative account for all platforms and eliminates local aliases.
Correlation of High-Risk Applications and Usage			
Threat analysis and vulnerability management programs lack the correlation of vulnerable applications and real-world usage.	Organizations cannot prioritize vulnerabilities based on user behavior and application usage.	Track application usage with granular details and map the results to known vulnerabilities.	Control applications via whitelisting, blacklisting, and greylisting based on vulnerabilities, age, and risk.

(*continued*)

Table 23-1. (*continued*)

Challenge	Need	Solution	Benefit
Removal of End-User Administrative Privileges			
Security best practices, threat reduction, and compliance regulations require the management of privileged rights.	Remove administrative rights from all end users while allowing them to maintain productivity.	Implement a least privilege solution that can target applications and operating system tasks for privileged rights—without providing the end user with administrative credentials.	Risk reduction by avoiding baseline drift, malware mitigation through the removal of rights, lower total cost of ownership, regulatory compliance, and fewer administrative accounts.
Removal of Server Administrative Rights			
Security best practices, threat reduction, and compliance regulations require the management of privileged rights and session activity monitoring when accessing servers.	Remove administrative or root privileges from administrators, while allowing them to maintain productivity on server-based operating systems.	Implement a least privilege solution that can target applications, databases, and operating system tasks for privileged rights—without providing the administrator real local or domain credentials.	Risk reduction by enforcing change control, malware mitigation through the removal of rights, regulatory compliance, and full session management.

(*continued*)

Table 23-1. (*continued*)

Challenge	Need	Solution	Benefit
Removal of Application-to-Application Passwords			
Applications, services, and databases need credentials or certificates to operate correctly as their processes need authentication against local or remote resources.	The ability to remove stale and static password assignments within applications and replace them with API calls or programmatic replacements.	Implement a password management solution capable of replacing passwords within applications or substituting API calls within applications to remove user-defined or hard-coded passwords or certificates.	Passwords or certificates used between applications are no longer hard-coded or stale, and can be managed by a password management solution.

(*continued*)

Table 23-1. (*continued*)

Challenge	Need	Solution	Benefit
Change Control Workflow Requires Approvals			
Change control requiring administrative or root privileges mandates approval from team members before execution.	Instrument a workflow that contacts team members, requires approval or denial of privileged access to a host in order to complete privileged tasks governed by change control.	Implement a password management or least privilege solution that has a workflow engine (internally or compatible with third-party solutions) that can track, report, and provide access once approvals have been granted.	Change management, security best practices, and workflow approval and requirements can be met for privileged access.

(*continued*)

Table 23-1. (*continued*)

Challenge	Need	Solution	Benefit
Reduction of Threats for Infrastructure Access			
Nonserver-based infrastructure, such as routers, switches, firewalls, load balancers, cameras, security systems, iDRACs, etc., typically have the same password across multiple devices (password reuse) or have stale passwords, leading to unnecessary risk and exposure.	Provide a mechanism to manage infrastructure passwords, ensure they are all unique, and automatically rotate (manage) them periodically to ensure they do not become stale.	Implement a password management solution that is capable of discovering and classifying infrastructure devices and managing (rotating, etc.) passwords periodically for any managed account.	Risk reduction and consistent security best practices for unique passwords per device and automatic rotation of passwords to prevent leakage or stale passwords from being compromised.

(*continued*)

Table 23-1. (*continued*)

Challenge	Need	Solution	Benefit
Automatic Login with No Credential Exposure			
Provide access to a resource without exposing the credentials. How do you control what happens to a password once it has been released?	The ability to log on to a resource (application, operating system, database, etc.) without exposing the credentials and providing an attacker with the opportunity to copy and reuse the credentials.	Implement a password management and/ or a least privilege solution that can automatically pass credentials to a resource for authentication without exposing them to the end user.	Users are logged in automatically, and the session can be monitored for malicious activity.

(continued)

Table 23-1. (*continued*)

Challenge	Need	Solution	Benefit
Document Privileged Activity for Audits and Compliance			
Determine what a user did during a session and alert on any potential inappropriate activity, especially when using administrative or shared accounts.	A solution that can record video, keystroke log, and record application activity in a reportable and indexed format for review by security teams and auditors.	Implement a technology that can provide this capability (session record, keystroke log, and application activity) in line with an active session, or using agent or proxy technologies. The results should be stored in a database, encrypted, and protected so that they could be used for forensics or a court of law, if required.	Session activity can be reviewed for mistakes, malicious activity, training, or even breach forensics.

(*continued*)

Table 23-1. (*continued*)

Challenge	Need	Solution	Benefit
Provide an Access Broker to Cloud Resources			
Limit risk exposure to cloud resources by restricting privileged access to only trusted users, resources, and locations.	Implement security processes and technology that can control privileged access to cloud resources, ensuring they do not get compromised from remote threat actors.	Implement a cloud access service broker (CASB) or remote session proxy that can manage connections via user, credentials, location, and even context-aware time of date.	This adds a layer of security for environments to properly access and control cloud resources, while restricting potential lateral connectivity.
Manage Third-Party Access Risk			
Ensure partner, contractor, and authorized third-party access into the company, cloud, or other resources is used correctly by nonemployees, even temporarily.	Provide complete context-aware access of users, location, and time and date access to resources. Document all activity for auditing and forensics.	Implement a password management solution that controls and monitors nonemployee access with granularity needed to review any session activity.	Limit the exposure of nonemployee access and mitigate risks from stolen credentials, rogue sessions, and lateral movement by unauthorized personnel.

(*continued*)

Table 23-1. (*continued*)

Challenge	Need	Solution	Benefit
Break Glass			
Provide out-of-band access to systems during a crisis. Note: This is covered in detail in a prior section.	Privileged access can be granted in the event of an emergency.	Implement a password management system capable of releasing emergency (break glass) credentials in the event of a crisis and document all activity and usage to ensure proper resolution.	Ensures that crisis situations can be resolved quickly, even if key personnel are not available, or in the event of a disaster.
Minimize Data Exposure			
Controlling access to sensitive data when users or administrators have been granted privileged rights to a system, application, or database.	Provide a vehicle to monitor commands, data displayed, and output for malicious activity that might expose sensitive data.	Implement a password manager and least privilege solution that can perform command-line filtering, alert on activity, and search for displayed results that might indicate excessive data exposure.	Users and administrators can be blocked from issuing sensitive commands and teams can be alerted if data is visible from sensitive sources.

(*continued*)

Table 23-1. (*continued*)

Challenge	Need	Solution	Benefit
Granular Role-Based Access			
Operating systems and applications may not contain granular permission controls to restrict inappropriate access.	When possible, restrict commands, child processes, applications, and operating system functions even when the user is executing with privileged rights.	Implement a technology that can monitor individual commands, child processes, scripts, and applications and perform an action if they are executing, including blacklisting the task from executing.	The results minimize the attack surface for operations that may not inherently have role-based access built in.
Rogue Accounts			
Privileged users may have the ability to create rogue local, domain, or application accounts against company policies and security best practices.	Prevent out-of-band access and potential malicious activity by preventing the creation of rogue accounts.	Implement a technology that can monitor local, domain, and application account creation and, based on policy, even deny the accounts from being created in the first place.	Risk reduction by controlling account creation to authorized business processes only.

(*continued*)

Table 23-1. (*continued*)

Challenge	Need	Solution	Benefit
Service Accounts			
Service accounts have privileged access on the local system and, in some cases, such in the case of Windows domain accounts, access to off-system resources. Given the complexity of managing these credentials and the potential impact on operations, they are often configured with nonexpiring passwords and are rarely changed.	An automated method to discover, rotate, and restart distributed service account passwords, while minimizing the impact on dependent applications and processes.	Implement a password manager that can perform centralized discovery, password management, and intelligent restarting of services across the enterprise.	Stored passwords are no longer hard-coded and can be cycled on an ongoing and frequent basis, all while reducing downtime of application and related services. This reduces the risks associated with backdoor access by employees and contractors, as well as with numerous password hacking techniques.

(*continued*)

Table 23-1. (*continued*)

Challenge	Need	Solution	Benefit
Controlling Access Availability			
Administrative accounts are "Always-On" or allow for persistent access creating a risk surface based on time during which a threat actor can exploit an administrative account.	Apply ephemeral properties to administrative accounts and provide access just in time to satisfy business requirements.	Based on business requirements and honoring internal change control and workflow, administrative accounts are only available for a period of time required to complete a task.	The risk surface based on time for administrative accounts, especially those not used frequently, can drastically be reduced.

(*continued*)

Table 23-1. (*continued*)

Challenge	Need	Solution	Benefit
Dynamic access control is not a specific use case, but may be implemented to provide added security in any of the previously discussed scenarios. Organizations that want to control when a user should have access to specific resources and systems can be limited by the native access models. For example, third-party vendors should not be able to access their passwords after working hours, or server administrators should not have access to the financial application server during month-end payroll processing, or from remote locations.	The bottom line is that many organizations have internal and external entities that need to access the network regularly. There is an issue with this: how can you be sure that the credentials used for access are being properly managed? As seen all too often, hackers will leverage external company credentials to find a route in. Organizations need the ability to overlay a more flexible and dynamic access model on top of the native access constructs of the underlying systems and applications.	Implement a password management and/or session management solution(s) that provide dynamic access policy constructs. Dynamic access models evaluate all the parameters at the point of the access request to make sure the appropriate decision is made regarding access. Evaluation criteria can include: Who is trying to log on? What system are they trying to access? Where are they logging in from? What level of access are they requesting? What is the day of the week? What is the time of day?	Applying context to each access request/session reduces risk by enabling the organization to incorporate best practices to privileged access that can help protect your organization from a breach. For example, if we know that a break glass account is for emergency use only, let's only make it available outside of normal business hours. Also, if we would normally expect that account to be accessed via a remote worker working from home, let's also make sure the request is coming in via the VPN concentrator.

(*continued*)

Table 23-1. (*continued*)

Challenge	Need	Solution	Benefit
Incident Tracking			
Remote management and ticketing systems lack the visibility into incidents and unplanned resource allocation.	The ability for authoritative sources for change control and incident tracking to have awareness and approvals of out-of-band access and changes.	Implement a privileged access solution that integrates activity with ticketing, help desk, and other call center solutions for workflow and documentation.	Any and all access is documented with tickets, and a documented process for access can be achieved.
Onboarding of a Remote Workforce			
Employee, vendor, or contractor remote access is not managed through established controls and processes.	Establish security controls for remote workers in accordance with established guidelines and access restriction policies.	Automatically onboard accounts and configure them for remote access to internal resources, simulating, as much as possible, an in office experience.	Remote access workers are automatically onboarded to support teleworking and eliminate risk associated with virtual private networking (VPN) technologies.

(*continued*)

Table 23-1. (*continued*)

Challenge	Need	Solution	Benefit
Onboarding of Remote Access Accounts for Privileged Access			
Privileged remote access accounts are not managed through established controls and processes.	Establish security controls for remote access accounts following established guidelines and access restriction policies.	Provides discovery and automatic onboarding of accounts configured for remote access, whether on-premise or from external connections.	Remote access accounts are automatically onboarded for privileged account management and have passwords that are managed, rotated, and tracked for inappropriate access.

(*continued*)

Table 23-1. (*continued*)

Challenge	Need	Solution	Benefit
Session Management for Remote Access			
External connections to on-premise resources, or cloud environments, do not fall under session management policies for auditing and reporting.	Connections established to on-premise resources can originate outside of the perimeter and could circumvent session monitoring policies.	Session management, including session recording, keystroke logging, and lateral movement detection, can be performed at the connection demark, through the privileged session proxy, or at the endpoint itself depending on the compliance requirements.	Regardless of remote access entry point, session management can be enforced irrespective of network path or resource accessed.

(*continued*)

Table 23-1. (*continued*)

Challenge	Need	Solution	Benefit
Privileged Remote Access			
Administrator or root remote access requires user interaction to retrieve credentials for privileged access.	Technology used to retrieve privileged credentials for remote access is susceptible to attack vectors, including screen capture and memory-scraping malware.	Provide seamless privileged remote access to resources, with no user intervention, to retrieve and apply credentials without the end-user exposure to the account.	Seamless connectivity, ease of use, and a mitigation strategy for malware that attempts to obtain credentials from an end user's asset during a privileged session.
Remote Access Risk Assessment			
Remote access is granted to an authorized user regardless of risks and threats associated with the target or source asset.	Creating an asset risk system based on industry standards to measure threats and risks and use the associated data to determine connectivity and privileges associated with remote access.	Provide threat and risk assessment data from configuration and vulnerability assessments to the privilege and remote access engines to determine remote access connectivity state.	Remote and privileged access can be denied to insecure assets or from high-risk sources based on asset cybersecurity hygiene using industry standard scoring.

CHAPTER 24

Deployment Considerations

Any time you embark on an enterprise project, the costs, return on investment, risks, benefits, threats, and workflow (to name a few) should be considered. When deploying a PAM solution, the realization that it may impact the entire organization needs to be addressed with everyone who may potentially be impacted—from employees to vendors. This means that not only administrators will be affected, but also end users who may lose administrative rights. This can affect rank and file workers and executives, all the way through contractors (although I hope your business never gives temporary employees admin rights; sadly it happens). Deciding where to start, how to deploy, how to educate, and the measurable outcome are challenges that must be addressed up-front. If they are not, internal politics, user resistance, and shadow IT may completely circumvent the reasons for embracing PAM in the first place. This chapter covers some of the deployment considerations all executives, security professionals, and operational teams should consider, discuss, and address along their PAM journey.

© Morey J. Haber 2020
M. J. Haber, *Privileged Attack Vectors*, https://doi.org/10.1007/978-1-4842-5914-6_24

Privileged Risk

Lack of visibility and awareness of all the privileged accounts and credentials across an enterprise poses a monolithic challenge, especially for those companies that rely on manual processes and tools. Privileged accounts, many long forgotten, are sprawled across most organizations including desktops, servers, hypervisors, cloud platforms, cloud workloads, network devices, applications, IoT devices, SaaS applications, and more. Different teams may be separately managing (if managing them at all) their own set of credentials, making it difficult to track all the passwords, let alone who has access to them and who uses them. An administrator can easily have access to more than a hundred systems, possibly disposing them to take shortcuts in order for them to maintain their credentials.

With this proliferation of privileges scattered throughout the environment, where do you start? In some cases, organizations will start with the end users and target desktops and remove administrator rights to mitigate threats like ransomware. In other cases, they will start by protecting the *nix server environment supporting critical business applications, like trading floors or banking systems. In some, they will need to adhere to third-party vendor monitoring as a compliance requirement. Perhaps they have a nearer-term need to focus on a subset of assets to respond to an audit finding, such as properly securing and managing assets connected to the secured PCI network segment. Whether you begin with servers, desktop, networking devices, and/or other connected devices, your decision is a function of risks, complexity, and cost. Ask yourself where the biggest pain is first, what is the risk of tackling it first, and can it be successful? Once you understand the risk and pain, you start by "ripping the Band-Aid off" or "picking the lowest-hanging fruit" to prove success and gain experience.

For many organizations, quantifying this risk from day one through the sustainment of the solution is a problem. How do you actually measure privileged risk? This will vary from organization to organization and is generally modeled after the regulatory compliance requirements governing your organization. A fault in a control, therefore, gives you an indication of risk. After all, it is not like a CVE[1] with a CVSS[2] score; measurements you choose to use need a defendable basis.

Privileged Credential Oversight

Even if IT successfully identifies all the privileged credentials strewn across the enterprise, this does not by default translate into knowing what specific activities are performed during a privileged session (i.e., the period during which elevated privileges are granted to an account, service, or process and actively being used). Privileged access to a superuser account should not amount to ceding carte blanche to the user. Moreover, PCI, HIPAA, and other regulations require organizations to not just secure and protect data but be capable of proving the effectiveness of those measures. So, for both compliance and security reasons, IT needs visibility into the activities performed during the privileged session.

Ideally, IT should also have the ability to seize control over a session should inappropriate use of the credentials occur. But, with potentially hundreds or concurrent privileged sessions running across an enterprise, how does IT expeditiously detect and halt malicious activity? While some applications and services (such as Active Directory) can log user actions, and while Windows servers using logon events within Event Log data can reveal some behavioral anomalies, expect full coverage of privileged account activity to require a complete implementation of PAM, not just managing passwords. And contemplate the use cases needed to track oversight, auditability, and the necessary infrastructure when designing your deployment and workflow. Credential oversight needs its

---

[1]Common Vulnerabilities and Exposures—https://cve.mitre.org
[2]Common Vulnerability Scoring System—www.first.org/cvss/

own security to prevent misuse of stored sessions, and potentially large quantities of storage if session archives are required to be stored for long periods of time.

Shared Credentials

IT teams commonly share root, Windows Administrator, and many other privileged passwords so workloads and duties can be seamlessly shared as needed. However, with multiple people sharing an account password, it may be impossible to trace actions performed with an account to a single individual, complicating auditing and accountability. For a successful deployment, assess how often this problem occurs and where it needs to be addressed with PAM. Simply put, determine how often and where in your environment users are sharing privileged accounts and how you can eliminate this poor behavior with PAM. This is true for every user that has a privileged account—from server administrator to network infrastructure engineer to help desk technician.

Embedded Credentials

Privileged credentials are needed to facilitate authentication for app-to-app (A2A) and application-to-database (A2D) communications. Applications, systems, and IoT devices are commonly shipped, and often deployed, with embedded or backdoor default credentials that are easily guessable and pose a formidable risk until they are brought under management. These privileged credentials are frequently stored in plain text, perhaps within a script, code, or a file on the device, or even in documentation. Unfortunately, there is no universally efficient method to detect or centrally manage passwords stored within applications or scripts. Bluntly, every implementation is different. Securing embedded passwords requires separating the password from the code so that when it's not in use, it's securely stored in a centralized password safe or secret store. For a successful deployment, identification of all the embedded credentials is critical when implementing PAM and how you handle fault tolerance when they are removed ensures there is no interruption to your business once you do.

SSH Keys

IT teams commonly rely on SSH keys to automate secure access to servers, bypassing the need to enter login credentials manually. SSH key sprawl presents a substantive risk for thousands of organizations, which may have upward of a million SSH keys and present viable backdoors for hackers to infiltrate critical servers. Look at your own environment and ask, where are SSH keys, how are they being managed, and what do you do when they expire? Realistically, PAM can manage SSH keys, so environments never get in this situation. It all starts with a discovery of keys and an automated process to bring them under management. This is a deployment consideration that is often overlooked as teams focus on password management for end users, while neglecting to address those SSH keys used by administrators and applications.

Privileged Credentials in the Cloud

The challenges of visibility and auditability are generally exacerbated in the cloud. They are, after all, not your computers and you have limited "rights" for visibility. Cloud and virtualization administrator consoles (as with AWS, Office 365, Azure, etc.) provide vast superuser capabilities, enabling users to rapidly provision, configure, and delete resources at a massive scale. Within these consoles, users can spin up and manage thousands of virtual machines, containers, and other services (each with its own set of privileges and privileged accounts) with just a few clicks.

One predicament then arises around how to onboard and manage all the newly created privileged accounts within "everything" that has been created and, just as important, correctly deprovision them once a resource is decommissioned. On top of this, cloud platforms frequently lack native privileged session monitoring capabilities that work at a granular level to audit exactly what was done. And, even for those organizations that have implemented some degree of automation for their password management, if not architected with the cloud in mind, there's no guarantee a password management solution will be able to manage cloud credentials adequately through all of these resources. For a successful deployment, determine how many cloud services your organization is using, who has privileged access, and how the resources are being accessed, maintained, and monitored. And, remember to ask about the entire workflow, including new account onboarding as well as account offboarding. Many times, the latter is overlooked and your PAM implementation is bogged down with junk accounts it is trying to manage.

Functional Accounts

The concept of functional accounts is used within privileged access management (PAM) and identity and access management (IAM), referring to accounts used to perform automated account management functions, regardless of being local, centralized, within an operating system, application, on-premise, or in the cloud. Simply put, functional accounts help to manage other accounts. Functional accounts have elevated privileges and, in many implementations, domain administrator or root privileges across multiple resources. Management functions can include, but are certainly not limited to, account creations and deletion, password rotation, account enablement or disablement, and group membership placement or revocation.

A good functional account architecture limits the reach of each instantiation and prefers multiple functional accounts governing zones, resources, assets, and applications vs. a few that have nearly godlike, or domain privileges, across the entire environment. These accounts typically also fall outside of any just-in-time management for identity and privileged access management solutions since they must be considered "always-on" in order to perform their automated functions. The latter makes it easy to understand that if a functional account is compromised, repercussions are quite pronounced, and every account under the functional account's control (managed account) is in jeopardy too.

As an example, consider a deployment of Windows resources within your environment. The resources could be servers or laptops. In this scenario, a functional account would manage all of the privileged and service accounts assigned to the resource and linked to other systems that must share the same credentials. They can be rotated and checked in and out on-demand, or based on a workflow. All management for these accounts, whether they are local or domain-joined, is accomplished via the functional account. The goal is to ensure the credentials are always unique, never become stale or dormant, and are changed frequently enough to mitigate risks of the privileged credentials being stolen or misused.

If you consider the power and purpose of functional accounts, there are several things that administrators and end users should always heed:

- Functional accounts should never be associated with any identity. They operate independently.

- They are strictly used for automation from an IAM and PAM solution. They should not be used by other applications.

- They should never be used for any daily work. Ever!

- They should be managed like any other highly privileged account and passwords or certificates combination and be rotated periodically to prevent them from becoming stale. This must be done with great care to ensure dependent management functions do not break due to a missed password change or error.

- Functional accounts should be excluded from any just-in-time IAM or PAM initiatives.

- Whenever possible, they should be local accounts and not domain accounts. However, certain applications and implementations will necessitate exceptions. Follow this simple rule: if it can be managed or implemented without using a domain account, that is probably a lower-risk method.

Functional accounts are a necessary concept to place privileged accounts under management. While they have elevated privileges to perform their functions, they must be treated as a high security risk and deserve protection that even exceeds that of domain administrator credentials. IAM and PAM solutions can manage these expectations for an environment, but some basic do's and don'ts should always be honored when considering your deployment.

Applications

Traditionally applications only had to store credentials when trying to authenticate against external resources. Some examples are remote databases, file shares, or directory stores. Ensuring that developers securely store these credentials has always been a challenge. Unfortunately, developers have created a large number of applications over the years that store these credentials in plain text (or even poorly hashed) within the configuration files of the application. With the explosion of cloud computing and SaaS and IaaS offerings over the last 5 years, applications are increasingly interacting with many platforms, and not just a single external resource. It is common for configuration files to have many credentials to connect to other external resources, including API keys. One of the promises of zero trust is to eliminate this credential storage model and use a third-party policy engine to broker authentication. Often, API keys are not seen as the sensitive piece of information that should be protected by developers. This is evident by the number of applications where effort is put forth to securely store credentials, yet API keys for cloud resources are left in plain text and, sometimes, even posted in public Internet forums. How many times have developers pushed code to GitHub with API keys included or accidentally exposed API keys while posting source code to Stack Overflow? The carelessness is shocking.

As with traditional resources, when investing in the cloud, we need to push developers to achieve the highest application goals, but with the least amount of privileges. This philosophy is hard to abide by with most public APIs. With traditional usernames and passwords, it is often possible to create role-based access with limited privileges. Developers need to be aware that API keys usually grant applications access to the entire environment. This is contrary to the principle of least privilege. Exposure of an API key cannot be contained to the minimal amount of functionality that the consuming application requires. SendGrid is one of the exceptions to this and does an adequate job providing fine-grained control to limit the functionality that the API key is allowed to consume.

As enterprises continue to migrate workloads to the cloud and advocate for more secure coding, API security and vendor platform security will continue to mature. PAM has a place by ensuring that privileges are not Boolean and any programmatic application access also has a fine-grained privileged model. When considering your PAM deployment, consider how applications authenticate and specifically whether they use API keys. These should not be hard-coded in your applications, but rather centrally managed in a secret store.

Application-Specific Password

There is one thing certain about securing privileged access, by the time you read this book, something will have changed. Since the original release of *Privileged Attack Vectors* in 2017, concepts like one-time passwords (OTPs) and behavioral authentication have spiked in popularity, while other methods have withered in failure or otherwise fallen into disuse. One new promising concept that was introduced to the mainstream consumer community in 2019 was application-specific passwords. This has not translated yet to the enterprise, but there are definitely merits in the concept that will probably lead to commercial implementations soon.

The concept behind application-specific passwords is simple—an identity has only one account and, therefore, only one username. This is different from the traditional one identity to multiple account model. However, each account can have multiple passwords where each password is unique per application. A user effectively logs on to a management console and generates a random password for a new application. The user registers the application with a unique name like "Outlook" and has a finite amount of time to create an account and authenticate from that application. The application is then fingerprinted, or a key exchanged, during the initial authentication to trust the application. If the password is attempted to be used by another application due to it being stolen or some form of password reuse, it is denied access and the application-specific password potentially locked out. While this creates a potential management nightmare for a user with hundreds of accounts, it does solve key privileged access management problems from lateral movement to password reuse. It is a newer concept worth keeping an eye on and a deployment consideration since most enterprise password management solutions cannot interact with this paradigm yet.

CHAPTER 25

Privileged Account Management Implementation

Organizations increasingly recognize that properly securing and controlling privileged credentials ranks as one of the best defenses against attacks from external hackers as well as from malicious insiders. For optimal results, a privileged access management solution should protect identities, accounts, passwords, and keys at all stages of the privileged attack vector kill chain (Chapter 1) by implementing comprehensive layers of control and audit. The overall objectives for your implementation should include the following:

- **Reduce** the attack surface by limiting the use of privileged accounts and by controlling privileged access to resources across the enterprise. This is especially true regardless of whether the remote access session starts from trusted internal resources or from authorized external entities.

- **Monitor** privileged user, session, and file activities for unauthorized access or changes that inappropriately affect the organization's sensitive data or normal business operations.

© Morey J. Haber 2020
M. J. Haber, *Privileged Attack Vectors*, https://doi.org/10.1007/978-1-4842-5914-6_25

- **Analyze** asset and user behavior to detect suspicious or malicious activities, and to help secure operations in accordance with security best practices and regulatory guidance.

- **Low Impact** approach for maximum adoption of PAM across the enterprise, and to protect privileges without obstructing productivity or overburdening operations.

Implementing an end-to-end privileged access management solution should follow a defined process to minimize costs and distractions, and to speed results. When managing privileges as an attack vector, applying this simple, ten-step approach helps manage risk and provide predictable and documentable results (Figure 25-1). The result of this ten-step process is measurable as you embark on your PAM journey.

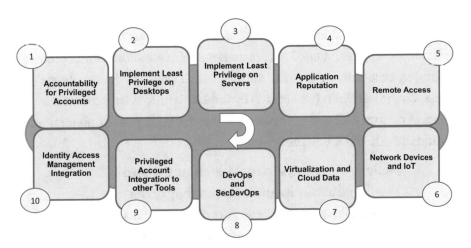

Figure 25-1. *Ten Steps for a Successful Privileged Access Management Implementation*

Throughout the process of selecting and deploying your privileged access management solution, keep in mind these steps are just a guide and do not necessarily need to be followed in sequence. However, it is highly recommended every organization starts with step 1 because, if you have no idea where your privileged accounts are, you have no way of measuring success for any step that you may choose to do next. Figure 25-2 provides a simple graphic for explaining the scope for step 1 within your entire organization considering all the roles and resources that need coverage.

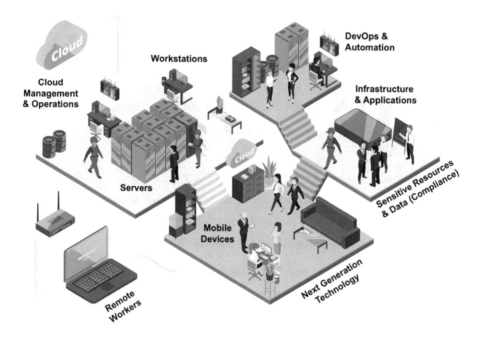

Figure 25-2. *Scope of Discovery Within a Typical Enterprise*

Step 1: Improve Accountability for Privileged Accounts

The most logical starting point for gaining greater control over privileges is by improving accountability over privileged passwords. In simple terms, discovering every place privileged accounts exist throughout your IT universe and determining which ones are being shared, by whom, and why they are being shared. Ineffective management of shared accounts is a problem that has significant scale and risks. You don't have to look much further than recent breaches to understand the implications or the challenges. As a reminder:

- Systems can have embedded or hard-coded passwords, leaving opportunities for misuse. These need to be discovered for management.

- When human interaction is required for credential entry, it can lead to credential exposure. Discovering where manual entry of privileged accounts is occurring will assist with automating privileged credential injection.

- Passwords and keys are needed for application-to-application and application-to-database access and should never be hard-coded. These should be identified and placed under management

- End-user passwords are generally static, so there must be protections against passwords being leaked or reused outside of the organization. Discovery of local administrative credentials will identify assets that should have those rights removed. Least privilege should be implemented as a mitigating control.

- Manual password rotation is unreliable and time-consuming. Humans will always make mistakes by missing an account password change or reusing a password. Discovery and automation of management for these accounts removes the human element.

- Manual auditing and reporting on access is complex and error-prone. Discovery of all privileged accounts and automation will help ensure reporting, auditing, and analytics are as accurate as possible.

So, how exactly do organizations ensure accountability of shared privileged accounts to meet compliance and security requirements without impacting administrator productivity?

The answer is something we have touched on several times: automation. Automating privileged account discovery provides accountability that helps drive password and session management, the removal of administrative rights on endpoints (least privilege), and the management of privileged remote access sessions. By improving the accountability and control over privileged access, IT organizations can reduce security risks and achieve compliance objectives. With this goal in mind, consider these additional five subrecommendations for the accountability of privileged accounts:

1. Full network scanning, discovery, and profiling with auto-onboarding of privileged accounts.

2. Provide discovery of privileged accounts through third-party integrations and API calls.

3. Build permission sets dynamically according to data provided during discovery assessments.

4. Apply granular access control, workflow, and auditing for any discovery process to ensure accuracy.

5. Enforce role-based access to discovered data to ensure results are not misused against the organization.

With these requirements, organizations can discover all the accounts in their environment, place those accounts under management, and satisfy auditor requests that accounts are now managed or properly offboarded.

Step 2: Implement Least Privilege on Desktops

Once accounts and assets have been discovered and are being consistently managed, the next step to complete privileged access management is implementing least privilege on end-user machines. That is the removal of local administrative rights potentially invoked by the local or remote user. As a security best practice, organizations should reduce the risk on desktops before servers (such as Microsoft Windows Server, Unix, or Linux as indicated in step 3) as the endpoint is typically the last mile of security, but the primary target for a threat actor. Some organizations may choose to reverse this order and do servers before desktops. This depends on the organization's business requirements and risk appetite, but as discussed, step 1 should be done first to even determine the scope of any deployment.

To that end, the process for IT to restrict or disable end-user privileges potentially can be complex and time-consuming, but it must be done to support audit or compliance mandates for the removal of unnecessary administrative rights. When environments have standardized desktop images and applications, the process is relatively trivial. If every machine is different, then prioritizing which users, roles, and assets to manage first becomes a larger business and technical discussion. And although users should not be granted local administrator or power user privileges in the first place, sometimes certain applications require elevated privileges just to execute correctly. So, how do IT departments reduce the risk of users having excessive privileges and subjecting the organization to potential exploitation or compliance violations without obstructing their productivity?

The answer is only through least privilege access for applications. This requires a rules-based PAM technology to elevate application privileges without elevating user privileges. By eliminating end-user desktop administrator privileges and instrumenting application control, applications can operate with the required privileges, but neither impact the user nor provide them with excessive privileges that are a liability.

To aid in this step, consider the top ten subrequirements for desktop least privilege management:

1. Default all users to standard user privileges, while enabling elevated privileges for specific applications and tasks, without requiring administrative credentials.

2. Enforce restrictions on software installation, usage, and OS configuration changes based on privileges assigned by rules.

3. Eliminate the need for end users to require two accounts to perform appropriate administrative tasks.

4. Make dynamic least privilege decisions for applications based on that application's vulnerability, risk, reputation, and compliance profile.

5. Match applications to rules automatically based on asset- or user-based policies.

6. Report on privileged access to file systems for all users and document system changes during privileged sessions to prevent malicious tampering.

7. Monitor sessions and log keystrokes during privileged access to determine whether or not a local user is using privileges appropriately.

8. Provide a technique for using real domain or local privileges when required, including multi-factor authentication for applications that must authenticate to a remote directory store.

9. Integrate with other privilege solutions to achieve a uniform approach to password management and remote access.

10. Leverage an integrated data warehouse and data analytics across the privilege universe for accurate reporting, regardless of where privileged activity occurs for a user.

Step 3: Implement Least Privilege on Servers

In current information technology environments, business-critical, Tier-1 applications are attractive targets for threat actors. They contain the sensitive data and applications attackers want to compromise, but rarely can a threat actor effectively target the most sensitive resources first. Obtaining privileged user credentials via other assets can provide access to these sensitive systems through privileged attack vectors and lateral movement. Having root passwords, superuser status, or other elevated privileges is important for users to do their jobs. Unfortunately, this practice also presents significant security risks stemming from intentional, accidental, or indirect misuse of those privileged credentials. This is especially true when those credentials are shared or have weak passwords leading to trivial access of Tier-1 systems. The impact can be felt on a server class operating system from Windows to Unix and Linux. For server-based operating systems, privileged attack vectors become exaggerated due to the following:

- Role-based access controls are inefficient and incomplete (such as native OS options), lacking the ability to delegate authorization without disclosing passwords.

- Default tools are not secure enough (such as open source sudo or local administrator accounts) to address risk or compliance requirements and lack the ability to record sessions and keystrokes for audits.

- The default operating system cannot restrict activity inside scripts and third-party applications, leaving a shortcut to unapproved applications.

- Open source solutions and native tools do not offer an efficient migration path away from sudo or shared accounts if it is being used throughout the organization.

Therefore, how do IT organizations limit who has access to root accounts to reduce the risk of compromises without hindering productivity? We are literally full circle again on the observer effect.

Organizations must be able to efficiently delegate server privileges and authorization without disclosing passwords (or even the credentials required) for root, local, or domain administrators, or other accounts. Recording all privileged sessions for audits, including keystroke information, helps to achieve privileged access monitoring requirements without relying on native tools that are deficient.

Therefore, the top ten subrequirements for server privilege management capabilities include the following:

1. Industry-standard support for authentication solutions, including OAuth, SAML, and other multi-factor solutions.

2. Advanced control and audit over commands at the system level, even when they are obfuscated in scripts or renamed.

3. A flexible policy language and rules to provide a migration path from native tools with the features needed to manage virtually any business requirement.

4. Extensive support for many Windows, Unix, and Linux platforms.

5. Recording and indexing of all sessions for quick discovery during audits.

6. Brokering privileges transparently, ensuring user productivity and compliance.

7. Change management of all settings and policy configuration, allowing full audit of who has changed what, version control, and rollback of all existing configuration files.

8. REST API for easier integration with third-party products.

9. An architecture that provides high availability and seamless disaster recovery.

10. Leverages an integrated data warehouse for centralized reporting and analytics across all managed systems.

With this capability, you gain complete control over root and administrator access on any type of server operating system and meet virtually any business or regulatory requirement for privileged access.

Step 4: Application Reputation

Application whitelisting, blacklisting, and greylisting are forms of application control and a subset of application reputation services. Once shared credentials are under management and end users have the privileges they need to perform their jobs (and nothing more), organizations can move to a better understanding of risks to help make better-informed privilege elevation decisions. The challenge, though, is that most risk assessment solutions do little to help security leaders put vulnerability, attack, malware, and application risk information in the context of business. Saddled with volumes of rigid data and static reports, the security team is left to manually discern real threats and determine how to act upon them when users execute an application.

Therefore, for step number 4, consider expanding your application management initiatives to include application reputation and application control services. With these capabilities implented, automated decisions on whether or not an application is too dangerous to execute can be based on:

- The source location of the application by determining if it was loaded from a trusted share vs. downloaded from the Internet or copied from a secure location on the file system

- Real-world threats based on known hashes for vulnerable or exploitable versions

- Improperly digital signing/signing using a stolen certificate

- Outdated versions or a missing security patch

- Software not licensed to the organization therefore blocking shadow IT

Based on these criteria, information technology and security teams should adopt privileged access management policies to compensate for the risk. That is, the application should be measured against the threat and the runtime of the application should be:

- Denied execution

- Automatically limit the privileges assigned to the application (i.e., no child processes or denied access to the file system)

- Event logging and alerting, including automatically opening a support ticket based on the application and risk

This not only stops exploits from becoming a privileged attack vector, but also blocks drive-by social threats that can leverage vulnerabilities within the environment until mitigation or remediation steps are available.

Step 5: Remote Access

As we have discussed, almost all attacks involve some form of remote resource access. Only an insider initiating an attack directly on a system's terminal is not engaged in remote access. In addition, the vast majority of these attacks come from true external threats and can involve threat actors that are specifically targeting your organization all the way through remote contractors, vendors, and even remote employees. Remote access, especially for privileged accounts, provides an entry point past traditional perimeter defenses that a threat actor can leverage to fulfill their nefarious mission. With these characteristics in mind, privileged access management should manage remote access sessions by:

- Automatically injecting authorized credentials into a session without ever exposing them the to the user

- Providing secure connectivity deep into an organization or the cloud without the need for dedicated clients, special applications, or protocol tunneling

- Allowing for complete privilege monitoring to determine if the session was appropriate

- Enforcing a workflow that applies just-in-time access and includes ticketing solutions to grant the appropriate privileges

- Integrating with a variety of third-party services, from directory stores to SIEMs, for visibility and authentication within an environment

- Providing connectivity as a bastion host, eliminating the need for VPN solutions and costly VDI deployments

- Support for all major remote access protocols, including RDP, SSH, VNC, and HTTP(s), as well as agent technology to provide secure remote access connectivity to any type of device

If you consider steps 1 through 4 of this chapter for identifying privileged accounts and managing the endpoints and applications on them, the next logical step is controlling who can access them remotely and with what specific privileges. It is a logical progression. Secure the target and then secure who can access it, especially if the communication needs to originate from outside of your organization.

Step 6: Network Devices and IoT

The most common username and passwords for network and Internet of Things (IoT) devices within an enterprise are not necessarily the defaults that come with the device. Most administrators change them, but they may choose one that is easily guessable. According to Forbes[1] in 2019, the top ten most hacked passwords are (m is for millions):

1. 123456 (23.2m)

2. 123456789 (7.7m)

3. qwerty (3.8m)

4. password (3.6m)

5. 1111111 (3.1m)

6. 12345678 (2.9m)

7. abc123 (2.8m)

8. 1234567 (2.5m)

9. password1 (2.4m)

10. 12345 (2.3m)

In parenthesis is the number of times they have been compromised in the wild. This list not only pertains to network devices, but any device in a corporate environment. It is important to mention here because, with potentially hundreds or thousands of managed network and IoT devices in an environment, assigning a complex, unique password to each device and securely storing each password is a logistical nightmare without a password management solution. So, it's not uncommon for

---

[1]These Are The World's Most Hacked Passwords—www.forbes.com/sites/kateoflahertyuk/2019/04/21/these-are-the-worlds-most-hacked-passwords-is-yours-on-the-list/#46172ebf289c

administrators to choose a simple, common, and guessable password and assign it to every device for ease of management. Unfortunately, threat actors can easily guess or brute force these devices to gain access. In addition, as we have discussed, the second most common privilege flaw is reuse of the same password across the entire infrastructure. And rarely are these passwords changed en masse. This holds true even if you have outsourced the management or have had employee turnover. These oversights and shortcuts lead to a variety of malicious activities, including recent vulnerabilities we've seen that can exploited to replace the device's bootstrap loader with a piece of custom malware.

To summarize, here are some key risks that stem from a simple lack of privileged account management on network and IoT devices:

- Default or common passwords that are misconfigured

- Shared credentials across multiple devices for management simplicity

- Excessive password ages due to fear of changing them or lack of management capabilities

- Compromised or insider accounts making changes to allow exfiltration of data

- Outsourced devices and infrastructure where changes in personnel, contracts, and tools expose credentials to unaccountable individuals

- Professional services provided by a vendor that sets the passwords and which are not changed after their engagement is complete

Any one of these could lead to excessive risk for your infrastructure. As such, organizations should look beyond desktops and servers when planning their PAM journey by including any network or IoT device. Additionally, with newer privileged access management solutions, organizations can move beyond the Boolean "access" or "no access" authorization models commonly used in many network devices. That means organizations now have access to proxy gateways that can enforce command whitelisting and blacklisting, session monitoring, and active alerting, and can control and limit root access.

Finally, a new generation of distributed denial of service attacks, often leveraging IoT, has emerged that represents a significant risk to all organizations. The number one vulnerability with IoT devices is the use of hard-coded, default, and weak passwords. Even when administrators change default passwords, most credentials can be still guessed via brute force attacks. While newer laws like CCPA plan to restrict this practice, there are still millions of devices already deployed that are susceptible to these attacks. Therefore, it is recommended to get all of these devices under management and ensure each one has a unique and complex password stored in your PAM solution and is properly managed for session (or remote access) activity.

Step 7: The Cloud and Virtualization

With the growing use of virtualized data centers and cloud environments for processing, storage, or application hosting and development, organizations have opened up new avenues for threat actors to access sensitive data and cause disruption. Organizations must secure access to these environments to mitigate security risks, while meeting the cost and efficiency promises of hosting more applications and services in the cloud.

Like traditional desktops and servers, unknown or undermanaged virtualized and cloud environments can create a significant security gap that opens networks to security breaches, data loss, intellectual property theft, and regulatory compliance issues. The first step in getting control over these assets is discovery as defined in step 1. There are several techniques used to discover assets in virtualized and cloud environments, including the following:

- Performing standard network discovery or scanning from a host machine with "line of sight" access to the virtualized environment. This should support discovery using IPv4 and IPv6 fingerprinting.

- Querying the hypervisor or cloud management platform to retrieve the inventory of virtualized assets, including containers, or configuring an active notification upon inventory updates.

- Using agents that are preinstalled on the base image library or that are installed during the normal server provisioning process.

- Querying a third-party asset management solution that provides a record of authority for what is operating in the environment.

Once cloud and virtualized instances are identified, they must be managed to limit exposure. From a privileged access management perspective, the options to secure these assets are similar to traditional desktops and servers, but with a few extra unique characteristics:

- Utilize a password management solution to manage the passwords across all virtualized machines, containers, and deployed management interfaces.

- Use a remote access solution with privileged session monitoring capabilities to control and monitor virtual machines and application-specific management console access.

- Use native delegation capabilities of the underlying hypervisor to reduce the privileges associated to users interacting with the system. This can include zero trust as well.

- Use a privilege management agent with a least privilege architecture to reduce exposure to administrator, root, and privileged developer accounts. This is especially important when linked with DevOps.

- Integrate with the native cloud or virtualization API for management of accounts and identities that can interact with hosted services.

- For virtualized non-Windows systems, consider using a directory bridging technology to centralize authentication and credentials in a single platform-agnostic directory store, like LDAP or Active Directory.

Now that the resources are under control, what about the hypervisor and cloud management platform itself? Here, again, inappropriate or malicious activities at this management level could have a devastating impact on the business. This includes administrators of your VMware, Microsoft Hyper-V, Amazon AWS, and Microsoft Azure environments. To counteract this threat, organizations again have several options:

- Use a privileged password management solution to automatically manage the passwords across all hypervisor and cloud management platforms. This encompasses everything from cloud-specific management consoles to API keys.

- Use a remote access and privileged session monitoring solution to control and monitor all user-based cloud management activities.

- Use native or third-party delegation capabilities of the hypervisor and cloud management provider to reduce the privileges associated with users that are interacting with the system.

- The cloud and virtualized resources are essential to any organization embarking on a PAM journey and utilizing these technologies to streamline costs, provide quicker time-to-market of services. Privileged attack vectors are arguably a higher risk in these environments, and managing them should become part of your standard operating procedure.

Step 8: DevOps and SecDevOps

For commercial application developers, or programmers who create automated DevOps processes, consider how beneficial it would be if you never have to enter credentials to begin your automation processes, or hard-coded passwords or keys in scripts to perform tasks. If DevOps tools automatically retrieved the current and proper credentials or queried a management solution to prove authorization (zero trust), any risks to automation based on privileged attack vectors could be mitigated. Management tools for services, remote access, and infrastructure would automatically recognize the logged-on user or automated process, the asset they are executing from, be fully context-aware, and seamlessly request and pass credentials for the needed functions. Privileged access management solutions for password management and secrets storage make this capability a reality using an Application Program Interface (API) to set, retrieve, and process credential and password requests. Some of the benefits of this approach for DevOps are the following:

- **Secure Applications:** Privileged access management APIs are designed to provide better security for all applications that require automation to enter credentials for normal operations. Developers can call a PAM API and retrieve the latest credentials for any user, application, infrastructure, cloud solution, or database to authenticate, perform automation, and ultimately release the credentials upon termination of the task. This can trigger automatic, randomized cycling of the password or additional automated processes to meet business objectives. Developers and IT never see, or know, the latest credentials for any given DevOps task, nor are the credentials ever hard-coded.

- **Privileged Attack Vector Mitigation:** Using a PAM API secures the runtime of applications and avoids hacking techniques like pass-the-hash that may be looking for persistent privileged credentials in memory. This approach is far more secure than single sign-on (SSO) since the password is constantly being rotated per task, application, or session, even if it is shared through multiple DevOps processes.

- **Developer Simplification:** This approach improves the agility and responsiveness of developers and IT by never requiring the entry of credentials for connectivity, automation, and execution of DevOps tasks. A simple API call is all that is referenced to ensure that the right credentials are always used.

Step 9: Privileged Account Integration
Third-Party Integrations

It is no secret that IT and security professionals are overloaded with privilege, vulnerability, and attack information. Unfortunately, advanced persistent threats (APTs) often go undetected because traditional security analytics solutions are unable to correlate diverse data to discern hidden risks. Seemingly isolated events are written off as exceptions, filtered out, or lost in a sea of data. The threat actor continues to traverse the network, and the damage continues to multiply. So how do security and IT operations teams gain an understanding of where threats are coming from, prioritize them, and quickly mitigate the risks?

By integrating privileged account data with other sources of security information, teams can identify a potential security incident typically missed by single sources of security information alone. Based on basic correlation, analytics, machine learning, or even artificial intelligence, integrating privileged account data with other solutions can pinpoint specific, high-risk users and assets by correlating low-level privilege and threat data from a variety of third-party solutions.

Therefore, consider privileged account information as a single source of privileged management data. In addition, all PAM solutions should be capable of providing the following ten subcategory integration methods:

1. Correlate low-level data from a variety of third-party solutions to uncover critical threats natively, or via certified third-party connectors.

2. Correlate system activity against application risk data and known malware.

3. Report on compliance, benchmarks, threat analytics, what-if scenarios, and resource requirements.

4.   View, sort, and filter historical data from multiple perspectives based on integrated role-based access.

5.   Integrate with SIEM solutions and provide support for common protocols like Syslog and SNMP.

6.   Profile IP, DNS, OS, Mac address, users, accounts, password ages, ports, services, software, processes, hardware, and event logs to accurately judge the risk for an asset or application.

7.   Group, assess, and report on assets by IP range, naming convention, OS, domain, applications, business function, and Active Directory.

8.   Import from Active Directory, LDAP, IAM, or set custom permissions to provide efficient account integration.

9.   Support multiple workflow, ticketing systems, and notification to coordinate with IT and security teams.

10.   Provide archiving and auditing capability of all collected privileged account information for modeling, threat hunting, and forensics.

By unifying privileged access management and other IT management solutions, IT and security teams have a single, contextual lens through which to view and address user and asset risk by activity, asset, user, and privilege.

Directory Bridging

Next, as a critical privileged account integration, please consider step 3 again for a moment. Once you have greater control over privileged access in server environments, the next logical step is to bring those systems under consistent management, policy, and single sign-on. Unix, Linux, and Mac have traditionally been managed as stand-alone systems, each a silo with its own set of users, groups, access control policies, configuration files, and passwords to remember. Managing a heterogeneous environment that contains these silos, plus a Microsoft or cloud environment, leads to inconsistent administration for IT, unnecessary complexity for end users, and a vast sprawling of alias accounts. These are known threats and areas of interest for a threat actor.

Therefore, how do IT organizations achieve consistent policy configuration to achieve compliance requirements, a simpler experience for users and administrators, and less risk from improperly managed systems?

The ideal solution is to centralize authentication for Unix, Linux, and MacOS environments by extending a directory store like Microsoft's Active Directory with single sign-on capabilities to these platforms. By using a directory bridge and extending Group Policy to these non-Windows platforms, IT environments gain centralized configuration management for accounts and stop the sprawl of local alias accounts.

The top four subrequirements for any bridge solution should include the following:

1. No requirement to modify a directory stores schema to add Linux, Unix, or MacOS systems to the network. This provides stability as the technology evolves.

2. Provides a pluggable framework with an interface similar to Microsoft's Management Console (e.g., Active Directory Users and Computers, ADUC) on Linux or MacOS, and full support for Apple's Workgroup Manager application to allow for seamless management with tools administrators are currently familiar with (low friction).

3. Single sign-on for any enterprise application that supports Kerberos or LDAP.

4. Allows users to leverage their Active Directory credentials to gain access to Unix, Linux, and MacOS, consolidating various password files, NIS, and LDAP repositories into Active Directory and removing the need to manage user accounts separately.

These concepts will enable simplified configuration and policy management for non-Windows systems and enhance the user experience by consolidating the number of credentials any one user needs to remember. Therefore, the lower the number of accounts, the less to correlate during an audit per identity, and the lower the risk surface for a threat actor to target.

Step 10: Identity and Access Management Integration

Identity and access management (IAM) plays a critical role in an organization's identity governance strategy. As organizations grow, so do the number of applications, servers, and databases used. Access to the organization's resources is typically managed through IAM solutions, which offer capabilities like single sign-on, provisioning, role-based user management, access control, and governance. But securing an organization's sensitive data and applications requires more. Provisioned users, regardless of privileges, can leave an organization exposed if activity of their usage is not monitored and documented properly. Identity and access management solutions help IT teams answer: "Who has access to what?" But, to achieve complete user visibility, privileged access management solutions are required to address the remaining questions:

"Is that access appropriate?" and "Is that access being used appropriately?" That is, PAM solutions should be providing more visibility and deeper auditing of the access and use of privileged accounts. Many times, IAM solutions will add users to a system or applications group, but will not provide the details as to the session activity nor keystrokes collected during the privileged session. As such, PAM extends the visibility of the IAM solution to further tighten security and audit controls. Figure 25-3 provides an illustration of this integration.

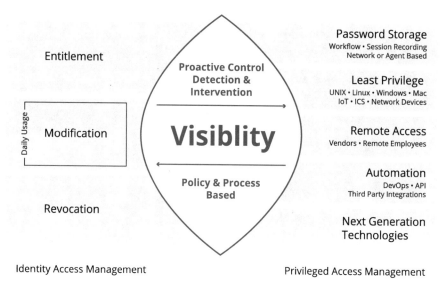

Figure 25-3. *IAM and PAM Integration*

As organizations mature along their PAM journey, they will more clearly understand how identities can be used as an attack vector and why the integration of PAM and IAM provides the best level of protection for any organization today against identity- and account-based attack vectors.

CHAPTER 26

Machine Learning

Machine learning (ML) is becoming increasingly prevalent as a tool to solve complex information security problems. It is an approach that allows computers to acquire intelligence in the way that humans do using algorithms based on artificial intelligence. With this, machines can learn from repeated interactions with situations and events to develop correlations and predictions about current and future behavior. Machine learning algorithms are able to discern information from a data series without dependence on a previously determined relationship or characteristics. Learning occurs as it does with humans and animals, and relationships are further strengthened by repetition and reinforcement. This approach has grown in practical terms with the increase in computer processing power and the reduction in compute cost, allowing the aggregation, ingestion, and analysis of very large datasets and events. In this way, machine learning enables a level of learning and intelligence that mimics the ability of a human, since the ability to analyze data at this volume and speed is impractical for the human brain.

Machine learning is considered a derivative of artificial intelligence (AI) and should not be confused with AI as a technology or theory. Machine learning is best characterized as fixed algorithms within AI that can learn and postulate, while true AI is a step above that actually develops new algorithms to analyze data. This is more akin to a human learning a new task with no previous frame of reference. Therefore, artificial intelligence is more associated with the interpretation of information that is learned to drive conclusions or make decisions, while, to work

© Morey J. Haber 2020
M. J. Haber, *Privileged Attack Vectors*, https://doi.org/10.1007/978-1-4842-5914-6_26

effectively, machine learning must already have awareness of the scope of data being processed. Because of this relationship, many machine learning implementations are part of, or lead to, an artificial intelligence application when the scope of the project is fully understood.

Machine Learning and Information Security

Due to the considerable volume of data created by modern information networks, machine learning can be a useful way to supplement human analysis of security events to identify indicators of compromise. This value is self-evident due to the inability of humans to interpret raw security event data, which can easily overwhelm even advanced security tools when there is a high quantity of data. Machine learning can help security analysts by detecting when an attack has taken place, evaluating network traffic and flow, assessing vulnerabilities and exposure, and correlating the information with privileged access. This is particularly useful in situations where resources are very dynamic and ephemeral and where nuanced rules like privilege management security policy are being used to determine if an event was malicious or not. Machine learning can be used to assess threats and the output can be utilized to create and maintain a threat database. This database can be supplemented by other external sources, but will serve as a contextually relevant tool to assess what threat actors have potentially impacted in an organization and to what degree. Machine learning is useful because it can create initial relationships and then strengthen or weaken those relationships based on continual learning and analysis. In addition, it can also apply context and attribution to threats to provide a richer picture of them, while also helping to reduce both false positives and false negatives.

The Human Element

Human security analysts also have varying levels of effectiveness in their roles. An analyst starting a shift will generally be more effective than one that is near the end of their shift. This problem is even more pervasive in emergency break glass or crisis situations, where the heat of the moment can limit visibility, dull senses, impair the ability to interpret information, and lead to false conclusions. Repetitive work is frequently the enemy of security analyst effectiveness. Machine learning can greatly reduce analyst burnout due to the need to make decisions based on the repetitive review of events, logs, and alerts. Machine learning can be implemented initially with analysts serving as validators for machine learning decisions and then expanding the ability of ML to operate unsupervised in controlled circumstances. This releases the security analyst to handle more complex tasks and to act as the final arbiter of processed decisions. In time, the machine learning capability can be relied on to handle entire classes of security events, but once this is implemented, it needs to be continually validated at future intervals to ensure that the approach is still effective and not prone to errors. The human element is critical for oversight of any machine learning implementation when measuring privileged risk.

Attack Vectors

Machine learning can also be utilized by security organizations to quickly identify and address malicious attacks. Events can be processed quickly that lead to the identification and interpretation of "low and slow" attacks that the average SIEM solution may miss due to basic correlation based on time. Frequently, anomalous events, which could actually be an indication of initial compromise, are readily lost in the white noise of very chatty security and network devices. Similarly, lateral movement actions can enable threat actors to hide within substantial network traffic, so a machine learning approach will baseline the network traffic so that anomalies will stand out as opposed to being obscured. Baselining makes machine learning approaches inherently customized to each individual company's network, growing more specialized and accurate over time. For privileged access management, machine learning is especially useful in helping to determine if a user's behavior should be considered malicious or benign based on all of these characteristics.

In addition, machine learning can be a useful tool for analyzing endpoint assets and their associated behavior. As more companies adopt a bring your own device (BYOD) approach (covered in Chapter 16), utilizing machine learning allows the traffic and events from noncorporate-owned devices to be uniformly analyzed and an overall threat management system developed despite the diversity of the endpoint devices. Since endpoint security and managing administrative privilege is an inherent part of privileged access management, machine learning is useful because it can determine if a user behaves correctly based on prior work history, and it can assess whether current behavior is consistent with allowable limits and boundaries based on policy. If either is violated, automation can quarantine access or raise an escalation to begin additional forensics to determine if the behavior is definitively inappropriate.

To that end, many organizations rely too much on vulnerability and signature-based tools that identify established and documented threats in their environments, but struggle with the detection of zero-day and new threats within acceptable timeframes. These capabilities are useful because they provide an ability to detect and respond to new and unique threats well in advance of them appearing in commercial security offerings. This is also useful detecting threats facing remote workers and in operational technology environments that are largely unsecured or not considered worthy of investment in standardized security tools. These unsecured networks are increasingly becoming the favorite targets of modern threat actors and considering the changing location for workers a modern solution to mitigate the risks.

Machine Learning Benefits

Machine learning can be a useful supplement to an identity and privilege management approach, but should be considered just one tool in the toolbox and not a panacea. Nothing will completely replace the need for security analysts and audits, and forensic information should be readily available for the need to dig deep or to hunt for adversaries. Machine learning tools should also be well understood when implemented, and not managed as a black box. Like any tool in a system, ML tools need to be tuned and optimized to work with the other solutions in your ecosystem. The human element should always look at how many events are yielding true and false positives and how this is improving over time. Overall actionable events should also decline with continued use of this technology as it has time to discover and mitigate threats. One thing that is certain is that machine learning and artificial intelligence approaches will continue to evolve due the ever changing landscape and the need to protect resources outside of corporate governance.

CHAPTER 27

Conclusion

Privileges as an attack vector represent the lowest-hanging fruit for a threat actor. While architecting and securing any environment can be relatively complex, these top 20 recommendations can help any organization achieve their goals and minimize risks to the business:

1. **Use Standard User Accounts**: Enforce that all users have a standard user account. Administrators across all platforms should log in with their standard accounts as normal practice and never use administrative accounts when using services like email or banking. They should only log in with administrative rights when they need to perform administrative tasks. And any activities performed while using administrative rights should be controlled and protected using PAM end-to-end.

2. **Never Share Credentials**: The risks of shared credentials and passwords, whether between peers or vendors, just elevate the risk of the password being misused and potentially leaked to a threat actor. It also makes auditing activity to a single user difficult, if not impossible.

3. **Never Reuse Passwords**: If one resource is compromised, then every other resource with the same shared password is at risk, even if the account or username is different.

© Morey J. Haber 2020
M. J. Haber, *Privileged Attack Vectors*, https://doi.org/10.1007/978-1-4842-5914-6_27

4. **Never Store Passwords in Clear Text**: Passwords should be kept secret. They should never be exposed in plain sight, no matter how they are stored.

5. **Secure Passwords**: If passwords need to be documented, they should be in an encrypted file, secured file system, or locked away in a physical safe as required based on business requirements.

6. **Minimize the Number of Aliases**: Making identities trackable and not hackable is key to correlating user activity to a single person.

7. **Minimize the Number of Administrative Accounts**: The lower the number of privileged users and their associated accounts, the lower the privileged risk surface and, consequently, the less to monitor and audit for privileged activity.

8. **Frequently Rotate Privileged Passwords**: Privileged passwords should be rotated after every use for privileged activity or on a regular schedule for electronic accounts. This keeps them from becoming stale and part of a password reuse attack, and less likely to be leaked over time.

9. **Ensure Passwords Are Complex**: Privileged passwords should not be easily readable by humans. Complex passwords that are not recognizable words or phrases help ensure they cannot easily be transcribed or verbally discussed. Every password should be complex, but some should be more complex than others to remove the human risk

element from the equation. This includes even using letters from foreign languages to strengthen complexity.

10. **Require Multi-Factor Authentication**: Implement multi-factor authentication for access to internal systems, applications, and sensitive data. While implementing static multi-factor based on whether a system or application is good, getting too restrictive can become frustrating for users. Look for solutions that can also restrict access based on the risk associated with the environment or activity. For example, if someone tries to launch a sensitive application after hours for the first time, or tries to run a sensitive command on a server that is missing critical patches, consider stepping up the security and triggering to reauthenticate with multi-factor to be certain the identity is who they claim to be.

11. **Implement Application Reputation Controls** (whitelisting, blacklisting, and greylisting): Implement policy to allow known good applications and log or deny potentially deviant applications. If possible, restrict launching of end-user applications with critical known security vulnerabilities.

12. **Enforce the Principle of Least Privilege**: If a user does not need access to systems, applications, resources, or data, remove their privileges. Remove administrator rights on desktops for all users and servers where administrators should be performing only specific tasks.

13. **Automate Password Management**: Control and audit requests for administrative passwords and launching of privileged sessions. Require unique passwords across all privileged systems and accounts.

14. **Eliminate Embedded Passwords**: Replace hard-coded passwords in applications, in service accounts, and in automation tools supporting DevOps. Consider concepts like just-in-time access to only allow credentialed access for those fine instances when deemed appropriate.

15. **Use Context-Based and Adaptive Access Controls**: At some point, people need access to do their jobs. However, that access should continue to be locked down, monitored, and validated. Restricting access based on static elements, like time of day or subnet, is good, but restricting access dynamically based on risk (i.e., does a ticket exist for the access, does this request adhere to normal access patterns, have I received recent alerts from my threat detection layers, etc.) adds greater protections.

16. **Monitor All Sensitive Privileged Session Activity** (especially to crown jewels): Any type of privileged activity to the crown jewels should be session recorded, keystroke logged, and monitored for inappropriate activity. If possible, the initial session review should be automated to rapidly identify a potential threat.

17. **Understand Obligations to Auditors and for Compliance**: IT and security professionals perform multiple diverse functions to secure a business. They should not do them as a checkbox for compliance. Understanding the exact nature of the requirement and the best way to meet the mandates can make everyone more secure and, ultimately, auditors happy (if there is truly ever such a thing). And just remember, being compliant alone does not make you secure. However, making your organization secure generally does make it compliant.

18. **Implement Threat and Advanced Behavioral Monitoring**: Implement privileged access security event monitoring and advanced threat detection (including user behavior monitoring) to more accurately and quickly detect compromised account activity, as well as insider privilege misuse and abuse.

19. **Segment Your Network**: Group assets, including application and resource servers, into logical units that do not trust one another. Segmenting the network reduces the "line of sight" access attackers have into your internal systems. For access that needs to cross trust zones, require a secured jump server with multi-factor authentication, adaptive access authorization, and privileged session monitoring. Where possible, go beyond standard network segmentation. Segment based on the context of the user and privileges, and the resources,

applications, and data that they are accessing. This is also known as micro-segmentation. If possible, even consider zero trust for your newest initiatives to segment authentication.

20. **If You Are NOT Having Fun, You Should Get a Different Job**: If a security professional is unhappy, they are not doing their job correctly. All the preceding items are potentially at risk, and so is the business. Security professionals need to be happy with their work, satisfied with the environment, and challenged on a regular basis. Security is ever-changing, complacency in security is death, and being unhappy will let the latest threat walk right past you. A threat actor does not care if you are happy or not, they just want your administrative accounts.

Final Thoughts

Surrounded by a team of professionals focused on privileged access management, I am constantly involved in what would be considered research activities that include ongoing outreach to customers, customer advisory boards, peer collaboration sessions, and industry analysts that are all motivated to solve real-world challenges.

We have entered the roaring 20's that ushers in a new era for privileged access management and new environmental safety concerns worldwide. Computing has become more distributed and there has been an explosion of privileged accounts managing everything from our desktops to the cloud. Most critical cybersecurity breaches today involve the exploitation of improperly managed privileges that threat actors use to infiltrate our environments and move laterally across our networks. The risk surface is undergoing a rapid expansion as the number of privileged accounts multiplies and recent events have spurred a sudden and massive explosion in the remote workforce. It begs the question, "How can you protect your organization amidst this vast, expanding universe of privileges, and with so many people potentially working from home?"

As we have discussed, the solution takes us far beyond the legacy PAM approaches of just storing passwords in a password vault. The modern approach to PAM secures every user session and privileged activity across your entire privilege enterprise. Fittingly, this holistic PAM practice is called Universal Privilege Management.

The Universal Privilege Management model encompasses securing and managing privileges across your entire landscape—from password management to least privilege management and all the way through secure remote access. Only by enabling this holistic approach and enabling the three core PAM disciplines (Privileged Password Management, Endpoint Privilege Management, and Secure Remote Access) can you adequately address the privileged attack vector problem.

Threats have changed, but today's best PAM technology, paired with the know-how, is up to the task of mitigating the risk. Hopefully, this book has helped arm you with the right "know-how," and I would like to wish you success as you embark on your privileged access management journey. Stay safe, stay healthy, and never share or reuse your passwords.

Index

A

Accounts, 24–25
Administrator/Root User, 19, 20
Advanced persistent threats
        (APTs), 88, 355
Adware, 82
Anonymous access, 27–29
Application monitoring, 144–145
Application programming interface
        (API), 53, 163, 197
Application-specific
        passwords, 334
Application-to-application (A2A)
        privilege automation, 197
    API, 163
    benefits, 163
    credential management, 164
    database administrators, 163
    develop access, 164
    features, 165
    password reuse attacks, 165
Application-to-database (A2D),
        156, 328, 338
App-to-app (A2A), 156, 328
Architecture, PAM
    active/active, 174
    active/passive, 175

cloud-based deployments (*see*
        Cloud-based deployments)
maturity model, 177–181
on-premise deployments, 182,
        183
paradigms, 174
third-party failover, 175, 176
Artificial intelligence (AI), 170, 361
Attacker *vs.* hacker, 6, 7
Attack vector, 10
    definition, 65
    firewalls and endpoint
        protection solutions, 65
    guessing, 66, 67
    malware, 65
    password resets, 75–77
    security questions, 71–73
    techniques, 84
Australian Signals Directorate
        (ASD), 275–277
Automate password
        management, 370

B

Biometrics, 89, 95
Black box approach, 171
Blank passwords, 29–31

© Morey J. Haber 2020
M. J. Haber, *Privileged Attack Vectors*, https://doi.org/10.1007/978-1-4842-5914-6

Printed in the United States
By Bookmasters